SOCIAL DIVISIONS AND LATER LIFE

Difference, diversity and inequality

Chris Gilleard and Paul Higgs

First published in Great Britain in 2020 by

Policy Press
University of Bristol
1-9 Old Park Hill
Bristol
BS2 8BB
UK
t: +44 (0)117 954 5940
pp-info@bristol.ac.uk
www.policypress.co.uk

North America office:
Policy Press
c/o The University of Chicago Press
1427 East 60th Street
Chicago, IL 60637, USA
t: +1 773 702 7700
f: +1 773-702-9756
sales@press.uchicago.edu
www.press.uchicago.edu

British Library Cataloguing in Publication Data
A catalogue record for this book is available from the British Library

Library of Congress Cataloging-in-Publication Data
A catalog record for this book has been requested

ISBN 978-1-4473-3860-4 paperback
ISBN 978-1-4473-3859-8 hardcover
ISBN 978-1-4473-3862-8 ePub
ISBN 978-1-4473-3861-1 ePdf

Cover design by Robin Hawes
Front cover image: BP3H9H Alamy
Printed and bound in Great Britain by CMP, Poole
Policy Press uses environmentally responsible print partners

Contents

List of figures and tables

Figures

Tables

Preface

This book is concerned with the social divisions of later life. It is not primarily a critique of inequality in later life, or a polemic for greater social justice in old age. Rather it is an attempt to illustrate how later life has become a more diverse social location than ever before. That diversity includes inequalities and differences that are structured by the social relations of work, the organisation of households and the changing nature of the economies of contemporary developed societies. However, it goes beyond this, exploring both what structures divisions and what structures difference. We have added the role of the body as a marker of division and difference in addition to the classical structural accounts of social division. While the disability movement has sought to reframe bodily impairments in terms of unequal access, and the anti-ageism movement has sought to critique the ideology of bodily decline by which age is culturally, politically and socially represented, we have considered the body as both a site and a source of social division that has acquired much greater salience within our ageing societies. We have also sought to identify how later life serves as both a site or social location of social divisions and an intersection mediating between social differences and social divisions. Just as class operates differently during working life, compared with how it operates before and after working life, so too we argue do other divisions, like gender, ethnicity and disability. Using later life as a lens to interrogate the nature of social division and social difference is as important as using social division and difference to illuminate the changing nature of later life. By emphasising this reciprocity, we hope to show that age and ageing are also matters of importance to social theory and the social sciences more generally.

1

Social divisions and social differences

Growing social divisions within society have become a matter of renewed concern as the forces of the financialisation, globalisation and marketisation of the economy have come to form the prevailing explanatory narrative underlying change in the contemporary world (Krippner, 2005; Stockhammer, 2012, 2015; Anttonen and Meagher, 2013). While terms such as divisions, inequalities, exclusions and oppression provide much of the social text for these narratives, there is often a lack of precision in the way they are used. In writing a book about the divisions of later life, it is necessary to begin by examining these terms and their employment within the social sciences. 'Social divisions' has been used in a number of ways to describe or represent the structuring of society and its social relations (Carling, 1991; Morris 1995; Anthias, 1998; Payne, 2007). Most uses tend to emphasise the presence and operation of objective structural differences between social groups and their consequences for the stratification of opportunity and advantage. Under this ambit are the ways in which social structures impact on the lives that people live, the opportunities and obstacles they face, as well as the ways they find to make sense of themselves and their place in the world. These latter issues constitute the subjective realisations of social division that exist both in the context of and in contrast to the objective institutional structures that realise such divisions. The former concerns issues of location or position, the latter identity and belonging.

The term 'social differences', on the other hand, is less focused upon hierarchies of inequality and disadvantage. Like divisions, it is concerned with the categorisation of persons. But unlike social divisions, it incorporates processes of creating and maintaining distinctions and structuring the separation between common selves and distant others. Identity and subjectivity play more of a critical role in sourcing social difference, while social divisions imply an externally ordered hierarchy of resources, power and status. This book aims to draw attention to both difference and division in addressing the diversity with which later lives are experienced, lived and socially realised. Consciousness of age or agedness constitutes a social difference, of course, but the consciousness of age does not necessarily map onto the structural divisions in power resources and status that exist between younger and older people. Institutional structures that draw upon chronological age as a criterion for access may impose some sense of an age identity, but this may be quite separate from the structures that institute inequalities between 'age groups'. Some social structures, in short, may emphasise structure and inequality, while others may emphasise distinction and identity. Yet others may draw attention to the social exclusion of particular groups or communities arising from difference. Many other divisions between people exist, of course, which may have important social consequences, without them necessarily being framed as 'social' divisions, such as the place or region where one lives. The extent to which most of the former constitute stable divisions offering limited opportunity for change in their social location, through personal agency, is one defining facet that makes some differences and divisions 'social' rather than 'personal', but exceptions can always be recognised.[1]

In the not too distant past, old age itself could be seen as a product of social division. The provisions for old age were coterminous with those based on the relative impoverishment and marginality of those deemed 'old'. In contemporary circumstances, however, where later life has become a universal expectation, old age serves less as a category or class than as a social and cultural location, or more accurately a series or set of interlinked locations as often associated with advantage as disadvantage.[2] Within those locations, old and new social divisions and social differences can be found, which reappear, are rejected or revised, or which take on a different form in later life. This complex locational intersectionality realises and reflects the transformation of later life, from the residual category of old age to this multifaceted arena of potential agency, identity and inequality now associated with post-working life. It is the realisation of this transition that forms the focus of this book. While later life is still framed as the end product of various over-determining 'structuring' influences drawn from earlier in life, and which add up inexorably to old age, this book explores later life as a site of growing diversity. This diversity is constituted by both division and difference where discourses and practices oriented toward choice, autonomy, self-realisation and pleasure are becoming as prevalent as those oriented toward decline, hardship and inequality.

This does not mean that those features of later life are denied or ignored. They have long been recognised. Soon after the idea of life expectancy was formulated, in the late seventeenth century (Hald, 1987), it became evident that social and economic circumstances played a significant role in determining who might and who might not expect to 'enjoy' a long life (Antonovsky, 1967: 33). As forms of life insurance evolved and membership of friendly and mutual aid societies penetrated the lives of the middling sort, actuarial experience sharpened these understandings, paving the way for what might be called the realisation of old age through its institutional 'governance' (Bois, 1994; Lewin, 2003). During this period, old age came to be seen as the product of other social divisions that lead, at varying rates, to an end of life characterised by a lack of assets, capital and resources, whether through never accumulating any or through losing whatever little one had earlier acquired.[3] Determined less by chronology than by function, old age categorised 'those who were infirm, frail, and suffering incapacities of body or mind to the extent that they could no longer fully support or take care of themselves' (Roebuck, 1979: 417). During the course of the twentieth century things began to change. This change, which continues today, makes later life more than the mere outcome of lifelong, cumulative immiseration, but rather a distinct and diverse part of life's journey. Later life, in short, has become framed both by its continuities and by its separation, continuities that at times join and at times separate the lives and circumstances of older and younger persons. Many of the divisions and differences that are realised in later life can be understood as the reworkings and reframings of earlier life. Many, but not all; the intention is to pay equal attention to those that appear uniquely, or take on a more distinct role, later in life, as to those that constitute its continuities.

Divisions, differences, identities and inequalities

Social divisions are often constructed, somewhat tautologically, as inequalities. As such, they represent important determinants of the potential of individuals, as members of a social group, to realise the opportunities open to them as already structured social beings; or equally to find themselves excluded from such opportunities. They represent what Durkheim (1982) would call some of the most important social facts of society. Nevertheless their status as social facts does not mean they reflect an unequivocal consensus in how they are socially represented. Anthias, for example, has proposed delimiting the term 'social division' only to questions of social 'inequality'. For her, a social division involves:

> a classification of a population (i.e. a taxonomy of persons) and a range of systematic social processes which relate to that taxonomy, and which then serve to produce socially

> meaningful and systematic (although not unitary) practices and outcomes of inequality. (Anthias, 2001: 837)

This is similar to the position adopted by Payne, who argues for a better integration of social divisions into a unified model of inequality. He writes:

> While questions of difference, inequality and division lie at the heart of sociological analysis – for example, in the form of 'class', 'gender', 'ethnicity', etc. – these dimensions of difference have not been studied in an integrated way. The similarities and differences between these dimensions or 'social divisions' remain relatively unexplored, and the potential for a more comprehensive understanding of social inequality is as yet unrealized. (Payne, 2007: 901–2).

Payne proposes that social divisions reflect 'a society wide distinction between two or more logically interrelated categories of people which are socially sanctioned as substantially different from one another' (Payne, 2013: 348). These divisions are not just 'substantially different'; they also confer unequal access to desirable resources, which constrain life chances and lifestyles. Such divisions tend, in turn, to produce shared social identities, which are 'often expressed by reference from their perceived difference from those in an alternative category of the same division' (Payne, 2013). Payne leaves open the relative salience of, as well as the potential interrelationships between different types of social division, including those that emphasise binary comparisons versus those that rely upon multiple divisions, which may or may not be capable of numerical representation (Payne, 2007: 907). Thus, he allows ideas of social difference to become salient and not simply those of social inequality.

Seidman goes further. He argues that the social divisions experienced by many people establish not so much a position in a hierarchy as a sense of identity, which may or may not be accompanied by an awareness of the relative subordination that such identities confer (Seidman, 1997). That this may be translated into a politics of recognition rather than one of redistribution has itself been a topic of much discussion (Fraser, 1995; 2008), raising the question of where the boundary lies between cultural difference and material inequality (Calhoun, 1995). Best has gone further still, effectively ignoring inequality and privileging identity, distinction and the necessary presence of the other in creating the boundaries by which individuals, as social agents, are constructed (Best, 2005: 2). He argues that social categories emerge in mutual and opposing relations with other co-emerging categories, through processes concerned with the legitimation of social claims for recognition, resources and rights. For Best, any social division necessarily involves this element of subjectivity, of persons being conscious both of what they are and what they are not and the material realisations emerging from such divisions. Sceptical of the idea that social class (as the standard-bearer of social inequality) constitutes the dominant form of division within contemporary society, Best argues that 'in the latter years of the twentieth century, class analysis [has become] increasingly irrelevant … with concepts such as cultural identity … having a more significant impact upon our chosen styles of living' (Best, 2005: 74).

Such heterodox views have not gone unchallenged. Atkinson (2017), Ransome (2005) and Savage (2015) have all argued for the continuing importance of class as the key to understanding division (and thus inequality) in society. They seek some other resolution of the persisting tensions between structural accounts that focus on inequalities between groups and culturalist accounts that stress the 'dynamic' nature of community, identity and self-definition. Stressing the role of culture and subjectivity implies that while social divisions are both shaped by and in turn shape differences, and hence constitute potentially hierarchical forms, social differences per se do not necessarily embody or equate to social inequality. Although some proponents of cultural difference advocate this or even more extreme positions, most social scientists still see the existence of differential access to society's cultural and material resources as the underlying structure shaping and sustaining social divisions. While the analysis of social class is most often associated with this kind of formulation, issues of access, power and reward are now more widely accepted as being connected with other social and cultural differences that may be equal to or in certain settings more influential than those arising from class.

Social class itself is seen as having a more complicated relation to the distribution of power and resources than was once the case (Pakulski and Waters, 1996a). While terms like social divisions and social differences can help make these points, outside the UK these terms are less widely used and the commonalities and distinctions between them less often discussed. Considerable consensus does exist, however, that the conventional study of social stratification based upon class is at least an incomplete model for the analysis of economic and social opportunities as well as experience, lifestyle and cultural practices. Whether anything could replace, complement or qualify social class as the major source of difference and/or inequality in society is rather less clear. The French sociologist Ivaylo Petev, for example, takes a negative view of the role of class:

> Empirical research depicts a complex picture of lifestyles. Factors such as race, ethnicity, religiosity, gender, and age seem to have more influence than class … Lifestyles are stratified not in discrete class-specific patterns but into status hierarchies largely determined by the degree of cultural capital, typically measured by level of education … In turn, these cultural hierarchies are themselves decomposing due to the spread of education and the diffusion of cultural products … Furthermore, individuals tend to bridge class boundaries at the level of social networks that shape lifestyle preferences … Building on such evidence, the critique of class analysis promotes the idea that the association between social classes and lifestyles, if it did exist at some point, is today superfluous. (Petev, 2013: 634)

While the majority of those examining social divisions agree that social class is still relevant, whether the 'big classes' are easily 'converted into culturally coherent communities' is not so generally accepted (Weeden and Grutsky, 2013: 1757). Social differences and divisions have become more complex and, though persisting as a division, social class has become much more contingent, more culturally inflected and less consciously articulated as people's source of identity and position.

If social class still occupies its pride of place as a central element in understanding division and inequality, it needs to be set alongside other salient divisions and differences that separately and collectively offer a variety of ways by which diversity and inequality, identity and division are made evident within contemporary society. This is as true when considering the socially framed differences of later life as it is for those of working life. Given the extent to which people in later life are removed from the world of paid employment, it could be argued that occupation and labour force position play a much more limited role in shaping the divisions and differences of later life. At the same time, dealing with social divisions as a series of relatively autonomous social categories that bisect older people's lives may be pragmatically useful; however, it risks obscuring how later life is patterned by overlapping identities. These in turn are fashioned by intersecting structures, each of which is capable of being made more salient at different times and in different circumstances, before and during later life. These divisions, and the structures supporting them, shape but never fully determine the opportunities, lifestyles, experiences and exclusions that make up the nature of later life.

Intersectionality: identity and structure

Recognising the complexity interweaving within and between the various structuring influences in society, a number of writers have begun to explore social division and social stratification through what has come to be known as the 'intersectionality' approach (Crenshaw, 1991). Originally concerned with addressing the intersections of inequalities and oppressions faced by particular marginalised groups, notably African American women, intersectionality seeks to bring to the forefront the idea that the binary divisions that have dominated thinking about the structures of modern society are always mediated by and at times submerged within other divisions. Although the term has had as yet only a limited influence upon studies of social stratification in later life, the issues presented by intersectionality and its highlighting of the contextualising role of social divisions upon each other are likely to gain importance as the cultural norms established by the twentieth century nation state are transformed by what is described as a growing 'hybridity' (Bhabha, 1994; Wade, 2001).

This reflects demographic as much as it does economic change; economic as much as technological change; and cultural as much as social transformation. It may be considered the longer term outcome of what Wallerstein (1989) called the 'social revolution' that began in 1968 and whose locus of change was the emergence of 'youth culture' and its various 'sub-cultures'. The impact of that 'revolution' continues, but no longer so distinctively and more or less exclusively confined to the social world of 'the young'. In the subsequent half-century, the growing hybridity of life and lifestyles has extended its impact across successive generations, and is now reaching those whom one might call 'the newly old'. While this point will be expanded further in later chapters, here attention is drawn to some of the main parameters of the ensuing intersectionality, the ways the term has been deployed, and some of the limitations it possesses in providing an adequate analysis and understanding of social differentiation and social stratification in later life, in the early decades of the twenty-first century.

Most consider that the term was introduced into the social sciences through the writings of the critical race scholar Kimberlé Crenshaw (1991). The term was crystallised in a paper that she presented in the late 1980s concerning the intersection of race and sex (Yuval-Davis,

2006: 193). In it, she reflected the experience of a number of black feminist writers who considered that the women's movement, so important a part of the long 1960s' 'social revolution' had treated women's issues largely through the lens of white middle class women, as if their experience constituted a kind of universal position applying to all women whatever their circumstances. To many black feminists, this felt like a denial of the difference that race meant, for both men and for women, in their social relations and life experiences. Patricia Hill Collins (1990) further highlighted the interlocking systems of oppression that she saw framed around race, class and gender in American society. Extending these arguments beyond their North American origins has broadened the scope of the term, widening its focus from the powerful dividing line of race that so permeates the US to a much broader conception of the term. Based upon a conference entitled 'Celebrating Intersectionality?', the edited book, *Framing Intersectionality*, provides one starting point for this broader interpretation (Lutz, Vivar and Supik, 2016).

First, as one of the contributors to that volume notes, the geographical arena has shifted in which the term has been applied. The divisions of race, class and gender that formed the classic nodes of intersectionality have since 'been augmented with other dimensions of socio-cultural and economic inequality, including that of sexual orientation' (Kosnick, 2016: 121). This expansion of the term has however led to the criticism that it 'treat[s] … all differences as equivalent and hence interchangeable when they have different logics and operate at different levels' (Phoenix, 2016: 138). Others have argued that expanding its focus has led intersectionality to becoming no more than a 'buzzword' with limited analytical purchase (Davis, 2008). Others claim that it emphasises social 'location' over social 'process' (Choo and Ferree, 2010: 146), adding little to existing analyses of gender and race (Nash, 2008). At the same time, intersectionality does offer a way of thinking differently about the social divisions within society. From this perspective, intersectionality can be presented as neither an explanatory nor a purely descriptive term. Rather, as Crenshaw has put it, it serves as 'a prism refracted to bring into view dynamics that were constitutive of power but obscured by certain discursive logics at play' (Crenshaw, 2016: 231).

In this broad sense, intersectionality can be linked with other positions such as critical legal studies and queer theory that collectively seek to challenge what they identify as the binary nature of power and the accompanying essentialist assumptions about already instituted socio-cultural divisions. Further, intersectionality it is argued, helps 'de-marginalise' and mark particular groups of people whose position within society has been too easily overlooked or subsumed under other 'bigger' social divisions. Such a position implies actively avoiding a reliance only upon already existing theoretical delineations. Equally, it takes issue with the employment of already existing formal research methodologies that risk replicating the very hierarchies that are being interrogated. Consequently, the approach advanced by Crenshaw attempts to prevent the formalisation of intersectionality as either a methodological or a theoretical position. Instead, it advocates intersectionality as a methodological stance that, by focusing upon some key intersections between the various social divisions already operating within society, helps prevent their subsequent reification.

Adopting an even less formalised position, Villa has argued for treating intersectionality primarily as 'a heuristic framework … a kind of reminder to keep the complexity and intersection of many constituent categories in mind … [in short] a critical stance on categories' (Villa, 2016: 183). While some have argued that this kind of meta-positioning risks marginalising or minimising still further the questions of race and racialisation that provided the original stimulus for introducing the term, it can also be argued that privileging race over other divisions does no more than replicate many of the problems of earlier approaches that privileged first class, then gender and now race. Because of this, there is a necessary tension in such intersectional approaches. One stance can easily be seen to negate or neutralise others. Arguably, it is that very tension that forms part of its heuristic value, just as it risks dissolving all that seemed socially solid into subjectivity and hot air.

Bringing in the body: corporeality and chronology

If intersectionality has drawn attention to the complex interrelationships between social divisions and social identities based upon class, gender, race and ethnicity, the rise of the disability movement can be credited with helping bring the body into focus as a site and source of social division (Gilleard and Higgs, 2013). While issues of race and gender highlight the signifying role of the body as a marker of difference, the intersection between disability and age has proved more problematic in positioning the body as a site of division based not just upon embodiment and performativity, but upon the body as a source of unequal 'corporeal capital'. By bringing the body to centre stage in the analysis of inequality and social stratification, the disability movement has made the body both more salient and at the same time more problematic in analysing social difference. Treated as biological givens, age and disability have long been 'the most neglected of the big six social divisions' within the social sciences (Hearn, 2016: 94). Indeed, the idea that age and the body might be seen as primarily 'social constructions' and not biological givens very significantly post-dates the classic divisions of social theory, such as those concerning class, gender and ethnicity/race whose bodily markings, such as they were, constituted mere markers of what were essentially social processes.

While age and the body have been recognised as sites impacted upon by society and its institutions, considerations of how the social is actively involved in constructing age and the body is of relatively recent origin. While sociology's active engagement with the body can be dated to Bryan Turner's book, *The Body and Society* (Turner, 1984), Peter Öberg's 1996 paper on the 'absent body' (Öberg, 1996) marks another 'beginning' in the engagement between ageing studies and the 'somatic' turn in the humanities and social sciences (Tulle, 2015: 127). Although earlier 'precursor' studies can no doubt be found (Turner, 1991: 12), these two points of 'origin' provide at least some rough indication of the relative novelty this area has in the study of ageing, society, its divisions and stratification.

Disability studies barely pre-dates these latter developments. Emerging in the late 1970s/early 1980s, 'as part of a cluster of politicized identity-based interdisciplinary fields of study that arose from rights-based, social-justice-influenced knowledge building and disseminating initiatives' (Garland-Thomson, 2013: 915–16) disability studies has created a reading of the body that has proved distinctly problematic for the social sciences. The subsequent 'rediscovery of the body' in ageing studies has in turn created new problems for disability studies. By addressing these two problematics early on, the intention is to clear a path toward considering the body as a site and source of social division in later life and the problems that arise from adopting such a position. To begin with, however, the initial reluctance to include disability as part of the sociology of the body (as distinct from its position in 'medical sociology') should be acknowledged.

One of the first edited collections to introduce the topic of the body into the study of society, social processes and culture ignored 'disability' completely (Featherstone, Hepworth and Turner, 1991). Not only were there no chapters on the topic, but the term 'disability' did not even warrant an entry in the book's index. As Higgs and Jones (2008) noted other books on the 'sociology' of the body that appeared around the time ignored both ageing and disability. In the inaugural issue of the journal *Body & Society* the editors outlined six themes that they intended this new journal, directed toward the 'expanding interest' in the 'human body and the nature of embodiment', to address (Featherstone and Turner, 1995: 1). None concerned disability. Even in Frank's extensive 'decade review' of publications of potential relevance to a sociology of the body, age gets no mention while disability jostled alongside illness as a sub-theme concerning the 'medicalised body' (Frank, 1990: 134–144).

A major factor complicating the exploration of the body, impairment and disability within the social sciences has been the concomitant decentring of the body as a site of division and inequality that was promoted by the disability movement itself (Hughes and Paterson, 1997). The argument put forward by activists such as Oliver (2013) was that people with a disability are disadvantaged not by their bodies or by their bodily impairment but by their exclusion from society and its resources, such as education, employment, housing and transport. They argued that bodily impairments have been used as a 'cover' by society to justify its neglect of the rights of people with disabilities and deny them access to the same range of goods resources and services to which able-bodied people have access. The relatively 'disembodied' approach that characterised the disability movement helped create the gulf between a sociology of the body and disability theory that only began to be acknowledged around the turn of the century (Barnes, Mercer and Shakespeare, 1999; Thomas, 2007).

Like all new social movements, the disability movement was pioneered by young people, particularly young people attending college or university. They represented an articulate and informed section of youth attracted by the new social movements and countercultures of the late 1960s and early 1970s (Fleischer and Zames, 2001; Hahn, 2002). By focusing upon issues of education and employment, this movement, like the women's movement, and indeed like the movements supporting equal rights for gays and lesbians, ethnic and racialised minorities, was dominated by the concerns of those in early adulthood. Framed as a social identity, disability was considered most authentic when it was a stable source of difference, present from birth or at least early in life, before social identities were formed. Disability acquired later in life, like ethnicity or homosexuality practised late in life, was less identified as such. The aged body was never an icon for the movement. In order to shift emphasis away from the frailty of the body, it was important for these young activists to present disability as a signifier of desire, opportunity and potential. The young man or woman in a Paralympic-style wheelchair replaced the old woman in a bath chair as representative of the disabled wheelchair user for whom access to education, employment and transport was critical (Pullin, 2009).

This created a contrarian position – where the body was both site of, and mis-signified as the core of, the exclusions practised by society on people with mental and physical impairments. As Siebers (2001: 740) has noted: '[t]he disabled body seems difficult for the theory of social construction to absorb: disability is at once its best example and a significant counterexample'. He goes on to state:

> Society creates pain, but this creation backfires, producing a resource to struggle against society – this is the dominant theoretical conception of pain. I do not want to underestimate the amount of psychic pain produced by society; nor do I want to deny that psychic pain translates into physical pain. Clearly, the pain of disability is less bearable because people with disabilities suffer intolerance and loneliness every day. They hurt because the able-bodied often refuse to accept them as members of the human community. And yet most people with a disability understand that physical pain is an enemy. It hovers over innumerable daily actions, whether the disability is painful in itself or only the occasion for pain because of the difficulty of navigating one's environment. The great challenge every day is to manage the body's pain, to get out of bed in the morning, to overcome the well of pain that rises in the evening, to meet the hundred daily obstacles that are not merely inconveniences but occasions for physical suffering. (Siebers, 2001: 744–5)

This position permeates the social differences occasioned by the body. Suffering, as Levinas has noted, can serve to disrupt the unity of individual consciousness as well as the possibilities for collective action, for a communality of shared suffering (Levinas, 1994). While the potential identity conferring nature of disability which results from the emergence of the disability movement has undoubted merits, and benefits the circumstances of many people with impairments, its stabilisation as a social division mediating between the disabled and non-disabled can and has been criticised for emphasising a politics of suffering and paralysis (Brown, 1995: 55) while ignoring the social and temporal fluidity of impairment, disability and suffering (Garland-Thomson, 2014: 10–11). Herein lies its problematic, translating the corporeal into the dividing practices of embodiment and dissolving the subject into the social. Bringing the body back in has been an important step forward in the social sciences, but in doing so it has exposed to scrutiny the complex intersection of social divisions, social differences and the temporality that emerges with age (Dumas and Laberge, 2005).

Age, cohort and social change

This leads us to the final issue with which this introductory chapter is concerned, the role of age, time and period (or era) in shaping social division and identity. At the outset, it was noted that old age – or later life – represents a social division within the life course, a division that has long been acknowledged in society (Gilleard, 2002). Realising old age or rather realising a valued old age, was once the outcome of other social divisions such as those associated with wealth, work and status. The old age of the pauper, the servant or the labourer was irrelevant in framing more positive representations of age; it was merely the ragged end of ragged lives. The concern with managing a good later life – whether in the classical, medieval or early modern world of the West – was a concern confined to prosperous men and their actual or impending old age. Those left to labour or to beg were of at most only marginal interest. But while period or era operates independently of a purely 'stages of life' framework, altering the meaning, shape and circumstances of age and the life course, temporality on both counts plays a part in altering the structures that influence and shape social divisions (Bonoli, 2007).

To take a simple example, in contemporary society the status of being 'poor' is rarely the persistent fate of one group of persons, let alone of one individual or household.[4] More families move in and out poverty than remain permanently poor. As Layte and Whelan (2003: 172) note:

> The consistent finding across research from the USA, Britain, Germany and the Netherlands has been that there is substantial movement over poverty thresholds between years, and that poverty spells are shorter than research based upon cross-sectional data had previously thought.

Part of this temporal patterning of poverty reflects the variation of income associated with the differing stages of life – reflecting what has been called the institutionalisation of the life course. In nineteenth and early twentieth century industrial society, the chances of being poor were greatest in childhood and old age and least during the period of early adulthood (Rowntree, 1901). This 'life course' structure of poverty remained evident throughout first modernity (i.e. from the late eighteenth to the mid twentieth century (Rowntree, 1941; Rowntree and Lavers, 1951). Since the late 1970s, this life course patterning has gradually lost its shape. The decline of the male breadwinner model in determining household income, the expansion of and increasing fluidity of retirement and the growing variability in the structure of family and work relations have undermined the economic ordering of life's stages (Leisering and Leibfried, 2001).

As industrialisation has lost much of its former dominance, the nature and organisation of work has changed. Educational opportunities have expanded, standards of childhood health have improved and income diversity has grown. Within the habitus fashioned by post-war consumerism, new configurations have emerged which have led to increased fluidity in the delineation of social divisions through the growing 'biographisation' and 'temporalisation' of advantage and disadvantage (Leisering and Leibfried, 2001: 239). Class, as a source of social identity, has declined in importance as other social identities shaped less by the role of work have become correspondingly more salient. This includes identities based on lifestyle, gender, sexuality, ethnicity and race. While the social structuring by income status and wealth has not disappeared, changes taking place in contemporary society have established a greater diversity of influences impacting upon people's 'lived experience', 'forms of life' and 'access to resources'. These changes have in turn affected the salience of age and the stages of life. There is increasing recognition that later life is no longer what it once was; that periods or stages of life have less stable social meaning and more variable, contradictory forms of social representation. In short they have been affected by the new opportunities and the new challenges that mark the transition of 'second modernity' (Beck and Lau, 2005).

Ulrich Beck saw this aspect of second modernity as the rise of processes leading to or institutions increasingly supporting the 'individualisation' of society (Beck, 2002). His periodisation of modernity – the shift from 'first' modernity to 'second' modernity – has greatly influenced the authors' own work on ageing and later life (Gilleard and Higgs, 2005). The transformation of society from one form of modernity to another has been associated with a series of changes that cumulatively have eroded the role of the 'classical' divisions in society that formed the core of nineteenth and early twentieth century sociological thinking. While it would be a mistake to believe that those earlier structures of modernity have vanished or ceased to impact upon the lives of men and women in the twenty-first century, continuing to apply a framework based solely upon those earlier divisions, without recognising their temporal specificity, can lead to a misapprehension or misidentification of what has changed, particularly what has changed about later life. It is not just that old age is no longer 'synonymous with poverty' (Shragge, 1984: 196) or that it is no longer a brief period of 'half-life, characterized by economic insecurity, poor health, loneliness, resistance to change, and failing physical and mental powers' (Tuckman and Lorge, 1953: 260). Old age – or what we prefer to term 'later life' – has become a more complex social space, sharing in many of the liquidities characterising cultural, economic, political and social life today. Issues that previously scarcely figured in the way society thought about or understood itself now impact not just on working life, but on later life, forming both new continuities and new disjunctions with earlier working adult life.

Times change and age too is changing. In the process, the social divisions of second modernity are fragmenting the once homogenous social character of old age. These divisions continue changing, in form and in substance. They expand and diversify. Statuses and positions that once subsumed all stages of life from childhood to old age are no longer so stable or so determinate. While the divisions of gender and race may seem relatively unchanging, their importance has grown and their framing within the life course continues to change. Other divisions have emerged, such as those concerning the status of the body as social marker, while divisions that were once confined to particular periods of life have since penetrated all stages of life. These are not matters of social mobility, the relative mobility or stability of 'class' positions or opportunities. Rather they reflect the flux of second modernity, the individualisation that it entails and the permeation of chance, choice and circumstance through every phase of the lifecourse (Meyer and Bridgen, 2008). Temporality affects so many aspects of our social being. This is especially the case for the body, and the rise and fall of statuses and social divisions that are based upon corporeal identities, such as health, fitness, illness and impairment. These new divisions and the identities associated with them are less essentialised than the divisions of old, given the inherent temporal instability that is attached to them. Despite their temporality, however, they are not lacking in social significance both for accessing resources and in realising new opportunities (Heap and Fors, 2015).

Conclusions

The existence of social divisions seems a universal feature of society; the nature and significance of those divisions, however, seems more contingent upon time, place and the particular organisation of power in a society. More to the point for this book, as old age has become a common experience, so the social divisions within later life have become increasingly apparent. Once arguably the product of earlier social divides, later life has itself become a site for social divisions, divisions that reflect both differences and inequalities. Later life can be seen as emphasising older divisions that once were seen primarily in working life, while modifying others that cut across the life course and realising still others that seem almost like new divisions or at least divisions made more salient with age. Later life serves as both a location for, and an end point of, such divisions. As the depth and range of what constitutes later life shifts and expands, various aspects of these social divisions will likely change further, developing in and through the shifting intersections of one with the other.

Age and time (in the sense of lifetime, of secular or generational time and of the passing of time) modify the realisation of social divisions. As later life continues to change, it serves as the social location for ever shifting social divisions, blending past and present, while pointing, hesitantly, toward the boundaries of its future hybridity (Hazan, 2015). This, at least, is the premise upon which much of the book rests and the implications of which it seeks to explore. The various intersections of social structure, social relations and social identities in later life are what concerns us. Ageing – and particularly the ageing of developed societies – brings to light new problems and presents new challenges for society and for social theory. In exploring this emerging territory, we hope to consider these divisions as a way of understanding changes in the social nature of later life. In the process, we also hope that it may shed some light on the changing nature of social divisions themselves. Treating social divisions as both structured inequalities and as socially constituted identities, we have subtitled our book 'Difference, diversity and inequality' to capture these twin perspectives. We hope that by so doing, a choice is acknowledged in how a sociology of later life can be realised, represented and understood.

Notes

1 One might consider height as an example of a stable division separating advantaged tall people from disadvantaged small people. Height, however, is less integrated as a collective representation of social division, unlike physical disability or obesity. Outside such individual, constitutional differences, we could also have included religious affiliation or residential location. While both religion and place of residence can be changed through personal agency, the everyday reality is that making such changes is subject to considerable social restrictions. We recognise the role of religion and residence as potential social divisions distinct from if not

unrelated to the categories of ethnicity or class. We have chosen to exclude these latter arenas as much for reasons of space and our limited knowledge as because they seem subject to the exercise of personal agency.

2 The fact that later life (or old age) is now considered as a position of advantage and power as often as of disadvantage and marginality is reflected in the 'generational politics' that contrasts the advantaged 'baby boomers' with the disadvantaged 'millennials' (see, for example, Kohli, 2015; Bristow, 2016; Erk, 2017; Pickard, 2019).

3 Writing at the end of the nineteenth century, Joseph Chamberlain concluded that 'one half at least of the working class are condemned to end their days as paupers' (Chamberlain, 1892: 727).

4 The proportion of US households aged 65 and over that were permanently in poverty during the post-recession period, 2009–17, for example, was roughly one-quarter that of the much larger proportion who 'transitioned' in or out of poverty during this time (Fox and Pacus, 2018: Appendix 1, p 31).

2

Social class and inequality in later life

Social class and its related inequalities have been a mainstay of research in the social sciences. Research into class-related inequalities has existed alongside, but has often not been connected with, the concerns of class theory. Despite both approaches seeming to depend upon one another in order to give substance to their claims of social significance, a strange lack of engagement continues to exist between the two traditions (Scambler and Higgs, 1999). In contrast to the limited work on social class theory, social class-related inequalities have been extensively researched, particularly in relation to health, where the connection between class, health and mortality has been well established (Antonovsky, 1967; Bartley, 2004). Even though this research has been criticised for its lack of theoretical justification and categorical imprecision (Cartwright and O'Brien, 1974), it continues to bask in the glow of its underpinning the analysis of the 'Black Report' (Whitehead 1992), establishing what the UK Conservative government came to term 'health variations'. Its influence has continued, with regular assessments of its impact (MacIntyre, 1997), as well as acknowledgement of its role in creating the burgeoning field of health inequalities research (Bouchard et al, 2015).

While the field of inequalities has eschewed highly theorised concepts of class, ideas of social gradients or status abound (Marmot, 2006) along with the assumed psycho-social pathways to ill health created by such gradients (Wilkinson and Pickett, 2010). In the UK, policy recommendations such as those contained in the Acheson Report and the Marmot Review have focused on strategies to overcome inequalities even if this has been described as 'a labour of Sisyphus' (Bambra et al, 2011). The lack of a clear understanding of the structuring of social class links together the two strands of thinking about inequality in all its disparate forms (Goldthorpe, 2010; Scambler and Scambler 2015; Wemrell et al, 2016). Those concerned with these issues are confronted with the fact that while the nature of social class analysis has long been a central issue in the study of society and its social divisions, class remains, in the words of one contemporary analyst, 'a slippery concept' employed through a wide range of potentially disparate indices (Bottero, 2015: 15).

At the same time, existing almost as if in a parallel universe, contemporary writing continues the long tradition of updating the sociological theorisation of class that originated with Marx and Weber, the so-called 'founding fathers' of the sociological canon. A host of writers such as Bourdieu (1989a), Goldthorpe (2010), Mann (1973), Poulantzas (1975), Tilly (1998) and Wright (1979) have contributed to furthering thinking about class, though without achieving any obvious resolution. As these debates have continued, adjustments have been made accommodating more culturally located social divisions such as those associated with ethnicity, gender and sexuality (Atkinson, 2015; Bottero, 2004; Rothman, 2015; and Savage 2000). In addition to the growing interest in these other forms of social division, various arguments have suggested that class has lost much of its centrality in 'structuring' society (Kingston, 2000; Pakulski and Waters, 1996a, 1996b). Ulrich Beck has gone so far as to claim that class has become a 'zombie' category, dead but still living amongst us (Beck and Beck-Gernsheim, 2001). As with the earlier debates of the 1960s, the death of class argument has often been overstated (Dahrendorf, 1959; Bell, 2000) even as its relative salience is questioned (Wood, 1998).

Class remains one of the principal leitmotifs through which 'the turbulence associated with the disappearance of "society as usual"' can be explored (Esping Andersen, cited in Gilleard and Higgs, 2005: 149). This applies as much to the changing terrain of later life as to the stage of working life. Understanding the nature and place of class within later life presents some formidable challenges, both in the conceptualisation of class and in its social realisation in later life, over and above those applying to contemporary working life (Formosa and Higgs, 2013). This chapter starts by looking in some detail at the conceptualisation of class and how it has been utilised in understanding the inequalities of later life. It also considers alternative approaches to thinking about class, based less upon gradations and hierarchies of occupational status than upon those more 'status-like' aspects of social, economic and cultural life that emphasise consumption, distinction and the fashioning of lifestyle and identity. This more cultural framing of class places class less as an outcome of the underlying relations of production than as a set of multiply determined practices that collectively make and remake 'class' as an active system of categorisation that reverberates throughout the life course.

Relational versus gradational systems of social class

The impact of social class on later life is a frequently researched issue in social gerontological research. Like research on health inequalities, this work is largely atheoretical, employing a variety of measures chosen for pragmatic reasons. While reference is sometimes made to the need to use a 'theoretical' structure on which to base indices of class (Galobardes et al, 2006a), this requirement is more often than not overlooked in favour of empirical approaches. When measures of class are selected to 'best' represent socio-economic position, 'best' is usually taken to mean demonstrating 'most statistical power' to account for or explain the most variance in whatever aspect of later-life inequality is being explored (Grundy and Holt, 2001; Galobardes et al, 2006a). Such an empiricist framing of social class is arguably rather less dominant in Europe than in North America, where a typical definition of social class 'refers to a system of stratification based on access to resources such as wealth, property, power, and prestige, [where] a combination of these factors is usually conceived as one's socioeconomic status' (Moya and Fiske, 2017: 9).

Within the empiricist tradition, the term 'socioeconomic classification' or 'socioeconomic status' is often preferred to class. This is because of the former's atheoretical neutrality (Rose, Harrison and Pevalin, 2014: 4) and its umbrella-like capacity to cover whatever particular 'range of indicators and interconnected concepts [of] socioeconomic disadvantage' researchers have to hand (Galobardes et al, 2006b: 99). In adopting this kind of approach, it is customary to assign an index or quantum of socio-economic status to individuals, which, applied to people reaching or already in 'post-working' life, is typically represented as 'the stocks of resources across life domains that are accumulated and/or dissipated over the life course' (O'Rand, 2006: 146). Social class as marking the distinct social relations of economic life is replaced by some pre-judged quanta of individual human capital in what Eric Olin Wright has described as a 'gradational' rather than a 'relational' model of class (Wright, 1979).

This distinction between relational and gradational models of class, as Estes, Swan and Gerard (1982) acknowledge, provides a major site of debate on the nature of social class in later life.[1] In comparison with studies focusing on inequalities among people of working age, it also has some rather different implications. While the gradational model is easier to apply to any group or population for which data on individuals' wealth, income, past or present occupation, neighbourhood and education (or some combination) are available, relational models emphasising status group divisions or positions within the economy of relative advantage, control and power are almost invariably derived from an individual's position within the workplace. Since such relational models require explicit reference to occupation and place in the workforce, it is difficult to assign a relational class to older retired people in the absence of their location within the productive economy. The option is either to treat the retired as a largely undifferentiated, pensioned off 'reserve army of labour' (see O'Brien, 2010), or to 'assign' them a class position based upon their past occupational history, typically their last position before retirement, on the assumption that class in later life is nothing but the spin-off of an earlier class position (see Lopes, 2015). An alternative, less frequently employed approach is to treat older retired people as a kind of 'rentier' class, living off the returns of notional or actual 'pension pots' contributed to by a combination of living and dead labour (see Higgs and Gilleard, 2006). Here distinctions can be made between those whose retirement income derives largely from such returns from capital – in the form of active private pensions, property and/or from other forms of investment and property – and those whose income derives largely from the state's redistribution of earned income in the form of public pensions or social security. Although potentially illuminating, this particular relational model of class in later life (contrasting retirement income as rentier capital with pensions as deferred wages) has been largely eschewed by researchers.

Given the difficulties applying relational models of class to later life, gradational models of socio-economic status have more often been adopted when stratifying the retired population.[2] These models require no pre-ordained classes at all, only some system for assigning a numerical position to a given sample or population of older people. Always openly quantifiable, such methods are capable of assigning 'research subjects' to any one of a potentially infinite number of collapsible or divisible social categories, derived from some combination of more or less quantifiable indicators (most often including measures of income and years of education). While decisions of what to categorise, how to categorise and how many categories to employ may trace their origins to sophisticated class-based schema such as the National Statistics Socio-economic Classification (Rose, Pevalin and O'Reilly, 2005), they soon turned into socio-economic status variables rather than distinct class relations. The consequence is a 'wide disparity among stratification researchers with respect to the logic and contents of the derived scales applied in actual data analysis' (Ganzeboom and Treiman, 1996: 202). Unsurprisingly, then, many prefer to avoid any notions of relational categorisation, choosing instead dimensional measures in making up what is then termed a socio-economic gradient.[3] Such gradational models have the benefit that they facilitate testing hypotheses based upon the decomposition of shared variance between whatever SEP (socio-economic position) indices that have been selected and whatever 'outcome' variables are the study's focus. The results are unsurprisingly predictable, if somewhat tautological, leaving open any number of theoretical explanations of what might explain the demi-regularities of disadvantage carried through into later life.

Class as gradational status: cumulative (dis)advantage theory

One of the more widely adopted gradational models of socio-economic status is that embodied by the cumulative advantage/disadvantage hypothesis (Crystal and Shea, 1990; O'Rand, 1996; Dannefer, 1988; 2003). Cumulative advantage/disadvantage theory postulates that economic and social advantages and disadvantages accumulate over the course of a life, leading to a growing inequality between those starting life with much advantage and privilege and those starting without any. Drawing upon R.K. Merton's work (1968), Dale Dannefer first described this as the Matthew effect of ageing, whereby, quoting from the New Testament's Gospel of Mathew, 'unto every one that hath shall be given and he shall have abundance; but from him that hath not shall be taken away even that which he hath' (cited by Dannefer, 1987: 216). Gradational indices of socio-economic status can be derived whose 'accumulation' constitutes a kind of quantum of class growing and expanding over the course of life.

Within this gradational model, the effect of age and retirement can be represented as the drawing down of the cumulative stock of capital that an individual or individual household has acquired during working life. In this human capital model, education forms a kind of investment whose returns are realised with cumulative benefit over the course of working life; ageing, by contrast, represents the expenditure of resources (of material assets, of physical prowess and of social position). Hence the income and wealth, the education and training and the social networks accumulated prior to retirement are seen as jointly determining a person's socio-economic status or their stock of human capital at and in retirement. The maintenance of a class location in retirement is determined 'in the last instance' by the structures of earlier life, but it is not necessarily over-determined by those structures, since variation exists in the choices made along the way (for example, in the investments in human financial and social capital the individual made or the decision to stay on or leave higher education, and so forth, and the unforeseen expenses incurred from misfortune and misinformation). The stability of those market choices and of a person's life circumstances will consequently affect the accumulated assets, capital and resources with which the person or the household enters old age, leading to a degree of invariance between past and present capital before and after working life.

Despite the scope for such individual 'agency', the individualised basket of resources accumulated by an older person are thought to be influenced by the initial stock of human capital granted them from birth. This is capable of progressive attenuation (or enhancement) by a range of potentially separable patterns of advantage and disadvantage accumulated during the life course. Many breaks and disjunctions might be envisaged, depending upon the particular culture, economy and society in which an individual life course is traversed. Adopting this kind of contingent approach favours a model of potential agency set against the presence and nature of stability in society, in work, in education, in healthcare, in housing and in the organisation of social welfare. While it might once have been unusual for an individual household to move outside its historical position within the socio-economic structure, the circumstances of modernity have enabled new degrees of social flux, rendering the social realisation of the cumulative advantage hypothesis as much a matter of individualised fortune as the over-determined order of privilege and power. This approach represents in some sense the application to ageing studies of Gary Becker's theory of human capital (Becker, 1962, 1993), amongst whose defining premises is that '[p]eople need to invest in themselves during their whole lives' (Becker, 2002: 8). It is perhaps more resonant of the social imaginary of power, progress and position embodied in North American society than the class-based framework still holding sway in Europe.

Gradational measures have been used extensively to develop, test and evaluate 'cumulative (dis)advantage theory', which has become the 'master narrative' in the study of social division and inequality in later life (Ferraro, Shippee and Shafer, 2009). Given its distinctly pragmatic base and its flexibility for interpretation within a suitably 'individualised' framework, it is unsurprising that cumulative advantage theory has been so widely researched in the USA. That the results of such research lack consistency is perhaps unsurprising, given the changeable circumstances surrounding lives in contemporary society, as well as the variable nature of what constitute advantages and assets in the face of the various challenges and opportunities that later life presents.

Rephrased as 'cumulative inequality' theory, the basic tenets of this model have been outlined in reverse form by Kenneth Ferraro, who states: 'disadvantage accumulates over the life course, thereby differentiating a cohort over time' (Ferraro, 2007: 336). Ferraro and Shippee (2009) identified five core theses underpinning the cumulative [dis]advantage/cumulative inequality model. The first proposes that '[s]ocial systems generate inequality, which is manifested over the life course through demographic and developmental processes' (p 334), the second that '[d]isadvantage increases exposure to risk, but advantage increases exposure to opportunity' (p 335), the third that '[l]ife course trajectories are shaped by the accumulation of risk, available resources, and human agency' (p 335) and the fourth that '[c]umulative inequality may lead to premature mortality; therefore, non-random selection may give the appearance of decreasing inequality in later life' (p 336). They then added a fifth axiom, to avoid making this a rather over-deterministic formulation, arguing that researchers need also to be aware 'of turning points as times during the life course when major change occurs in how the person responds to a risk or an opportunity' though this does not exactly constitute a thesis or tenet of the model, but more a kind of caveat (p 335).

Some of the early US studies of income inequality across the life course failed to support the argument. In a study of inequality across the life course, the Gini coefficient of income inequality[4] was found to be higher among the youngest age group (0–6 years) than among the middle aged, while that of college-age groups (18–24 years) was found to be higher than among both the middle aged and the young-old (65–74 years), hardly evidence of a cumulative pattern of growing inequality predicted by the model (Crystal and Shea, 1990: Table 1, p 440). Using a quasi-longitudinal design, Prus observed a non-linear pattern of change among a Canadian 'pre-boomer' cohort (people born around 1925). He observed an inverted U curve, with income inequality rising more or less steadily from the forties to the early sixties, but then declining markedly as the cohort aged into their late sixties and seventies (Prus, 2000). In a review of cross-national studies of income inequality in retirement during the mid-1980s and early 1990s, Pederson observed that (a) 'people belonging to households with heads above 60 are almost nowhere a particularly disadvantaged group in terms of household equivalent income'; and that (b) 'overall income inequality measured by the Gini coefficient and other summary indices … among elderly households shows wide differences among developed countries', with the US showing 'by far the largest inequality coefficients and income differentials' compared with other countries where a 'taming' of inequality was generally evident after retirement (Pedersen, 1999: 125–6).

Have matters changed in the aftermath of the recent global financial crisis? Has the combination of austerity, neo-liberal policy and pre-existing inequalities lead to a further bifurcation between the haves and the have nots within the retired population? Not according to one recent OECD survey. The report's authors found that 'inequality among people starting their working life is now … much higher than among today's elderly, which is in stark contrast to patterns observed in the past', when inequality was thought to grow with age (OECD, 2017: 27). Employing other measures of human capital – such as health, well-being and wisdom – also shows few signs that cumulative advantage/inequality has led to inequalities widening after, compared with before retirement (van Zon et al, 2016). Most recent evidence continues to show that ageing – or rather later life – is less likely to be a site or source of inequality (or polarisation) compared with working life, where generally it was, and has become more so, before and after the Great Recession (OECD, 2017: 129; Poterba, Venti and Wise, 2018; Whelan, Russell and Maître, 2016).[5]

Other aspects of cumulative inequality may acquire more significance as people age. Young children's mental and physical capacities start off relatively independent of the income or wealth of their families, but grow more closely connected with their family's social status as the linkages between their assets and capitals grow closer over time. Individuals reaching retirement age are consistently advantaged (or disadvantaged) across a range of circumstances, by this growing confluence between their financial, functional and social resources. Evidence that the overall matrix of resources (corporeal, cultural and material) demonstrates a stronger 'positive manifold' in later life than it does earlier in adult life is however limited, as is evidence that the distribution of composite indices of 'resourcefulness' manifests any greater bifurcation or polarisation in later life. While the cumulative advantage/disadvantage model of growing inequality continues to stimulate research in social gerontology (and in life-course research more broadly – see Levy and Bühlman, 2016), the empirical evidence supporting its extension into later life is not strong. The possibility remains, of course, that a greater polarisation takes place at the margins (a point we will explore later) between the poorest and richest, in later life, not captured by distributional measures like the Gini coefficient, or that a stronger positive 'manifold' of general socio-economic advantage/

disadvantage emerges in later life, even when no single parameter demonstrates widening inequality.

Some evidence seems to favour this latter interpretation (Hoffmann, Kröger and Pakpahan, 2018) but even if it were possible to show a tightening interconnection between different forms of assets and capitals, that would not of course constitute proof of the gradational model of class. It could equally well reflect the general hypothesis that Dannefer first argued, that a widespread, non-specific process of intra-cohort differentiation takes place across the board increasing with age (Dannefer, 1987; Nelson and Dannefer, 1992). This might be not so much the dynamic of an underlying socio-structural process working itself out across the life course [but] a consequence of age's ever widening dispersion of competencies and capacities, bringing further fortune to the already fortunate and further misfortune to the unfortunate, with socio-structural factors reflecting no more than another facet of this 'Matthew effect', amplifying the constantly increasing inequalities that age and chronology incurs, outside as well as within the body (Dannefer, 1987: 225).

Relational classes in later life

Unlike gradients, relational classes constitute distinct 'social identities … defined against those who are other/not-me' (Bradley, 2014: 431). They are not infinitely divisible groups of individuals possessing differing amounts of assets, capital and resources, but classes set apart by their different and competing interests and access to power. While many in mainstream sociology have sought to base their approach on such theoretical models of class identity and class interest (for example Goldthorpe, 1997, 2010; Breen, 2005; Wright, 2005), they also seek to underpin their arguments with the analysis of quantitative data and in so doing rely upon classificatory schema based on individuals' membership of occupational groups, placing occupation at the core of both interests and power (Bergman and Joye, 2001; Rose and Harrison, 2007; Lambert and Bihagen, 2014). As a result, the classificatory systems selected by relational class theory leave as many problems as they claim to solve (Marshall et al, 2005). Retirement from the productive economy makes the notion of framing relational classes in terms of identities and interests within the dominant system of production less coherent and sustainable than such framing during working life.

Many different groups end up being designated 'unclassified' or 'unassigned' when relational classes are measured by such occupational schemes, not only the retired population. In their commentary on and critique of relational class schema, Bergman and colleagues have drawn attention to the difficulties associated with empirical research using and validating particular coding schemes (Bergman et al, 2002). They note, for example, that such scales (a) 'have little to say about the majority of the population including the unemployed, home workers and the retired'; (b) that attempts to substitute codes or categories for the majority of 'unclassified' persons lack any substantial validation; (c) that 'work has primacy over the definition of someone's social standing'; (d) 'that while some schemes recognise the multidimensionality of stratification in terms of educational achievement, employment status, authority etc. they tend to be unidimensional in their implicit assumptions about resource allocations'; and (e) that large-scale social change 'in the form, function and centrality of work' render such scales of limited relevance (Bergman and Joye, 2001: 44). Such problems are well known and have been widely discussed (see for example Savage, 2000; Marshall et al, 2005) but it is useful to be reminded of these ongoing debates and the difficulties they pose in using relational class indices in empirical research into class and later life.

Within a Marxist model of relational classes, different assessments have been made of how fractured such class divisions can be. Since capitalism as a dominant economic system is considered by Marxists to create only two fundamental classes, each with mutually antagonistic interests, this division aligns all segments or divisions within society with the interests of either capital (that is, the bourgeoisie) or labour (that is, the proletariat). Other strata occupying positions between these two key classes benefit or fail to benefit from aspects of this division of economic surplus according to the degree to which their social location allies them with workers or capitalists. This zero-sum relation to power is fundamental to the Marxist model and any patterning of inequalities throughout life must necessarily reflect this antagonism. The accumulation of advantages within one class requires the accumulation of disadvantage within the other antagonistic class. Over time this should lead to a polarisation, more than mere inequality; a polarisation that arguably should have crystallised into a more fundamental inequality at the end of working life compared with that at its beginning.

Marxist models assume that society is a class society because of the exploitation of labour power and the appropriation of their product. Irrespective of any further fractioning, society remains divided between the competing interests of capital and of labour, a division that more or less ignores considerations of age or stage of life. Anything that can be won back from the owners of capital in the form of pay rises, better working conditions or more generous pensions is seen as a reappropriation of lost surplus value.

Although few contemporary Marxist class analysts have pursued this issue in any depth, in the 1970s and 1980s state retirement pensions were seen by Marxist thinkers as part of what was termed the social wage, wrestled from the capitalist state as part of welfare amelioration (Walker, 1983; Myles, 1989). Even now, there remains an assumption that class division continues into retirement, with reliance upon or relative independence from state pensions (or social security) being a critical outcome of competing class interests. The neo-liberal agenda to diversify later-life income and expand opportunities for home ownership has undoubtedly muddied the waters of such Marxist class analysis. The diversity in sources of income (and housing wealth), the expanding base of those with an active interest in the fortunes of capital and only a historical interest in past labour have rendered the idea of a growing polarisation in retirement less rather than more likely.

Multiple assets and resources sustain later life; resources dominated as much by patterns of lifecycle redistribution that even out incomes in later life as they are by wage-related pensions. The consequence is that incomes in later life are evened out more than at other points in the adult lifecycle (Causa and Hermansen, 2018: Figure 8; OECD, 2017: 30). Income in retirement itself plays a relatively more attenuated role in determining levels of hardship, perceived financial security, quality of life or stress in retirement than it does in working life (Arber, Fenn and Meadows, 2014; Whelan, Russell and Maître, 2016; Foster, Tomlinson and Walker, 2019). Although there is noteworthy cross-national variation in these redistributive effects, there seems to be 'a converging pattern over the decade, indicating convergence at lower levels of income polarization, inequality, at-risk-of-poverty, and social exclusion in Europe as a whole' (Wang et al, 2015: 23). While there are undoubtedly 'winners' and 'losers' in the patterning of economic fortunes in the twenty-first century, those patterns do not suggest that such patterning is any more evident among the retired population, nor are there any indications that inequality among those in later life is growing.[6]

Nevertheless, despite the evidence, the idea of 'two nations' or 'two worlds' in retirement continues to have purchase (Crystal and Shea, 2002; Crystal, 2018). The 'two worlds' assumption of a growing polarisation between the 'haves' and the 'have nots' has been a constant trope since the nineteenth century, a trope that was first extended to the circumstances of the retired population in the post-war era of nearly universal retirement. It is still propounded at least as often in social gerontology as in the rest of the social sciences, if not more so. The haves – the minority – are thought to retain positions allied with the interests of the owners or controllers of capital (for example, people retiring with large private pensions, substantial property interests and direct or indirect 'rent' in the form of dividends, share options, or actual property rental income). The have nots – the majority – continue to share the interests of those whose life chances and opportunities are and were derived from work and wages, receiving pensions directly or indirectly in the form of deferred wages, or state-mediated transfers, contingent to varying degrees upon what they earned during their working life. This selective disadvantaging is seen as further entrenched by devalued occupational pension schemes that seek to reduce their obligations or fail altogether while the personal pension schemes of the executive and professional classes continue to thrive.

Since the late 1980s, however, household incomes have shown little evidence of growing polarisation. In the last two decades, income polarisation has scarcely changed (Wang, Caminada and Wang, 2017; Wang et al, 2017). Income inequality in the UK is lower among retired households than it is among other types of households, at least for the several decades for which data is available, while retired householders' median income has grown faster throughout the first two decades of the twenty-first century than those of working age households (Cribb, Keiller and Waters, 2018: Figure 2.6; Webber and Mallett, 2018: Figures 2 and 3). Of course, one cannot generalise data about inequality or polarisation in later life to all societies, not even to all ageing societies. Differing patterns of later life income and wealth continue to evolve in different countries and research remains very limited. Nevertheless, income diversity seems more characteristic of the retired population than any growing polarisation between a well-off and an impoverished minority, with little hollowing out of those retired households of the 'middling sort'.

Unlike in working life, where wage income plays a more determining role, the combination of income and wealth from multiple sources in later life places later-life households in a rather different position. As income and wealth become less tightly tied to the wage market economy there is less income inequality and less income polarisation. Intergenerational transfers (taxes on working age people returned as welfare benefits or state pensions related to the cost of living, for example), variable returns from capital (in the form of occupational or private pensions held by pension funds that are invested in contemporary markets – through bonds, stocks and shares and so on), changing patterns of inheritance (of housing assets, in particular) as well as differential systems of deferred wages (in the form of occupational pensions based on defined benefits versus defined contributions) all play a part in restructuring the relationship between capital and class in later life. Retirement also places less constraints on consumption compared with working life, enabling greater discretionary power mediating between household income and expenditure, further reducing the over-determinacy of income in shaping lifestyles and later-life opportunities. As retirement becomes a more 'do-it-yourself' project reflecting the institutionalised individualism of second modernity, the ties that link wage labour, wealth and the conditions of life, assumed by relational class analyses, grow weaker not stronger.[7]

This is a marked change in society. Reading de Beauvoir's impassioned account of the hardships of later life during the 1950s and 1960s, one can well understand why concerns were expressed at that time that two nations were being created in later life (de Beauvoir, 1977) and one can well understand why social gerontologists at that time feared that 'each social class is destined for a specific kind of old age, reflecting the existing class relationships of a given moment in history' (Guillemard, 1975: 217). Equally one can understand why claims continued to be made that 'social class of origin' determined the kind of old age one might suffer (Walker, 1981). Life in old age for the majority was indeed bleak set against the background of 'les trentes glorieuses'. But the insistence that 'the traditional Marxist definition, which analyses the class structure of the capitalist mode of production by basically contrasting the two antagonistic classes – capitalist and proletarian – must be upheld' in later, as in earlier life (Guillemard, 1982: 228) seems no longer suited to the conditions of later life in the twenty-first century. Across Europe, at least, income inequality in retirement has remained at or below that of people of working age, and though evident in the latter decades of the twentieth century, this pattern has clearly continued into the first decades of the twenty-first century (Neugschwender, 2016: 47; ONS, 2017). Despite the warnings of those still predicting a future 'two nations in retirement' (Hudson and Gonyea, 2012; Crystal, 2018) half a century since such woes were realistically enough warned of by Titmuss (1955), such a division seems if anything less rather than more characteristic of later life. This is so whether viewed by measures of inequality, of polarisation or of relative 'disadvantage' (Iacovou, 2018: 346).

Arguably, much of the explanation for the limited role of 'classical' relational class analysis lies in the relative expansion of the domain of consumption over the domain of production in determining where the distinctions and divisions of society are most visibly projected.

This is arguably even more the case in later life, and here the nuances of status may be thought to play more of a role than those attributable to class (Chan and Goldthorpe, 2007). The consequence seems less a remodelled 'consumerist' bifurcation of class into a 'rags versus riches' dichotomy than a blurring of what and where the principal sites and sources of stratification and identity are to be found, compared with the relative uniformity by which those differences are expressed. Unsurprising, then, that the correlation between objective and subjective views of inequality has been steadily declining, that subjective views of inequality coincide less than ever with objective indicators and that few older people now employ 'class' as a source of their identity (Hyde and Jones, 2015: 83; Ricci, 2016: 13; Gimpelson and Treisman, 2018: 48).

Consumption and the articulation of class as distinction

Consumerism – not just the sheer quantity of expenditure, but the articulation of consumer modalities – is influenced by factors other than money. Drawing upon what Bourdieu referred to as 'cultural' and 'symbolic' capital, consumption provides an alternative way of approaching class and the social divisions of later life and in turn offers a different interpretation of these divisions. The interconnection between what could be described as relations based on production and those based on consumerism have been identified by Crompton and others as similar to those between the more economically defined class-as-structure and those more culturally determined fields where class-as-distinction is fashioned (Crompton, 2008: 99). Most closely associated with the cultural study of class is the work of Pierre Bourdieu. His most influential work on the subject examined the practices of 'distinction' in French society of the 1960s (Bourdieu, 1984). Less interested in the underlying economic factors creating class divisions, Bourdieu wanted to explore the 'differing conditions of existence, differing systems of dispositions ... and differing endowments of power or capital' (Brubaker, 1985: 761). While those differing 'conditions of existence' are generally connected to the material conditions in which a person finds themself (Bourdieu and Accardo, 2002), advocates of such a cultural reading of class have since gone further. They argue that neither the subjective experience of class nor the social relations of class are to be read off by an individual's position in a mode of production or by reference to the particular decile, quintile or quartile of the distribution of income and wealth an individual or individual household happens to occupy. For those adopting such a culturalist view, people 'do' class, embodying it less in their labour than through the various practices by which they spend their time. In short, this more culturalist approach to class operates as much in the field of culture, consumption and leisure as it does in the world of work and production. Retirement, in consequence, has become less of a disjunction than it once was.

Although Bourdieu did not write about later life, his theoretical work does provide many useful concepts that can be used to develop an understanding of how class operates in later life. Bourdieu developed ways of understanding how consumption and its associated choices and lifestyle preferences not only involve discriminatory judgements but also create ways of transmitting those classifications to others. As Featherstone has written:

> Particular constellations of taste, consumption practices and lifestyles practices are associated with particular occupations and class fractions, making it possible to map out the universe of taste and lifestyles with its structured oppositions and finely graded distinctions which operate within a particular society at a particular point in history. (Featherstone, 1990: 11)

Bourdieu argued that cultural resources are increasingly important in how processes of inequality work because consumerism creates 'a social world where people are judged by their capacity for consumption, their "standard of living", their life style, as much as by their capacity for production' (Bourdieu, 1984, cited in Bottero, 2015: 22). For Bourdieu, as for other cultural theorists, classes emerge out of the distribution of various forms of capital, such as education, culture, geography, leisure, rather than being read out from one's alignment with the interests of capital or labour (Flemmen, 2013: 238).

This patterning of social differences and inequalities does not 'automatically' lead to the emergence of 'objective' classes as understood in classical sociological accounts. Rather, such classes are only possible social classes or 'classes-on-paper'. Bourdieu's non-reductive approach to class has been ably summarised by Flemmen:

> A society's class structure is to be seen as a multidimensional space, which objectifies the system of relationships between different positions. The basic structure of this space is shaped by the distributions of diverse forms of capital – economic, cultural and social – and the relations of strength that prevail between them. The structure of this space is homologous

> with a related, but distinct, space of life-styles, to the effect that positions in social space roughly correspond to distinct cultural tastes, preferences and outlooks. The structure of social space is continuous; it has no pre-defined sharp breaks or clear internal boundaries. (Flemmen, 2013: 328)

Bourdieu's writings on class, culture, and consumption have given rise to a particular school of thought in British sociology that has redefined the parameters of class analysis along more cultural lines (Skeggs, 1997; Sayer, 2005; Atkinson, 2010). Prominent among this group are sociologists such as Fiona Devine, Mike Savage and Alan Warde (Savage, Warde and Devine, 2005; Warde et al, 2009; Savage, 2015). Three assumptions developed from Bourdieu mark out their work: the accumulation over time of various forms of 'capital'; the interconnection of distinct lifestyles with these capitals; and the creation and maintenance of distinct networks or social spaces that link and are linked by these various forms of capital. As we have seen, such approaches treat consumption less as the simple outcome of class and the processes of class formation than as a constitutive element of its existence and continuation. Occupational or employment status of the individual or household is but one element in establishing an individual's or individual household's class position. Such an approach has been described as both much more contingent and much more dependent on 'class making', with the result that the boundaries of class remain always necessarily open (Flemmen, Jarness and Rosenlund, 2018: 127).

This more open-ended approach to the analysis of class means that people in positions outside the productive processes can still occupy a 'classed space'. Retirement from the productive economy does not exclude such households from the realm of class or from the activities of 'class making' (Higgs and Gilleard, 2006; Higgs and Formosa, 2015). While social class in later life relates to more than just the world of work and its historical legacy, this openness is not unstructured. Different forms of capital and the habitus they each support continue to play key roles in positioning older people in the 'class-making' practices of later life. But those are practices shaped in and of later life – not just the unthinking carry-overs of the past. A reluctance to accept the changed conditions of later life has led many authors to retreat to a rather unsophisticated reductionism that equates older people with unreconstructed class categories or indeed with residualised states of precarity. While it is possible to argue that this follows from Sayer's (2005) position of treating class as a moral category rather than an explicitly analytical one, it fails to address how later life realises its own class practices as well as the contradictions these contain, which are themselves worth studying in their own specificity.

Conclusions

The importance of social class as a source of social division in later life was rendered problematic after universal state pension systems were introduced. Subsequent developments in the nature of labour, in the conditions of retirement, and in the diversification of assets, capital and resources before and in retirement have impacted significantly on the marked polarisation that once characterised old age in the era of industrialisation. Once nearly all (male) workers retired from paid work with a later-life income more or less sufficient to keep them and their household from impoverishment old age began to be transformed. In that transformation lay the seeds for its later diversification. No longer a category of indigence, defined by those rendered impotent through age, old age became a social location capable within its own terms of increasing differentiation – both in its length and breadth. As further structural changes in the economy occurred and intra-generational occupational mobility expanded (Jarvis and Song, 2017) this social space has expanded, giving rise to new social divides and new social distinctions. The cultural models of class associated with the work of Bourdieu provide an alternative approach to class, especially for those 'people who don't have formal jobs including the retired carers and children' (Savage, 2016: 477). This 'capital, assets and resources' perspective appears more readily aligned with the segment of the population currently defined as retired and with all those, retired or not, occupying the social space that is 'later life'. It does so primarily by giving more weight to consumption and culture as constitutive components of class than by reducing old age to the residue of a past life, whether defined by former occupation and position in the productive economy or by the benefits of education received.

Bourdieu's approach permits consideration of the formation of classes as a more open and active process than that associated with the relational approaches to class based on the work of Marx and Weber and what might be called the 'productivist' model. For Bourdieu, class serves less as an over-determining structure than a social space where various class formations can be realised – giving more room for class making and lifestyle fashioning continuing beyond working life into retirement. The realisations of such class making and lifestyle fashioning are certainly not completely open; nor are their origins totally indeterminate. As Bourdieu was at pains to point out, the formation of classes is not arbitrary and material inequalities abound, alongside equivalent inequalities in social and cultural capital. What he recognised, however, was the multiple sources of 'class making' that operate within contemporary society – including those that emerge or evolve prior to as well as during later life. Consumption provides the critical dimension in such structuring. What people (or households) have to spend, how they spend it and why they choose to spend it one way rather than another serve as the principal arenas for the operation of class divisions throughout adult life. For Bourdieu, the practices associated with consumerism and discretionary spending shape much of the lifestyles of both young and old, not just reflecting but realising class.

Gradational models of class as socio-economic status or position dominate research concerned with inequality in health and well-being in later life. While there are technical problems in determining income and statistical problems in modelling its distributional properties, the gradational model offers a more viable alternative than either Marxist or Weberian relational models of class, or indeed Bourdieusian approaches in conducting empirical research into inequalities, especially when conducted with secondary data that may not have been collected with any particular model or theory of class in mind. This is particularly so when examining the associations between class and various other aspects of later life. What such models lack, however, is any explanatory power, in the sense of helping to explain how any particular distribution of advantages arises, how a household's place in that distributional nexus serves to influence life circumstances and lifestyles and where, if anywhere, these social divisions are realised and sustained and how they might determine a subjective sense of class. The choice of measures remains resolutely empirical and the findings unsurprisingly consistent in showing little sign that 'class' or 'socio-economic status' in later life reflects any growing inequality such as might be expected from the cumulative advantage/disadvantage model (Beckett, 2000; Huisman et al, 2003; van Ourti, 2003; House et al, 2005). So long as these findings remain critically dependent upon the rubber rulers measuring class (or more correctly, socio-economic position) one can postulate almost any conclusion from this research base from class 'not mattering' at all, to class mattering less with age, to class mattering more (Schöllgen, Huxhold and Tesch-Römer, 2010).

'Age-as-leveller', 'age as continuity' and 'age as accelerator' remain hotly contested variants in explaining or modelling late-life inequality. While these are active in generating research papers, they throw rather less light on understanding the structuring of late-life chances. While the social space where class or status divisions arise can be mapped in various ways, a substantive 'middle ground' of asset and capital diversity exists in most developed economies, where much of the 'new ageing' is taking place. Despite widespread claims, there is, to our knowledge, no evidence that after the great recession of 2007/8, this social location has been obviously hollowed out or shrunken by processes of post-recession economic polarisation.[8] Quite the opposite: the middle ground remains as extensive as ever. Indeed, it is more evident now than it was 30 or 40 years ago, in the era pre-dating so-called 'neo-liberalism'. It is this middle ground, the middle 80–90 per cent of the retired population of ageing societies where 'third age cultures' are established and elaborated, and where discretionary expenditure – or consumerism – most clearly fashions the distinct (and classed) 'later lifestyles' of the third age. Just because they do not map onto a progressive polarisation of later life (for which there is scant evidence), or obviously derive from the structural expansion of later life income inequality (for which there is equally scant evidence), such developments can no longer be ignored. They reflect critical changes in later life, changes arising from rising levels of income, an expanding array of goods and services and the growing salience of consumerism within and between retirement-age households.

Within the peripheries established by those at the top and bottom of the distribution of income and wealth, there is perhaps less change and fewer signs of the new ageing. Arguably those possessing the most capital, assets and resources are as little engaged with 'third age cultures' as, for very different reasons, are those in the meanest of circumstances. While income poverty might seem to be the defining feature of the bottom '5 per cent' (much as wealth may seem the defining feature of the top 5 per cent) other forms of lack – of family bonds, of health and functional capacity, asset ownership and resourceful neighbourhoods – may serve to ensure their exclusion more surely than a simple lack of money (DeWilde, 2004; DeWilde and Raeymaeckers, 2008). In our own work on the third age, we have paid most attention to the dynamic middle and its classed but classless consumerism. Less attention has been paid to the circumstances and experiences of those at the bottom and at the top. In both cases, 'class making' may be rather less evident – in the former because survivorship is the overarching concern, and in the latter because their interests, power and status are so well underwritten. Here issues of class and inequality merge with those of social exclusion, an exclusion characterising both, if for different reasons. Those at the bottom are involuntarily excluded from the range of goods and services that are otherwise accessed (or ignored) by most retired households. Those at the top are self-excluding, their well-off lives lying some distance from the everyday experiences shaping most older people's lives.

For various reasons, we have chosen not to frame social inclusion as a social division. In the first place, exclusion seems to involve both ends of the agency and structure divide, and in the second place, the term is fundamentally descriptive, not analytic. While describing a social location, it does not offer to understand it. Some well-off older people choose to keep themselves distant from the lifestyles of the majority, while others are unable to access the goods and resources that support the everyday aspects of cultural political and social life. Social exclusion seems a term applicable to both. Even were such ambiguity to be avoided by treating exclusion as applying only to those whose non-access and non-engagement is based upon a lack of assets, competencies and resources, the term offers little more than a set of descriptors. It may delineate inequality in a less narrowly economic manner, but it does not explain it. While there may be other valid reasons for studying social exclusion in later life, as a concept it plays little part in either interpreting or understanding the social divisions and differences that characterise later life in today's ageing societies.

Notes

1 While Wright contrasts 'gradational' with 'relational' models of 'socio-economic status' others use terms like 'attributional' and 'relational' to more or less similar ends (Goldthorpe, 2010).

2 Irrespective of age, most social science textbooks seem to favour gradational over relational models (Lucal, 1994).

3 The framing of socio-economic position or status as a 'gradient' has a long history in medical sociology and public health (see Daric, 1951; Stockwell, 1963).

4 The Gini coefficient measures the extent to which the *distribution* of income across individuals or households deviates from a perfectly equal distribution, taking values from zero (perfect equality in the distribution) to one (perfect inequality). Such indices of inequality are distinguished from measures of income or wealth *polarisation*, which refer to the degree to which income or wealth display a bi-modal distribution, a process sometimes described as the squeezing of the middle (Stiglitz, 2012). It is clear, theoretically and empirically that 'polarization and inequality are quite different phenomena', arising and changing more or less independently of each other (Chakravarty and D'Ambrosio, 2010: 60). For a fuller account of the differences between indices of inequality and of polarisation, see Walks (2013: 10–23).

5 Poterba and colleagues summarise their findings as follows: 'Low levels of wealth accumulation before age 65, rather than gaps in the safety net after 65 or rapid spend-down of accumulated assets, appear to be the primary determinant of low levels of wealth' (Poterba, Venti and Wise, 2018: 2). Noting the limited evidence

of polarisation in Ireland during the period 2004–11, Whelan has observed how 'income class effects account for a smaller proportion of variance [in levels of economic distress] for [the 65+] age group compared to the younger ones … in line with the decreased role of market outcomes at this stage of the life course' arguing that'= '[t]he "crisis" of the petit bourgeoisie is primarily a mid-life course phenomenon' (Whelan, Russell and Maître, 2016: 522). Tabulated data in the recent OECD report on inequality demonstrates how inequality, measured by the Gini coefficient, has hardly shifted among three successive cohorts of 65–69 and 70–74 year olds, despite evident rises in inequality among 40 and 50 year olds (OECD, 2017: Figure 3.18, p 129). Gini coefficient data accessed via Excel data file, Income Gini index by cohort and age group, OECD-wide averages).

6 The Resolution Foundation's most recent report, for example, indicates that poverty rates have fallen consistently among successive cohorts of newly retired UK households (Rahman, 2019: 12) with the consequence that 'while pensioners used to be concentrated at the bottom of the overall household income distribution, they are now roughly equally spread across it' (Rahman, 2019: 11).

7 Some authors argue that changes in home ownership have restructured the basis of class, away from labour and wage differentials, to financialisation and the returns on capital. According to Ray Forrest, these new forms of social (re)stratification vary societally, temporally and spatially and are currently most evident in what can be described as older, mature home ownership societies (Forrest, 2018: 4). As empirical support, see, for example, the emerging disparity between home owners and private renters reported in Japan, the UK and the USA (Forrest and Hirayama, 2018). Such suggestions are further supported by other recent research indicating that intergenerational transfers are more important determinants of household wealth than lifetime income, with capital assets like housing contributing more to wealth differentials than either earnings or employment (Fessler and Schürz, 2018: 542).

8 The idea of a 'squeezed middle' has been put forward by several writers, drawing attention to the growing amount of wealth owned by the top 1 per cent during the course of the this century (Pew Research Center, 2012; Stiglitz, 2012, 2014). Cross-national studies examining changing patterns of income growth across the distributional spectrum, however, have failed to observe any such squeeze. One review of this area concluded: 'neither of the polar "grand narratives" featuring so strongly in current debates – that high or rising inequality consistently boosts nor reduces real income growth for the middle – is true to the variety of experiences actually observed across the rich countries in recent decades' (Thewissen et al, 2015: 25). In the UK, income growth over the period 2000–17 has been greatest amongst the poorest fifth and least amongst the richest fifth of the population (ONS, 2018a). Elsewhere income growth during the period 2000–16 has generally been less at the extremes compared with the middle 80 per cent. In Ireland, for example, those in the middle of the income distribution (the middle 60 per cent) earned 51.6 per cent of the total income in 1994; this had risen to 52.6 per cent by 2004, although it fell back slightly to 52.3 per cent in 2013 (Savage, 2015: Table 2, p 8).

3

Ageing and gender

Sociological writing about class has been criticised for being gender neutral, in the sense that many writers focus on distributions of power, income and advantages that emerged from the workings of the productive economy, a set of institutions and processes that until recently was dominated by men's employment and the profitable returns on capital with scarcely any reference to the role of women (Marshall, 1994). In her seminal paper on women and class analysis, Stanworth (1984) went further and pointed out that this focus missed the importance of both women's employment and the role that gender played in creating the inequalities of power and reward. Retirement too was framed by the termination of men's formal engagement with the labour market. Women's domestic labour was less visible and was assumed to continue in a more or less uninterrupted fashion throughout their adult lives. This is evident in how women's experience of retirement was described as 'twice as much husband and half as much money'.[1] These *lacunae* in relation to the gendered nature of formal and informal work and its aftermath in post-working life began to be addressed by the social sciences in the wake of the second-wave feminism of the 1960s and 1970s (Barker, 2015). Only in the last decades of the twentieth century did the role of gender in shaping difference and structuring inequality come to greater prominence with a greater recognition of the gendered nature of later life (Calasanti and Zajicek, 1993; Garner, 1999; Hooyman, 1999). While the focus of this research was initially based on treating ageing as a woman's issue, attention has since explored men's ageing as a relatively under-researched and under-theorised topic (King and Calasanti, 2013; Thompson and Bennett, 2017).

This chapter examines gender as a structured social division, a source of inequality that runs throughout the adult life course. Its realisation in later life will be explored through four themes. The first addresses the interaction between men's and women's paid work and their subsequent economic position in post-working life. The second examines the role of the household economy in maintaining and modifying older men and women's social capital. The third considers the differential experience of health and well-being among older men and women, while the fourth deals with the different representations of gender in later life in literature, the mass media and the market. Exploring how these structures operate in the social relations of work, home, markets, media and healthcare can provide an understanding of the differences and similarities by which older men and women confront ageing. Such understandings of course leave unresolved the role played by the corporeality of sex and ageing as sources of difference. While wishing neither to deny nor to ignore the significance of the corporeal, the aim here is to focus on the social structuring of social divisions associated with gender.

Social science approaches to gender

Gender replaced sex as the preferred term to describe 'the social organization of the relationship between the sexes', relegating or rejecting in importance 'the biological determinism implicit in the use of such terms as "sex" or "sexual difference"' (Scott, 1986: 1053). The new social movements of the 'long' 1960s saw gender studies emerge as a distinct, cross-disciplinary field of study, attached to and often undifferentiated from 'women's studies'. Reacting against the dominance of a 'male-stream' perspective within the social sciences (Abbott, Tyler and Wallace, 2006) that had implicitly assumed that man and mankind served as a universal descriptor, those associated with second-wave feminism sought to rebalance this perspective by rendering visible the previous invisibility of women in social theory and social science (Marshall, 1994). Within feminist/gender/women's studies, a new emphasis emerged, on sex and sexuality, and the gendered division between productive and reproductive labour (McKinnon, 1982). Implicit in much of this research is the contested concept of patriarchy (Beechey, 1979; Walby, 1990a).

All writers on the subject attest to the multiple meanings associated with the term and the variety of explanatory mechanisms utilised to explain its existence and persistence (Miller, 2017). The term patriarchy is used to characterise the widespread disadvantages and oppression experienced by women. While some writers give this term more explanatory power, by treating patriarchy as both a system of power and a totalising ideology serving men's interests, others use it primarily as a general descriptor of all that advances, supports and upholds the interests of men over women. While some writers emphasise the exercise of power in legitimating men's dominance over women across all spheres of life, Walby (1990a) differentiates between sources of power that are exercised primarily within the 'private patriarchy' of the household and the institutional discrimination that operates within the 'public patriarchy' of markets, states and institutions (Walby, 1990b). Some feminist writing frames these systems of power as operating through explicit norms (or ideologies) that exclude women from positions of influence, while others frame them as operating through the institutional structures of the economy that limit or restrict women's capacity to exercise influence and gain resources, without explicitly and systematically excluding them. Although the utility of the term 'patriarchy' has been critiqued (Pollert, 1996), or used in somewhat inconsistent ways (Miller, 2017), it can be said that it has put a spotlight on thinking about the social divisions of gender as inequality, though arguably less illuminating when applied to difference.

Following the writings of Reinharz (1986) and Walby (1990a), three different approaches can be distinguished in feminist research. These are the cultural liberal, the Marxist/dual systems and the radical/intersectional approaches. These can be usefully extended to understanding gender in later life (Garner, 1999). The Marxist/dual systems approach, for example, has been concerned with the dually structured inequality in systems of both production and reproduction (Vogel, 2013), where the inequalities associated with the capitalist economy are compounded by the inequities of sexism and ageism that limit women's participation and exercise of power in both domains (Reinharz, 1986: 511). That impoverishment occurs more often among older women is considered the result of their living within an economy where well-being is heavily based on the mis/fortunes of lifelong wage labour. This creates a double jeopardy of impoverishment and exclusion that is based upon both age and gender. Captured more strongly by the cultural liberal standpoint is the exclusion or invisibility of older women, their relative absence from positions of authority, power and influence and the pressure for women to cling to the 'safety' of heterosexual marriage and middle age as protection against the indignities and vulnerabilities of becoming a single old woman. The standpoint of 'radical intersectionality' challenges all totalising representations of women's old age. Those arguing from this position point to there not being one but a number of old ages, which are selectively developed within the niches of men and women's able-bodiedness, their ethnicity, race and sexuality (Barrett and Toothman, 2017). While these intersections constitute distinct positions of disadvantage, inequality and oppression, they share an underlying gendered structuring of inequality within the economy, which ensures that women's interests remain, to varying degrees, contingent upon men's.

The Marxist/dual systems approach has focused on inequalities structured around differences in material advantage and power, reflecting in turn differences in men's and women's education, informal or reproductive labour, income and wealth. In contrast, the other two approaches have been equally if not more concerned with the objective devaluation and disadvantaging of older women and the processes fostering their internalisation in women's self-identity. The cultural-liberal perspective, for example, has emphasised the pervasiveness of ageism, the systematic devaluing of women's agedness by those, both men and women, not yet aged. The 'invisibility' of older women is framed less by the greater visibility of older men than by the greater visibility of images of younger women who are judged more valuable in a male-dominated society. Those who take this position argue that: 'the most important deprivations suffered by women as they age originate in the age-related social stereotypes that both restrict them and render them invisible' (Freixas et al, 2012: 48). Consequently, some of the earliest critiques within the women's movement were directed at the ageism of younger women rather than the material inequality characterising many older women's lives (MacDonald and Rich, 1983). As an ageing representative of the feminist movement, Carolyn Heilbrun observed wryly that: 'if younger women did not need me, would they bother with me? I think not' (Heilbrun, 1984, cited by Reinharz, 1986: 509). Carole Garner gave succinct expression to this culturalist perspective when she wrote:

> Much of western society's view of women's worth is associated with a socially defined physical attractiveness which clearly equates youth with beauty and values youthful beauty and the ability to attract men. Therefore, women lose their social value simply by growing old. Men are more likely to be evaluated and rewarded for what they do. As long as they are able to achieve, age alone has little bearing on social value. (Garner, 1999: 4)

Radical intersectional accounts avoid such generalities, drawing attention instead to the multiple positions older men and women occupy, rendering accounts of gender differences contingent upon other intersecting positions and identities, including of course the impact of ageing. Racial studies, for example, tend to focus upon black–white differences in old age, drawing attention to the inequalities within and between racialised divisions affecting older men and women. The intersectional approach seeks to give as much weight to such social divisions within each gender as to the overall differences between the genders considered in isolation from other social positions (Calasanti, 1997; Cronin, 2004; Krekula, 2007). These different perspectives or standpoints need to be set against broad areas of agreement that exist between these models. Dual-system theorists, for example, posit that the impoverishment and marginalisation of older women arises from an interaction between the capitalist economy and a patriarchal culture: some theorists of 'diversity' who adopt a more explicitly intersectional position have also applied a Marxist/dual-systems approach (Calasanti and Zajicek, 1993; Zajicek and Calasanti, 1998).

More recently, the focus upon older women's financial, health and social status has been expanded. Studies of gender and ageing have begun to consider the part played by 'hegemonic masculinity' in structuring later-life experience. The hegemonic masculinity deemed emblematic of men of working age can also compromise and disadvantage older retired men (McDaniel, 2003; Bennett, 2007; Springer and Mouzon, 2011; King and Calasanti, 2013). Widening the lens of gender in ageing studies represents a further questioning (queering) of the assumed and largely un-interrogated position of dominant groups, whether they be men, white, heterosexual or able-bodied people whose status has been the assumed and unexamined norm – the so-called unmarked category by which others are judged, and rendered 'other' (Brekhus, 1998). Interest has moved from purely structural inequalities to ones that concern the identities and subjectivities co-constructed within particular social divisions such as class and gender. The struggles within and between social groups over the exercise of agency have also become important, whether in the realisation and representation of identity, self-expression or experience. This cultural turn is, as argued earlier, part of the processes of social transformation represented by the shift from first to second modernity.

It is propelled by, and in turn propels, the rise of individualisation, of lifestyle consumerism and in fashioning identities that both distinguish between and destabilise the traditional social divisions of society. This shift might be seen as an 'unholy' accommodation with late-stage capitalism, diverting attention from the 'fundamental' classed division of assets, capitals and resources, submerging those issues under the so-called 'ideologies' of ageism, classism, racism and heterosexism. However, it also represents an acknowledgement of a politics and a social science concerned with issues of identity and recognition that previously were ignored or considered subordinate to the dominant ideologies of class and society (Fraser, 1995, 1997; 2000). Acknowledging this shift, we shall try to maintain a focus upon gender as both a structure and a subjectivity, a source of identity as well as a site of inequality, and importantly a point of intersection as well as of division.

Men's and women's socio-economic status in later life

Examining the broader set of circumstances surrounding the social divisions of gender in later life, we begin by considering the impact of labour market participation accrued during men's and women's working lives and the relative advantages and disadvantages this confers upon men and women after reaching retirement age. While originating earlier in adult life, these differences cannot be simply read off as the direct, unmediated consequences of working life. Rather, they need to be thought of within the changing context of later life, of family life and its economic underpinnings. Throughout the 1940s and 1950s, the majority of US citizens aged 65 and over, men and women, were poor, reflecting the minimal savings possible from lives characterised by the relatively low-paid labour during the first half of the twentieth century. Even so, older women's poverty was greater than that of men, since they were even more vulnerable because of a lack of personal savings, limited access to occupational pensions and a relatively high rate of widowhood with minimal survivor benefits (McLanahan, Sørensen and Watson, 1989: 110). In Europe, a similar pattern was evident. Women found themselves in poverty in later life much more often than did men, even though the overall rates of poverty were not then as high as those found in the USA, given the presence of state pensions (Korpi, 1975; Piachaud, 1983). Things changed significantly during the second half of the twentieth century but the gender gap remained. In less industrialised countries such as Greece and Portugal, where poverty rates among the retired and the older agricultural workforce remained high, gendered differences were less marked, set against more widespread hardship (Tsatloglou, 1990). Rising wages, improved pension coverage and more adequate welfare arrangements brought the majority of older people out of poverty, an effect masked by continuing inequalities within the older population. By 1990, state-mediated cash transfers had moved some 80 per cent of elderly US households out of poverty, while similar transfers effected such changes for less than 20 per cent of 'non-elderly' US households (Danziger and Weinberg, 1994: 47).

Significant minorities continued living in poverty and the women in such communities were likely to be more harshly affected. Nearly half (45 per cent) of African American households headed by older women, for example, remained poor, in contrast to less than 5 per cent of US households headed by older white men (Danziger and Weinberg, 1994: 35). Twenty-five years on, poverty rates of US men and women aged over 65 have become broadly similar (8.8 per cent versus 10.2 per cent) and the gap between older white men (4.1 per cent) and older black women (12.1 per cent), though still substantial, has declined. These changes can be roughly periodised. Between 1965 and 1990, there was an overall reduction in old-age poverty but with significant minorities still left in poverty. From 1990 to 2015, the decline in later-life poverty was less marked, but the decline that did occur reduced gender and racial disparities (US Census Bureau, 2015). These changes are illustrated in Figure 3.1.

European data show broadly similar trends. One recent report found that while the overall rate of poverty amongst older people in the OECD European region was no different from that of the general population, consistent gender differences remained, with older women experiencing higher poverty rates – by some 6 per cent on average – compared with older men (Haitz, 2015: 74). Haitz (2015: 74) attributed this discrepancy to earlier 'gender differences in the labour market and life expectancy' rather than to any gender bias located within later life itself, i.e. arising from structured inequalities in a country's pension system. Older women's shorter working lives, more frequent breaks

Figure 3.1: Poverty rates in the USA: working versus retirement age households and gender, 1991–2015

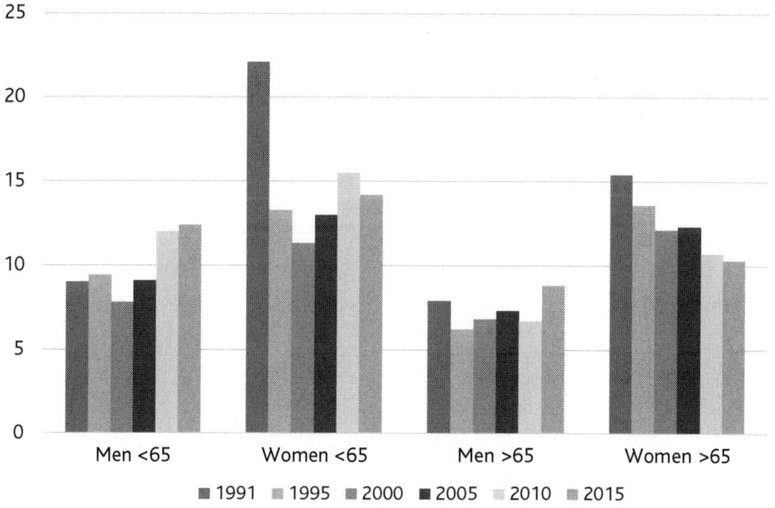

Source: US Census Bureau, 2015.

Table 3.1: Risk of late-life poverty in the European Union: men and women, 2000–15

EU-27	2000	2005	2010	2015
Men, 65+	14.0	15.8	12.9	11.7
Women, 65+	19.0	21.0	18.2	15.9
Excess female poverty in old age	36%	33%	41%	36%

Source: Eurostat, 2016.

in employment associated with childbirth and childrearing resulted overall in less 'capital, assets and resources' in later life although such differences were often masked at the level of household income so long as women were living with a male partner. Since older women lived longer than men, they became poorer because they aged longer alone. While rates of old-age poverty dropped from the 1960s to the 1980s, there has been considerable variability in the extent to which gendered inequalities have declined. Data from 14 European Union countries indicated that, in 1995, state and occupational pension schemes were preventing most older people from falling into poverty. Where overall inequality in later life was higher, however, the gender gap was also higher and even among countries with adequate pensioner incomes, single older women remained the group at highest risk of falling into poverty (Heinrich, 2000: 14).

Despite the 2008 economic recession, the relative economic status of older men and women has continued to improve. The Database for International Comparisons of Economies (DICE) illustrates the decline in later-life poverty among men and women between 1995 and 2015 (DICE, 2016). Most older people's incomes have kept pace and, in some cases have improved, both during and after the economic crisis (Eurostat, 2016). Gender disparities have remained constant, however, with older women still more likely to be living in poverty. This is shown in Table 3.1.

Median incomes in later life show a similar pattern. While older people's incomes have generally risen, older women's median income remains roughly 90 per cent that of older men's. Figure 3.2 illustrates this in terms of net income measured by standardised 'purchasing price standards' or PPS. By using PPPs to convert expenditure 'expressed in national currencies into an artificial common currency, the purchasing power standard (PPS) eliminates the effect of price level differences across countries created by fluctuations in currency exchange rates … [thus] truly reflecting the differences in the purchasing power of … households" (Eurostat, 2014).

Figure 3.2: Men's and women's net income: selected EU countries, 2000–15

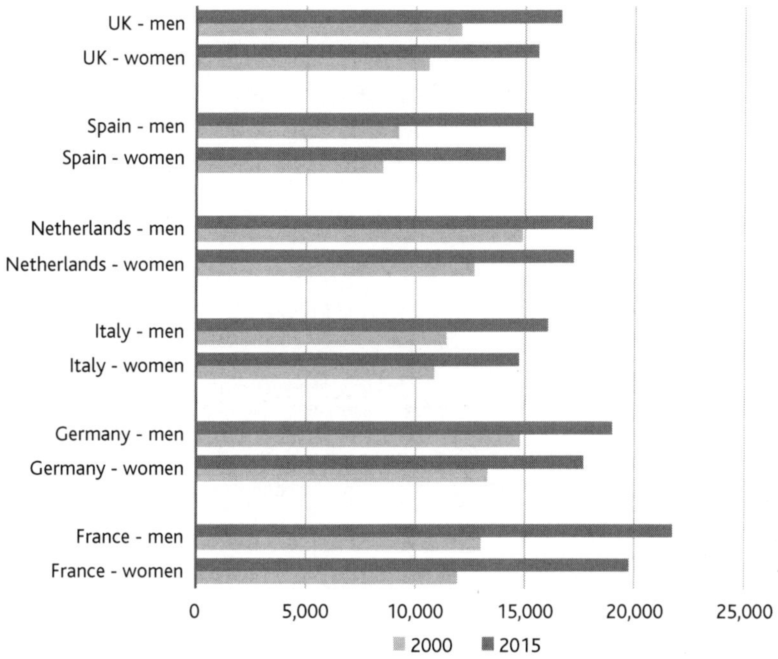

Source: Eurostat, 2016.

Although such figures illustrate differences by gender, they mask other sources of division that intersect with and qualify the impact of gender. If the median income of recently retired men and women (aged 65–74 years) is compared with that of longer retired male and female retirees (aged 75 and over), the gender disparity favouring men appears notably greater. This implicates other factors at work, including potential cohort or generational effects, distance from retirement as well as the changing structure of later-life households. Overall gender differences thus both conceal and reveal the long-term consequences of gendered income inequalities arising from the labour market, alongside changes in benefits and transfers, in later-life household structure and in later-life longevity (Figure 3.3).

When comparing men and women living alone, one has to bear in mind the fact that such 'single-person' households are realised in different ways. The position of the never married and frequently childless older man or woman, whose adult life has been spent in continuous paid employment, differs radically from that of the older widow or widower, most of whose working age life (especially for women) may have been spent outside the labour market. Drawing upon data from

Figure 3.3: Median income of men and women aged 65–74 and 75+ in selected EU countries, 2000–15

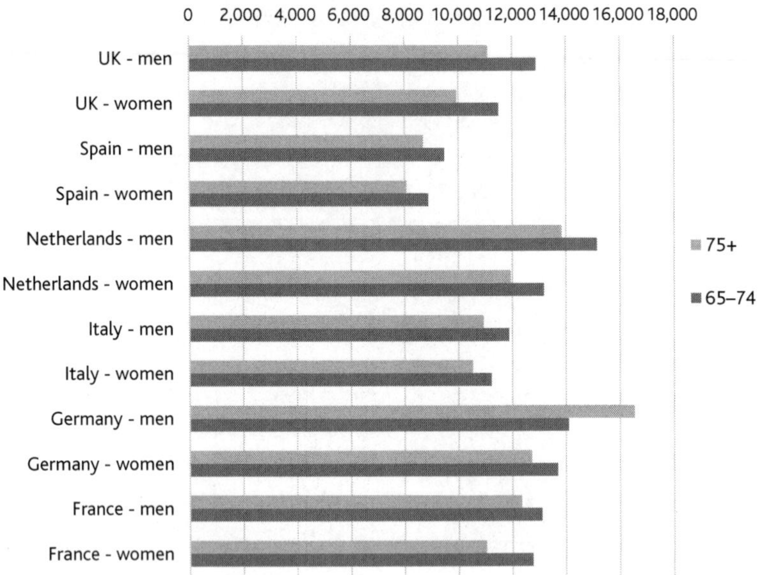

Source: Eurostat, 2016.

several European countries, Möhring (2017) observed how motherhood exercised a significant economic cost on older women's income, one that was greater in countries whose welfare policies were most closely aligned with the 'single male breadwinner' model, compared with countries more closely aligned to dual earners or other 'non-traditional' patterns of employment. Systems for 'compensation for caring', by contrast, made little difference. Given the lack of any 'fatherhood' effects, the more traditional the family household – heterosexual, male breadwinner, with childrearing and household maintenance delegated to women – the more economically unequal older women's status seems to be. While institutional arrangements designed to compensate for such a division of labour do little to shift this effect, Möhring's analysis indicates an apparent 'generation' effect, whereby more recent generations of older women (those born after 1940) faced rather less inequality than do their older compatriots (Möhring, 2017).

Such findings focus upon earnings and pension income. They tend to ignore other, broader considerations of what might be termed 'the overall household economy'. Recent studies examining gender differences in overall consumption, labour and the disparity between work performed and individual expenditure are more revealing. In one cross-national study, for example, Hammer and his colleagues estimated the combined impact of income from paid work and unpaid domestic labour over the life course in eight European countries (Hammer, Prskawetz and Freund, 2015). Up to age 60, they found marked discrepancies in earnings between men and women. This was evident in some countries (such as Austria, Germany and the UK) but not in others (for example, Finland, Hungary and Slovenia). When overall production (including both paid and non-paid domestic labour) was considered, the 'lifecycle surplus' (the gap between the estimated value of all productive activities and the costs of consumption) accrued by men and by women also varied across countries. A greater 'surplus' was accumulated by women (compared to men) in some countries (Slovenia and Spain); an equal surplus in others (Finland and Italy) and a greater surplus accrued by men in yet others (Austria and Germany).

Women occupying 'irregular' positions within the labour market end up in relatively poorer circumstances in later life, in most developed economies. Such positions are not typical however. In another cross-national study examining the net production and consumption of 'household labour' over the adult life course, Vargha and her colleagues observed a net reallocation of resources from women to men (Vargha, Gál and Crosby-Nagy, 2017) and in all 14 countries they studied, women did more for men than vice versa. That was until reaching old age. From that point, the gender gap became less and they found that the overall lifetime adult reallocation of household labour from men to women was relatively small. This was so particularly in comparison to the much more significant reallocation of labour taking place from adults of both genders (though women, most notably) to children (Vargha, Gál and Crosby-Nagy, 2017: 908).

While the gendered allocation of non-paid labour is unequally divided between men (where it is negative) and women (where it is positive), the net beneficiaries of such reallocations tend to be the children, not the partners/spouses. Even when men and women become net beneficiaries, as they do in their old age, their level of benefit remains substantially less than that accrued by their children. The household, in short, is less a site of gendered economic inequality in old age when the household economy (in terms of unpaid labour) becomes more salient, in contradistinction from the labour market where gendered inequality undoubtedly exists. Thus, although income in later life is clearly attached to income in working life, such conclusions must be qualified if 'inequality' is considered more broadly in the context of later life and its domestic economy. As noted in the previous chapter, the links between earned income and the 'deferred' wages of retirement are at best a demi-regularity, varying in extent from country to country.

Those countries with a Bismarkian pension tradition (where pensions are closely related to incomes) show a stronger link than countries with a more universal pension system, whether or not this is supplemented by voluntary, occupation-related, supplementary pension schemes (OECD, 2017: 40).

To summarise, during the last half-century, across both Europe and North America, the majority of retired households have moved out of poverty. This movement has benefited older men and women even as those least likely to have escaped later-life poverty remain households headed by divorced or widowed older women (Dermott and Pantazis, 2014). The reason why this discrepancy has continued arises in large part from the conditions of working life that still favour men, the long-term costs of childcare, the differential age of men and women at marriage and at death and the extent to which a country's welfare policies are still based on a male breadwinner model. While the institutional arrangements governing employment, childcare support and social security contributions can help mitigate some of the gendered inequalities of later life, such effects are relatively limited. The long shadows cast by the different positions that men and women occupy during their working lives, the impact of marriage and childrearing and the different expectancies of life in retirement remain, if less marked than they once were.

Still, such findings require qualification. Gendered inequalities are more prominent among older than younger retired households. They are most evident in single-person households but less between gay and lesbian householders. Over the coming decades, these discrepancies might well decline. As traditional models of family life, the gendered arrangements of work and welfare and the narrowing of the age gap in survival continue to evolve, men's and women's material circumstances in later life may grow less unequal (Chau, Foster and Yu, 2017). The more comprehensively the household economy is evaluated, the less marked the effects of gender itself are in later life. This is not to deny the existence of multiply determined locations of impoverishment in later life, but simply to point out that gender is only ever one factor in determining the inequalities of later life and one that is increasingly contingent.

Families, households and social capital

The complexity and diversity of older men's and women's lives can be represented in ways other than by their income, expenditure and household production. Arguably, the size, strength and stability of a person's social relationships contribute as much to their experience of and engagement with life and society as does their income. Changes in gender relations within retired households seem as often as not to result in older women's social life and relationships being relatively 'richer' than that of older men. The greater the distance from earlier working life and its public patriarchal structure, the less the social capital deriving from the networks of work seems to operate while relations outside of work – with family, friends and neighbours – become more significant (McLaughlin et al, 2010). Measures of 'social capital' provide one way of quantifying these differences. That is what this section focuses on. The term 'social capital' is, however, somewhat loose and the methods of assessing it vary as much as do those for assessing financial status. Although not often used as an index of gendered inequality, relational social capital can serve as an alternative way of assessing gender differences within the world of home, work and the market.

Women's social capital can be seen to be located, through a variety of circumstances, more often in the family, the home and the limited social space afforded by the relations of proximity, while men's social capital typically derives from the public sphere, of citizenship, of markets and of work. However, before examining this standpoint in more detail, we need to consider some of the approaches that have been made to assessing 'social capital' and the thinking lying behind them. Table 3.2 (drawn from Kreuter and Lezin, 2002) provides an outline of the principal understandings of social capital associated with particular social theorists and how it should be assessed.

Table 3.2: Definitions of social capital, adapted from Kreuter and Lezin (2002)

Author	Definition
Bourdieu (1985)	'The aggregate of the actual or potential resources which are linked to possession of a durable network of more or less institutionalized relationships of mutual acquaintance or recognition'
Portes (1995)	'The capacity of individuals to command scarce resources by virtue of their membership in networks, or broader social structures'
Putnam (1996)	'The features of social life – networks, norms, and trust – that enable participants to act together more effectively to pursue shared objectives'
Fukuyama (1999)	'A set of informal values or norms shared among members of a group that permits cooperation among them'
Paxton (1999)	'Social capital is the idea that individuals and groups can gain resources from their connections to one another'

From the outset, although 'social capital and networks are frequently seen as synonymous' (Ryan, 2008: 673), there are important differences between a view of social capital that is based upon collective representations of trust and ease of cooperation and one that is based upon the extent and strength of people's social networks (Paldam, 2000: 630). The former (trust, and so on) is typically represented by 'cultural' indicators of social capital, while the latter (networks) is usually treated as a 'structural' component of capital (for example van Deth, 2003: 83). Paldam (2000) has argued that measures of social capital can be operationalised at the individual level of capital (for example, the amount of trust or degree of cooperation an individual or household feels for others around them), or aggregated at the collective level (that is, the sum of trust or degree of cooperation collectively reported by a neighbourhood, area, region or country). Similar approaches can be made for individual and collective measures of the strength and depth of social networks, although it is generally much easier to employ the latter as measures to assess the relative richness of men's and women's social capital compared with the former.

Alternative approaches assessing the structural aspects of social capital pre-date the term, drawing upon older concepts such as 'social cohesion', 'social integration' or, more narrowly, 'social support'. Some have argued that this supplanting of the older terms by newer ones is itself a reflection of a subtle gender bias, with 'social capital' treated more as men's business while earlier terms like 'social cohesion' were more often confined to the domestic realm of home, family and neighbourhood. Fine, for example, has argued that male social capital is regarded pre-eminently as a market or civic quality, while female social capital is restricted to family and the domestic sphere (Fine, 2010: 72). He cites a point made earlier by Molyneux (2002) that the fascination with the concept of social capital that has become evident across the social sciences has had the effect of pushing to the background concepts of social cohesion and integration that arguably gave more centrality to the role of women and the domestic and familial spheres. The 'creation' of social capital within various facets of working life seems more productively carried out, for example, by men than by women, whether through instrumental or emotional mechanisms, unlike the generation of social capital in the form of social cohesion (van Emmerick, 2006).

Social capital has also been divided into what Putnam called bonding and bridging social capital, the former being the social networks based upon affinity and shared identity – what he calls 'a kind of sociological superglue' – the latter on networks that bridge different social categories, groups and identities, encompassing 'people across diverse social cleavages' (Putnam, 2000: 22–3). This distinction seems inherently gendered. Men's 'bridging social capital', for example, can be seen as forming through work and the various associations and relations connected with work. Such bridging capital seems to dominate that derived from women's more limited familial and neighbourhood networks and their focus upon social bonding by keeping families, friends and neighbours together (Lin, 2000). Removal (through retirement, illness or unemployment) from the domain of work, however, might be thought to deplete men's social capital, rendering them dependent upon the 'limited' social networks established and maintained by their wives. In effect, men upon retirement have to give up their more extensive bridging capital in exchange for the bonding capital developed maintained and controlled, more often than not, by women.

Research shows that retirement significantly depletes older men's networks but enhances those of older women (Cornwell, 2011a: 614). For single older men, the impact is even greater as there is no partner to supply an alternative set of relationships (del Bono et al, 2007). Since women are more likely than men to maintain contact with their children and siblings, living alone, though more common among women, has less effect on constraining their family contacts and hence their stock of social capital (Cornwell, 2011a). In short, the extent to which society disadvantages women in working life may be reversed in retirement because men's gendered advantage derives much of its status and power from the relationships of work. While some aspects of gendered inequality may be maintained through the cultural habitus of 'hegemonic masculinity' derived from work, such habitus are less actively realised in retirement, as they are no longer reinforced by the hierarchies of work or the previously dominant practices of corporeal vitality.

Removed from these domains, older men fall back upon the once devalued social capital within the domestic sphere, a sphere where male privilege has perhaps a more limited purchase, especially in later life. As men find themselves reliant on the social capital built and sustained by their wives, an inversion in the ordering and influence of male versus female social capital seems to take place. Evidence in support of this comes from studies examining men's and women's social networks before and after retirement (Cornwell, 2011b; McLaughlin et al, 2010; Shaw et al, 2007). At the same time, it begs the question whether retirement in the twenty-first century is still quite so patterned. Has women's greater amount of paid work experience and men's increased engagement with the domestic made such a crossover of capitals less evident? Further, are there differences among different social groups, in different ethnic communities and for same-sex compared with opposite-sex households?

In our previous work, we suggested that the cultures of the third age are characterised by, among other features, a shift in the focus of later-life social relationships, as relations with partners and peers – horizontal, intra-generational relationships – grow in importance, to rival the intergenerational relationships that traditionally had dominated later life (Gilleard and Higgs, 2005: Table 5.1, p 99). A meta-analysis of changes in the overall size of social networks found that while earlier studies saw older adults experienced a decreasing size of such networks compared with younger working age adults, more recent studies less often found such age-associated declines (Wrzus et al, 2013: 14).

Although few studies have focused directly upon such generational changes, there is some evidence of changing patterns of inter- and intra-generational relationships. In one study, Stevens and van Tilburg found that younger cohorts were

> more strongly affected by societal changes that have contributed to developing friendship, specifically same-sex and cross-sex friendship, more often and maintaining friendship longer than did older cohorts ... [and] that women have benefited from societal change more strongly than men in terms of friendship development and maintenance in later life. (Stevens and van Tilburg, 2011: 39)

As friendships take on greater significance in the formation of social capital during working lives, and as they are more often sustained into at least early old age (the sixties and seventies), the significance of social capital derived from intergenerational, intra-familial relationships created and maintained within the domestic sphere may decline. At the same time, it can be argued that women have also extended their intra-generational relationships by their greater participation in the workplace, establishing wider social networks, while losing few if any of their more traditional links with kith and kin (Norris and Inglehart, 2005).

Gender differences in social capital, whether viewed as the strength and extent of bonding and bridging social networks or in terms of social integration, trust and shared understanding, do seem to shift after retirement. The bridging capital conferred on men by work tends to decline with age and retirement, while the social bonding capital cultivated by women, and which is connected to relations with family, friends and neighbours, is more often retained. The theory of mutual social disengagement associated with Elaine Cumming can be reinterpreted as an over-generalisation of men's ageing, based on these observations (Cumming and Henry, 1961). Longitudinal studies of men's and women's social ties before and after reaching 'retirement age' demonstrate systematic differences, in terms of overall network size as well as in the pattern of 'bridging' and 'bonding' social capital (Addis and Joxhe, 2017). Studies that have ignored or sidelined gender have consequently produced conflicting patterns of longitudinal change. Those that have focused upon gender, however, show more consistent evidence that (a) older women maintain larger overall networks (McLaughlin et al, 2010); that (b) older women maintain more social bonding capital (Shaw et al, 2007); and that (c) women develop more bridging social capital by having more divergent connections within their networks compared with older men (Cornwell, 2011b).

With the rise of new social networks associated with internet-based social media, this field of investigation indicates new developments and new ways of assessing social capital within increasingly networked societies. As older people become more familiarised with the internet and social media applications, new as well as old relationships may become more common. This development is creating new possibilities for both new forms of community and new arenas for social divisions. No longer a product of a digital divide based primarily upon access, these divisions can be seen arising from differential patterns of connectivity, differing degrees of extensiveness in use and different styles of media socialisation between and within older men and women. From such developments one can envisage such divisions as that between the networked and the non-networked, and between the digitally included and the non-included. Such effects may lead to men's and women's later lives being more diversely distinguished by the changing outlines of social capital, formed not by the division of work and home, employment and retirement but by the penetration of digital connectivity as it continues through the twenty-first century (Nef et al, 2013).

Men's and women's health and well-being in later life

Income, wealth, family and social networks constitute some of the more important assets, capital and resources that differentiate the circumstances, lifestyles, opportunities and obstacles facing men and women in later life. Other assets, capital and resources contribute to

Figure 3.4a Men's and women's life expectancy at age 60, 1950–2015: high-income countries

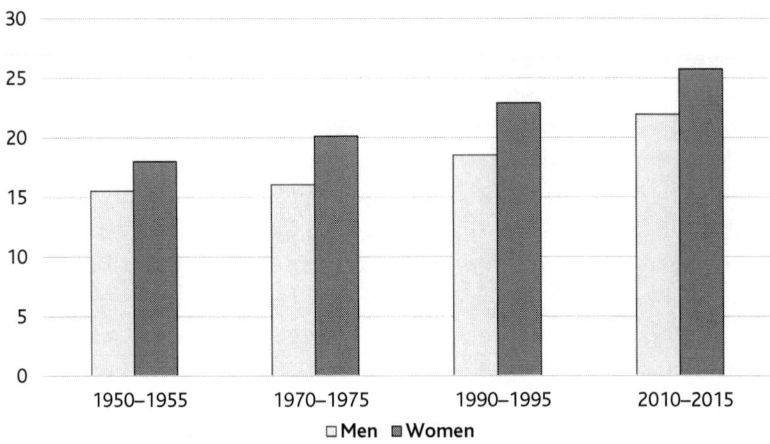

Figure 3.4b Men's and women's life expectancy at age 60, 1950–2015: low-income countries

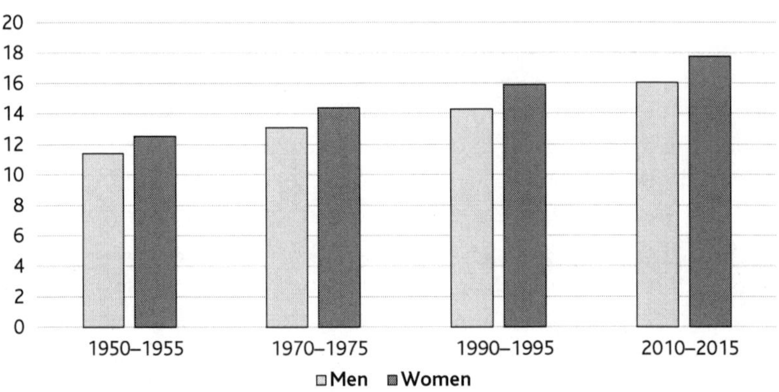

Source: DeSA (2018). *World Population Prospects: The 2017 revision*. UN Publications.

gender differences, not least the sheer quantity and quality of later life that men and women experience. In both rich and poor societies, inequalities exist in the sheer length of men's and women's lives, and the state of health in which those longer lives are lived (see Figures 3.4a and b).

In over half a century, little has changed. Both men and women are living longer, but men's later lives remain shorter. They are, however, spent in relatively better health. This has been termed 'the gender paradox' (Cooper et al, 2011; Pongiglione, De Stavola and Ploubidis, 2015). Observed consistently in many settings and societies, it forms a key feature in much of the health-related literature on gender and ageing (Newman and Brach, 2001). Despite improvements in the self-reported health status of women, the same pattern of gender disparities persists, with men experiencing greater mortality and women greater morbidity (Cummings and Jackson, 2008). Changes over time seem if anything to be accentuating the difference. One recent US study, for example, found that 'the percentage of years expected to be lived without disability' had increased for older men – from 78 per cent in 1982 to 81 per cent in 2011 – but has remained unchanged at 70 per cent for older women (Freedman et al, 2016: 1082). A recent German study observed opposing trends, however, with women's health in later life improving more than men's (Buttery et al, 2016).

Attempts to account for this paradox have varied. While most social scientists have focused upon socio-economic explanations in accounting for older women's poorer health, such explanations are rarely extended to account for women's greater longevity. The potential social antecedents of gender differences in mortality have not been as fully explored as attempts to explain older women's poorer health status. Longevity differences have mostly centred upon the corporeal, with explanations of men's and women's mortality differential focusing upon biological differences in the type and prevalence of diseases affecting men and women. Such research suggests that 'women have higher prevalence of non-fatal but disabling diseases [while] men have higher prevalence of fatal diseases and chronic diseases strongly related to mortality' (Pongiglione, De Stavola and Ploubidis, 2015: 7). The incidence of cancer, coronary heart disease, diabetes and chronic kidney disease is greater among older men, while the incidence of arthritis, depression and osteoporosis is higher in women (St Sauvier et al, 2015: 4). While the latter are seriously disabling conditions, the former are more likely causes of death (with shorter periods of disability). This effect is amplified by the greater co-existence of those former conditions with other forms of morbidity among older men (Chamberlain et al, 2015). While there seem to be few gender differences in onset, multi-morbidity seems to be more common among older women. This suggests that the gender paradox arises from the differential patterning of disease (and hence of survival rates) rather than differences in the rate of onset of disability and morbidity, differences which are difficult to explain in terms of socially structured antecedents (Rocca et al, 2015).

Turning from the epidemiology of specific diseases to more generalised measures of self-reported health, here there is more evidence of social influences. Arber and Cooper (1999), for example, have argued that after controlling for differences in age, disability and socio-economic status, older women report better health compared to men. They propose a different paradox: given their greater functional limitations and poorer economic position, why is it that women report better health than men do? (Arber and Cooper, 1999: 74). Perhaps, they suggest, older women are more resilient or possess more supportive social networks; perhaps they have learned earlier in life to treat their impairments and limitations as less important in assessing their own health; or perhaps they have invested less in (or relied less on) the physicality of their bodies. Such mediation or subjective 'discounting' of illness might even contribute to women's greater longevity. Whatever the mechanisms by which such discounting takes place, gender differences in subjective judgements of health remain and are clearly important, both personally and socially. There is considerable evidence, for example, that health contributes more to overall later-life well-being than all other factors (Halleröd, 2015: 580). Disability is a significant factor in social exclusion and the costs of long-term illness have considerable material consequences, even when nationally funded healthcare systems minimise the direct costs of treatment. Despite their significance, gender differences in the nature and extent of health inequalities in later life remain an under-researched and under-theorised topic.[2] As Rieker and Bird have noted:

> Sociological theory offers considerable insight into women's greater morbidity and the gendered patterns of psychological disorders. But for the most part, sociologists and other social scientists have not fully examined the diverse antecedents of gender differences in mortality or the types and prevalence of diseases/ (Rieker and Bird, 2005: 43)

Cross-sectional and longitudinal studies show greater heterogeneity in health status with increasing age (Deaton and Paxton, 1998; van Kippersluis et al, 2009: 824). This heterogeneity, however, seems less evident among older women than among older men (Santoni et al, 2017). While this might suggest that ill health exercises a relatively greater influence in creating differences (inequalities) among older men than it does among older women, this pattern of influence seems to be reversed in a so-called 'demographic crossover' when, in extreme old age, it is men rather than women who demonstrate less heterogeneity in their health status (Franceschi et al, 2000; Terry et al, 2008). Perhaps selective survivor effects are more evident among older men than they are among older women, although such explanations are most often framed in terms of differential levels of physiological or psychological 'resilience' rather than in terms of socially structured inequalities.

Because of the differential survival of older men and women, much of the infirmity and morbidity associated with later life has been represented through gendered imagery. Infirm old women have dominated the social imaginary of the fourth age throughout history (Pickard, 2016; Gilleard and Higgs, 2018). Older people live much of their later life without serious disability. Still, at the extremities of age, illness and impairment become a not uncommon fate. The gendered paradox of health and mortality marks women not men as the representatives of 'deep' or 'real' old age. In contrast with third-age lifestyles, where gender operates as a source of distinction as much as of disadvantage (Gilleard and Higgs, 2013), and in terms of 'successful ageing', which also show few gender inequalities (Depp and Jeste, 2006; McLaughlin et al, 2010), the fourth age seems drenched by such gendered imaginaries. In terms of representational meaning, such gendered differences colour ageing. A good part of that colouring lies in the representation of ill health and the meanings age and health have for older men and women (Russell, 2010: 187). The different social representations and personal meanings of age and agedness among men and women extend beyond issues of health and illness. Hence, it is to the issue of gendered representations of age in general that we next turn.

Gendered representations of age

Studies of gendered representations of age and agedness have expanded as part of the broader cultural turn evident in the social sciences (Twigg and Martin, 2015). This final section explores how age is represented through gender, and how age inflects representations of gender in contemporary life. The discussion concentrates upon the way gender contributes to the articulation of the cultures of the third age; through discourse, imagery and performance as well as how it is insinuated within the social imaginary of the fourth age. In doing this, we are turning from a more or less exclusive focus on the gendered structuring of social and material advantage and disadvantage to a concern with the representations of gender and ageing and how gender shapes later lifestyles. Gender provides not just a line of fracture or source of inequality in later life. It also serves as a source of distinction, one that while socially structured is also socially integrated into the broader culture and institutions of society. Gender, in short, is both part of and actively contributes to the reconstruction of ageing and later life taking place in our contemporary world.

This perspective is not new. Over two decades ago, Diane Gibson drew attention to the need to balance what she described as a 'phallocentric' focus upon older women as structurally disadvantaged and unequally aged, to recognise that there are many aspects of being an older woman that can and should be sources of celebration and strength (Gibson, 1996: 435). It is by no means clear how differences in the meaning of age map onto existing inequalities, or how exactly they contribute to Gibson's notion of the phallocentric representation of the problems of old women. While many descriptive accounts of the cultural and social representations of age and ageing have been published, their linkage with social divisions and inequalities are surprisingly neglected. There are reports on differences, for example, in older men and women's sense of anxiety about or fear of old age (Yan et al, 2011; Barrett and Toothman, 2017), their degree of comfort or discomfort with their bodily appearance and function (de Souto-Barreto, Ferrandez and Guihard-Costa, 2011) and in their relative sense of 'invisibility' (Meagher, 2014). In general, what differences there are suggest that older men are somewhat less negative and a little less fearful about their own ageing but also perhaps more 'defensive'. The question remains of how such representational differences should be understood and how their impact should be assessed. Should it be framed, for example, in terms of representational injustice? Or as variations in the relative cultural value of age possessed by older men and women (or its symbolic capital – see Bourdieu 1985)? Or simply as the degree of negative attitudes expressed by men and women toward their own and/or others' ageing (as measures of relative ageism – see Palmore, 2001)?

There exists clear evidence that negative stereotypes about old age can adversely affect the health and well-being of older people (Dionogi, 2015; Levy, 2003). We also know that subjective judgements of poor health exercise as powerful an effect on future health and longevity as do objective indicators (Idler and Benyamini, 1997). Yet we know little about the relative salience of gender in mediating these and other related effects (de Souto-Barreto et al, 2011: 509). Lacking any consistent analytical frame, global judgements continue to be made about the devaluing of older women and their 'disgusting bodies'; a 'disgust' it is claimed, that 'has led to a culture of inequality based on ageist and sexist attitudes to older women … that not only renders the older female invisible but also makes her the subject of detrimental cultural and social values' (Hodgson, 2018: 65). However, is this statement more opinion than analysis? The unmarking of gender in age and gender studies can too easily lead to treating the effects of 'ageism' as part of the effects of 'sexism' and, by implication, the assumption that 'sexism' itself contributes to 'ageism'. But just as arguments concerning structural inequalities in the material circumstances of men and women in later life fail to capture the intersectional contingencies of gender differences, so too can issues of voice and visibility be blind to such considerations.

Nancy Fraser (1995, 2000) has drawn attention to the distinction between divisions based upon distributional inequalities (such as those associated with social class) and those based upon differences in cultural and social 'visibility'. While not seeking to elevate one over the other, she sought to recognise how both contribute to defining the social location of a particular social group. The distinction for both domains is blurred and is linked to the overall structure of society and social relations (Fraser, 1997). Lois McNay raised a related issue when she distinguished between gender treated 'as a question of position within language' and gender treated primarily as 'a lived social relation' (McNay, 2004: 185). While gender serves both registers, neither representational value nor material assets exist in isolation from each other: talk, text and the material conditions of existence are connected. How gender is portrayed is connected to how gender relations are organised and realised; and these in turn inflect both what is imagined and what is said about such relations. However, without reference to the relational nature of gender (that is, the distinct positions occupied by men and women) writing about women's ageing can imply a gendered difference in ageing that masks its commonalities. For example, Richards, Warren and Gott (2014: 67) have noted how 'the growth in consumer culture has led to the dominance of images which sell older people a glamorous, ageless lifestyle', which they treat as a kind of inverted ageism reacting against the more pitiable or pathetic imagery of the past. While what they and others note is the extent to which 'positive' imagery is rendered conditional upon the kind of resources needed to fully enjoy 'third age' lifestyles, they fail to acknowledge how such positions cut across gender, rendering men and women equally susceptible to the demand to be forever fit, functional and fanciable.

What is perhaps more notable than matters of mass marketing is the differential 'marking' of age narratives that are made by the two genders. Several studies, for example, have noted a superficial 'immunity' to the impact of ageism, as reported by older men (Hurd Clarke and Korechenko, 2016; Ojala, Pietilä and Nikander, 2016). Hurd Clarke has suggested that while men experience their ageing body 'as a diminished or failing resource in terms of their declining abilities to be autonomous, strong leaders, women express dismay over their changing appearances as well as their decreased abilities to perform femininity' (Hurd Clarke, 2019: 41). There is some empirical support for such differences. One recent Australian study, for example, observed that older men's experience of ageism was influenced by whether or not they looked fit or seemed able to perform, while older women's perceptions of ageism were framed much more by what they called 'lookism' – that is, negative judgements of their attractiveness (McGann et al, 2016). Whether this adds up to male privilege or simply men's unwillingness to acknowledge and address the adverse effects of being viewed as old is an open question. Structures and subjectivities can be easily confounded.

Conclusions

This chapter began with a consideration of the salience of gender as a source of social difference and inequality in later life. Although gender in later life is more than the sum of cumulative advantages and disadvantages acquired by men and women during their adult lives, the shadow of past inequalities between men and women remains a presence in later life. These historical inequalities have rendered the lives and circumstances, assets and experiences of older women different from and, at least in some ways, harsher and more limited than those of older men. Outside the framework of the heterosexual pensioner couple, where arguably the divisions of working life become attenuated, older widowed or single women remain materially less well off, with lower incomes and less wealth compared with the position of single older men. Within the context of the domestic economy and the shared household, such structural inequalities are much less evident, hidden as it are by the broader effects established by the totality of such household assets, capital and resources. In later life, perhaps more than in earlier adult life, the heterosexual couple is advantaged. Examined through the framework of social capital, on the other hand, older women are in general better off than older men, even in the case of older men and women living alone. Even though intra-generational relations have come to complement and in some cases furnish alternative sources of social capital in later life from those based on kinship and intergenerational support, retirement still means that older men more often suffer a greater diminishment of their social capital than do older women and arguably it is women rather than men who create and capitalise upon these relatively new forms of relations replacing or competing with the social capital of kith and kin.

The importance of what has been termed 'the patriarchy' seems to become rather less salient after retirement. The habitus of power once gifted men during their working lives seems less pervasive. This affects the gendered relationships of later life. Studies of the relative contribution of retired men and retired women to maintaining the household economy suggest that there is a growing partnership in later life that makes retirement less the 'tragedy' that it once was, for men (Townsend, 1964). While it has often been stated that marriage benefits older men more than it does older women, this gendered perspective of care and support has arguably also become less critical, particularly in the early years after retirement, as more men and women enjoy equal if different opportunities for participating in third-age cultures. While this may not be true for the poorest pensioner households, there is little evidence that gendered differences are more notable or more significant among them, even if responses to such poverty differ between men and women (Dermott and Pantazis, 2016: 31).

Living well in later life is not the prerogative of one gender. In negotiating later life, in successfully managing age and realising and sustaining effective later lifestyles men and women share much in common, despite their different pathways.. At the same time, gender differences have consequences not simply for the maintenance of social distinction but for maintaining certain inequalities, in material resources, the richness or poverty of a person's social networks, in the experience of disability and morbidity and in the expectations and representations of age. Rather than treat these similarities and differences as essentially gendered, we would argue that many are contingent upon and realised within other contexts, including those framed by class, cohort, ethnicity and sexuality. All such divisions within later life arguably add to, rather than overshadow, the discourses and practices that constitute the common cultural fields of the third age. Equally they also deepen the indignities and suffering that exists in all lives lived under the shadows of the common imaginary of a fourth age. In the transition to second modernity, however, while many of those historical differences remain, some at least of their inequalities show signs of lessening.

Gender, moreover, is more than a division and inequality. Older men and women continue to represent themselves as gendered beings at every stage of adult life and resist their neutralisation as sexless, ungendered old people. While age may appear an equaliser, or even a neutraliser of gendered distinctions, older men and women continue to 'perform gender'.[3] This is nowhere more evident than in the lifestyles realised within the cultures of the third age. Performances of gender are achieved in a variety of ways, some through the framework of traditional masculinities and femininities, others through personal relationships realised in and through family and kinship and, increasingly, through friendships and new later-life partnerships. Many familial roles preserve gender identity while protecting older people from experiencing the alienation of age and the consequences of their declining public capital. Aside from their material inequalities, gendered differences in later life contribute positively to the variety of ways of performing and representing later life. The performance of gender can itself be seen as a way of resisting the neutralisation of identity and self that the fourth-age imaginary so often threatens. The various realisations and representations of masculinity and femininity in later life can be as much affirmative as oppressive, perhaps more so than in earlier adult life, where the pressure to accentuate difference between and emphasise the commonality within gender may be much greater.

That is not to deny the impact of inequalities between older men and women, or to ignore the very real differences in the way that age confronts and challenges men and women. These different confrontations that men and women experience, however, need to be placed within the context of other differences and divisions such as those associated with variation in ethnicity, health, sexuality and wealth. Subsequent chapters consider the role these other divisions play in generating, mitigating and maintaining some of those inequalities as well as in shaping the experience of later life itself. For now, we would emphasise that gender should not be deemed merely another structure doubling or tripling the jeopardies of age. It is more than that, both in its subjectivity and its structuring of the social locations of later life. Gender contributes to later life's inequalities and injustices, but it also and equally adds to its complexity, richness and diversity.

Notes

1 See, for a recent reiteration of this phrase, Sylvy Sylva's 2003 paperback, *Retirement is Twice as Much Husband on Half as Much Money*.

2 The difference between *health inequalities* and *health inequities* is an important one, but often ignored. While the former can be conceived of as functioning like indices of economic inequality – that is, as measures of the variance in the distribution of health – the latter refers more specifically to the unequal distribution of health that can be attributed to underlying socio-economic inequalities. If corrected or redistributed, the latter would result in a lessening of the health inequalities themselves (see Kawachi, Subramanian and Almeida-Filo, 2002: 647). These issues are further elaborated in Chapter 5 on disability and able-bodiedness.

[3] The idea that biological ageing neutralises sex or gender as a materially visible distinction has long been advanced. See, for example, the nineteenth century discussions of age as the neutering of sexual difference, in van Konratowitz (1998: 147–9). It is still evident, as the following comment shows: 'There are two times in human life when it's difficult to distinguish between males and females … when children are small and when adults are elderly' (Haselton, 2018: 200).

4

Ethnicity, race and migration in later life

Ethnicity and race have become increasingly salient categories of social division for both policy makers and researchers in contemporary society (Bottero, 2004). As regards their social location in later life, however, they remain more or less marginal to the immediate issues they present to social integration and social conflict in the wider society (Torres, 2019a). The presence of ethnic minorities is itself seen through the lens of migration, whether as the consequence of historical processes of de-colonisation or of contemporary global unrest and upheaval. This is so particularly in the European context, while in North America ethnicity and race have rather different meanings and points of reference. In contrast to ethnicity which, at least until recently, has been refracted through migration and the self-narrative of its modern emergence, in the USA race is more surely located as a pervasive divide cutting through society. Their exclusion from full participation in the economy, which continued, albeit in more diluted form, well into the twentieth century, has placed African Americans as a group apart, distinct from the position of other ethnic groups whose members have often been seen as those who 'built' society. These divergent histories are crucial in trying to understand the nature of ethnic and racial divides as well as the accompanying experiences within Europe and America and their various realisations in later life.[1] While they bring new meanings and interpretations to the concerns of old age, they do so in different ways, and through different historical trajectories in each of the two continents. In this sense, the divisions of race and ethnicity are themselves mediated by and intersect with the circumstances and experiences of age and agedness.

Before discussing the social divisions of ethnicity and race in relation to their specific realisations in later life, we should first consider what is being described by these linked but separable terms. Discussing how the modern state has sought to establish an appropriate organisation of ethnicity, race and migration, Ludi Simpson has made the following observation:

> In the UK, the motivation for government measurement of 'ethnic group' can be traced to aims of anti-discrimination,

> multi-culturalism, controlling immigration, and social cohesion, each of which demands different categories and analyses. The leading instruments of government measurement, the Census and national surveys, have not developed categories of 'ethnic group' in a refined instrument representing a single theory, but contain the conceptual confusion of conflicting theories, and will continue to do so. (Simpson, 2002)

Definitions of ethnicity and race, in short, are inseparable from the intentions of those in positions of power who apply these terms. This includes not just the state, but disciplines such as medicine, statistics, and the social and behavioural sciences that seek to analyse and examine difference (often in support of political goals). To this should be added the various forms of mass media that echo, rebrand and select the various representations of ethnicity and race with which to engage, inform and entertain the public (Kohn 1995; Malik 1996).

In so far as this book is part of that tradition, of viewing ethnicity and race as sources of difference, division, identity and inequality, we cannot separate ourselves from the definitional practices embedded within these disciplines. Terminological practices are inherently problematic but Cokley has perhaps captured something of what we intend by describing race and ethnicity as related but different categories of division when he writes:

> Ethnicity refers to a characterization of a group of people who see themselves and are seen by others as having a common ancestry, shared history, shared traditions, and shared cultural traits such as language, beliefs, values, music, dress, and food. Definitions of ethnicity are usually broad, intermediate, or narrow in scope … Broad definitions of ethnicity involve shared biophysical traits as well as cultural characteristics. When the definition of ethnicity includes biophysical traits, ethnicity is essentially being used interchangeably with race … Race refers to a characterization of a group of people believed to share physical characteristics such as skin color, facial features, and other hereditary traits. (Cokley, 2007: 224)

When focusing upon 'racialised' divisions, that is those racial identities that are ascribed to groups by others irrespective of self-identity (Winant, 1986), we mainly refer to US society where most research on race and ageing has been conducted. Primary reference is made to Europe, and especially Britain, when concentrating upon age and ethnicity, since ethnicity and ethnic classifications have played a larger role in framing social divisions in Europe. This split focus seems justifiable because the systems of categorisation in North America and in Europe selectively emphasise one or the other of these statuses with more work being performed around race within American society compared with Europe. As regards ethnicity, the focus is more upon the UK, arguably because more research work has been performed here compared with other European countries, not least because data on ethnicity is not always collected in other European countries.

Migration is a composite process, implicated in, but not necessarily dominated by, issues of race and ethnicity (Duvell and Jordan, 2003). This chapter draws upon the literature on migration only as far as it is relevant to ethnicised or racialised divisions. This means ignoring other aspects of migration relevant to ageing, including rural to urban and reverse migration and 'retirement migration' such as that from northern to southern states in the USA or from northern to southern Europe, neither of which map so clearly onto concomitant ethnic and/or racialised divides (Warnes and Williams, 2006). Because most of the migration that has taken place in the post-war, post-imperial period has rendered significant the dimension of ethnicity to the status of immigrants, juxtaposing communities and cultures rather than, as in the past, fashioning and fusing new forms of community, we focus upon it selectively through ethnicity and its implicit othering. At the same time, we are aware of the significance of other forms of migration in shaping later life, both in Europe and in North America.

Race, ethnicity and systems of categorisation

The national framing of ethnicity and race plays a large part in the organisation of social difference and its related divisions. In the United States, for example, race has been a constant source of differentiation since the country was established (Strmic-Pawl, Jackson and Garner, 2018). In Europe, by contrast, race has rarely been explicitly deployed in official categorisation, and even ethnicity has been applied inconsistently (Simon, Piché and Gagnon, 2015; Chin, 2017). In the United Kingdom, for example, various attempts were made in the post-war period to formalise and constrain the consequences of the post-war influx of non-Europeans, from the covert recording of the 'colour' of criminals, immigrants and job applicants, to more recent overt attempts to 'map' patterns of migration taking place across the country (Brown, 2016). By the end of the twentieth century, UK censuses adopted a framework to classify the social divisions of ethnicity that was crystallised in the 2001 census. Only from the start of the twenty-first century is it possible to chart the progress of these divisions and the populations that are subsumed under them. By this time, of course, many of the UK's so-called ethnic minority immigrants were themselves nearing or had reached retirement age. Their links to their post-war 'sending communities' – which in the UK's case were mostly ex-colonial Caribbean and South Asian countries – had attenuated. These new, non-European Europeans had married, had children and seen their own children marry and have children in their turn. They were becoming grandparents in what had once been a foreign land. The vertical links of kinship that had extended back to their childhood had undergone significant changes, reconstructing ideas of community and identity. A generation of people from black and minority ethnic communities were reorienting themselves to what had once been the 'host community', but which, almost un-noticed, had become, if not always for them, home for many of their children and grandchildren.

These divisions of ethnicity in the rest of Europe have been rendered more complex by the different ways 'post-colonialism' has been realised and the different administrative and welfare policies that have been adopted by the different European countries (Freeman, 2004; Gatrell, 2019). The French state, for example, juxtaposed its own imperialist legacy with its position as the champion of the Enlightenment values of liberty, equality and fraternity, by studiously avoiding such categorisation by the state. After the Second World War, a network of actual and potential French citizens emerged alongside citizens of what were also French 'possessions'. Long and bitter wars of independence were fought as the various nations colonised by the French state struggled to extricate themselves from its control, though not necessarily from Frenchness itself. People in other overseas possessions retained their rights and ties and remained resolutely, if differently, French. France thus contains a wide and heterogeneous population of European and non-European peoples whose inequalities remain more or less invisible given the absence of ethnicity and race as officially recognised divides.[2]

Germany, which lost its short-lived overseas empire after the First World War, had then exercised its influence by expanding its European territory through extreme militarised and politicised nationalism. After defeat in the Second World War, it was divided into two countries, neither of which witnessed any post-colonial influx of migrants. As part of its post-war reconstruction, however, West Germany encouraged migrant labour primarily from southern Europe and Turkey. These ethnic immigrants were treated as temporary residents, guest workers whose working life was expected to correspond with, and hence limit, their official residence in Germany. They were not expected to grow old in Germany. The result was a shared understanding that the guest workers would in due course return home, to Greece, to the Balkan states or to Turkey, where they would enjoy the fruits of their labour among their kith and kin, a delayed reward for their days of alien, alienated labour in a foreign land. Many did return, but many did not. Since the 1960s, the number of migrants aged over 60 still living in Germany has more than doubled every ten years (Ruspini, 2010: 6).

In Belgium, Holland, Italy and Spain, a combination of British, French and German approaches toward ethnic migration can be detected. As the former colonial subjects of Dutch East India and the Dutch Antilles, several immigrant groups came to live in the Netherlands as such 'ex-colonial' subjects; others however came over from North Africa, the Balkans and Turkey, as 'guest workers' on the same terms as the guest workers of West Germany. In Belgium, the influence of the French antipathy to engaging in explicit systems of ethnic categorisation 'has made the ethnic reference a taboo' from which it is still trying to break free (Perrin, Dal and Poulain, 2015: 191). What data exists suggests that the largest ethnic minority groups in Belgium are of Moroccan, Turkish and Central African origin (Congolese and Rwandan), with the latter only arriving as ex-colonial subjects. In Italy and Spain, where the classification of ethnicity is as studiously avoided as in France, there was much less post-war migration. In the decades after the war, both countries more often sent their own populations to other parts of Europe than they received incoming migrants. Consequently, both these countries came late to issues of diversity and are only now struggling with the consequences. Mostly they have not yet faced the problem of ageing ethnic, non-European migrants. Instead, they are confronted with a steady influx of relatively wealthy older northern European retirees (Hunter, 2019).

In eastern Europe, throughout the period of the Cold War, the borders of the state remained closed to all but visitors from other fellow-communist states. Many of these countries remained caught up with unresolved issues of ethnicity from much further back in their own history, particularly with ethno-nationalist minorities whose culture and history had long set them apart from that of the majority. Here the issues of ageing among ethnic minority communities are different again, whether it is the Roma in Hungary and Romania, Muslim Albanians in Macedonia and Serbia, Turks or Pomaks in Bulgaria or Ukrainians in Poland.[3] In such cases most of these ethnic divisions go back generations, and the hostility that periodically breaks out, as in former Yugoslavia, arises not so much in and through old age but in young adulthood, when the competition for respect and resources is greatest. In the Nordic countries, ethnic homogeneity has characterised their societies for much of their history and continued to do so throughout much of the second half of the twentieth century. The few non-Europeans who migrated to these countries during this period were mostly young adults, students, professionals and semi-professionals, whose numbers were low, who mostly contributed to the knowledge economy and who were by and large young, healthy and fit. Only in the twenty-first century has this changed and a growing number of still mostly young non-European migrants have entered as economic or political refugees seeking haven in the welfare systems these countries afforded. Older ethnic minorities within Finland, Norway and Sweden are not migrants but 'first nation' peoples, whose nomadic lives have been traditionally shaped by fishing, farming and herding activities that entailed a relative disregard for national borders. The ageing of such first nation communities poses an even more complex set of issues, which share to a degree the problems facing the ageing of first nation communities in North America.

Given this level of diversity, ethnicity represents not one but a variety of social locations. Each represents differing intersections with issues of socio-economic status, of gender, of religion and of racialized divisions of varying degrees for different cohorts, different age groups and different communities. This is in turn realised in the different ways each state has adopted the collection of information on ethnicity and the extent to which ethnicity figures in national social policies. Some, like the UK, have maintained detailed statistics of ethnicity and migration status, stratified more or less based on colonial history, while others, like France, have refused as a matter of principle to enumerate any such divisions even as they were being realised within the broader society. The differential patterning of race and ethnicity, between America and Europe, and between the different European states calls for much caution in framing any broad model by which to represent, let alone understand, the inequalities and divisions of 'host' and 'minority' communities. While this is true for every age group, later life adds further complexity.

Intra-generational conflicts between host and migrant communities in Europe are often inflected by intergenerational divides themselves established back in the 'long' 1960s. In countries like Britain, France and the Netherlands, age serves as an extra pivot around which these divisions are reconfigured. The ties of family are also the ties of ethnicity. But as young immigrants grow old, those self-same ties make return home to 'age in place' a much harder decision to make than was perhaps first thought, either by the immigrants themselves or by the states that first encouraged their immigration. If home is where the heart is, those hearts increasingly are split, creating divisions within families, even within the individuals themselves. Notions of a later-life 'return' have become less certain, as old age is being realised, metaphorically and factually, in 'another country'. The issues thrown up by ageing in and out of place need to be re-examined in the light of these changing conditions.

Age and race: difference, distinction, disadvantage

Recognising the differences between race and ethnicity is important when reconceptualising the social divisions of later life. Ageing in the context of the long-established black–white divisions in life expectancies in America is a very different matter from ageing in the context of migration to another country. The black–white 'racial' division in US society forms an implicit matrix against which subsequent, historically distinct patterns of migration to the USA need to be considered (Cole, 2016). However novel the ethnic divisions of post-war Europe might appear, they too arose in the context of already fashioned assumptions derived from no longer acceptable racist ideologies developed during and alongside the course of European modernity. The interconnection between race, migration and ethnicity in Europe and in America makes understanding the ethnic and racial divisions of later life complex, even as their invariable contingencies become more difficult to ignore. For there exists a thread beneath this diversity that implicitly distinguishes between the legitimate and the never completely legitimate other, those who 'belong' and those whose belonging is questioned, differently, by both sides. In some cases, this may reflect difference more than division, but it is a difference that is as difficult to realise in a fair and equal manner as the more evidently structural divisions developed by and within the economy.

The United States of America championed the idea of a multicultural, multi-ethnic, civic community as part of its foundational narrative. Its history of welcoming, assimilating and enabling immigrants from all parts of the world to make America their home and a place where they and their subsequent generations could expect to prosper was celebrated (King, 2000: 29). Those brought to the country as slaves were a significant and telling exception. Even after the abolition of slavery, African Americans continued to form a continually racialized, excluded minority without the kind of ethnic grouping afforded the Irish, Italian or Hispanic Americans. The history of African Americans seemed to mirror that of mainstream USA; their culture reflected within, mediated by, and eventually constitutive of the mass culture of the USA (Wolfe, 2016). This paradox of being part of, but apart from mainstream culture makes growing up and growing old as an African American a different experience from that faced by other 'immigrant' groups, including those with a similar skin colour who arrived later, as immigrants from Africa and from the Caribbean (Berlin, 2010). The social division between black and white Americans involve differences and inequalities distinct from those characterising other 'migrant' communities. As Newman has put it, ageing takes place for African Americans, in rather a 'different shade of gray' (Newman, 2003).

American culture developed within the context of an already existing black–white divide, reinforced by the legal, moral and social distinctions that were structured by the interrelated influences of labour and appearance. Within this historical matrix, an accumulation of differences has exercised its effects over the history of the African American community as well as within individual life courses. Inequalities in education, in family structure, in gender relationships, in occupational status and in wealth have continued throughout the twentieth and remain in the twenty-first century (Sullivan and Meschede, 2016). While this inequality of assets, capitals and resources has both common and unique effects, the historically located racialised division that still separates white and black America knits together class, race and gender into a nexus of inequality. Thus, older black Americans are less likely to have attended college, accumulated or inherited financial capital, are less likely to own their own home, have additional health insurance, or be the beneficiaries of an occupational or private pension. Older African Americans are more likely to reach later life with a history of homelessness and poverty, of imprisonment, with longer spells of being single or un-partnered, and having reached retirement age, are more likely to show signs of 'accelerated ageing', evidenced by higher rates of chronic ill health and 'frailty' (Moonesinghe, Zhu and Truman, 2011; Devi, 2012; Levine and Crimmins, 2014; Bandeen-Roche et al, 2015); all this on top of lifelong exposure to institutional and personal racism from their constant compatriots in the white community (Krieger, 2012).

One effect of such inequities is that in each and every US birth cohort since records began, proportionally fewer African Americans reach old age. Those who do are likely to experience poorer health, with fewer resources to manage the impairments and illnesses that accompany old age (Brown, O'Rand and Adkins, 2012; Kelley-Moore and Ferraro, 2004; Taylor, 2008). Despite the changes brought about by the civil rights movement, the heritage of racial division and racialised animosity has not vanished, nor have these changes brought about much reduction in inequality. In 2013, for example, older African Americans held a mere 20 per cent of the median wealth of white Americans; among the middle aged (45–64 years) the wealth disparity was double (Sullivan and Meschede, 2016: 59). As far as income is concerned, while older white and black Americans have seen their incomes rise steadily over the course of the last half-century, during the period 1967–2014, the income of white older Americans increased by 143 per cent, compared with an increase of 103 per cent for older black Americans. The result of this differential rate of material betterment is a widening in the degree of racial inequality in old age (Social Security Administration, 2016: 6).

Not only do older African Americans have fewer assets and resources, they also appear to derive less benefit from the assets and resources they do manage to acquire (Assari, 2018; Brown and Hargrove, 2017). Even if the division between African Americans and their white counterparts does not necessarily grow more acute with age, different experiences of age remain evident because of the different routes taken and the different type of obstacles faced by black and white Americans on their way to old age (Newman, 2003). If one envisages the divisions in old age as in part the accumulation of advantage, in part the amelioration of disadvantage and in part, the perpetuation of both, it is possible to view the racialized divisions evident in US society as a compound of all three. In the case of wealth – or assets more generally –the gap between black and white wealth grows wider with age (Sullivan and Meschede, 2014). As regards income, the gap seems to be perpetuated but does not widen in later life, while as regards expenditure, the gap actually lessens, not least because healthcare expenditures, which figure so large in US household consumption, are offset for both groups by Medicare's universal system of healthcare.

As regards exposure to and harm arising from racial discrimination, with age there seems to be some amelioration. While a fuller understanding of the impact of discrimination at successive stages of life is needed, research suggests that racism may affect people more acutely in early and mid-life adulthood than in either old age or early childhood (Gee, Walsemann and Brondolo, 2012). Discrimination based upon such stable characteristics as race (and gender and sexual orientation) generally seems to decline with age, while discrimination based on change, such as disability, obesity or sheer agedness, seems to increase (Sutin et al, 2015). Although older African Americans are exposed to more discrimination than their white counterparts, the impact of that discrimination seems paradoxically to be felt to be greater when experienced by older white Americans compared with that experienced by their black counterparts. The authors of this research suggested that older white Americans were less prepared for racial discrimination, having long experienced the working advantages of their whiteness, while the lifelong accumulation of discrimination experienced by older black Americans builds up greater resilience and resourcefulness in handling such experiences (Barnes et al, 2008). Differences in the degree of racial discrimination experienced and reported at different stages of the life course have also been found in another study. The authors of this study found that experiences of everyday discrimination rose from adolescence into adult life, but then declined in later life, implying that growing older renders the experience of discrimination less painful and less pervasive than earlier in adult life (Luo et al, 2011).

The divide that race represents neither originates from nor finds its terminus in old age. The cumulative disadvantage hypothesis, discussed in Chapter 2 on class remains a hypothesis which, if extended through later life, has at best only equivocal support, with most studies indicating that increasing age 'levels out' the health inequities of working life (O'Rand and Lynch, 2018: 76). Arguably, most of the disadvantages associated with blackness arise before but continue to grow during working life. For African Americans, reaching later life is less certain and once reached often proves harsher, especially for older men. However, the origins of such adversity lie not in but before old age (Kelley-Moore and Ferraro, 2004; Kim and Miech, 2009). It is very much the legacy of hardship accumulated during earlier life.

These effects have been realised cumulatively not just in terms of past life, but also over past generations. One author has used the term 'weathering' to describe these lifelong effects (Geronimus, 1992). As Geronimus suggests, 'Blacks experience early health deterioration as a consequence of the cumulative impact of repeated experience with social or economic adversity and political marginalization' (Geronimus et al, 2006: 827). Minimally evident very early in life, Geronimus' research group has shown how by the time adulthood is reached, 'stark racial disparities in health in clinical and subclinical conditions across a range of biological systems [are evident] among young through middle aged adults' (Geronimus et al, 2006: 830). What is also notable is that the effect upon health arising from systemic racism cannot simply be 'reinterpreted' or 'reframed' in terms of 'class' or 'socio-economic status'

(Phelan and Link, 2015: 324–5). As Turner, Brown and Hale (2017) have observed, the inequality in health status between black and white Americans is evident at every level of socio-economic position, while the benefits from possessing material and social resources to offset poor health are greater for white than for black Americans. This 'diminishing returns hypothesis' means that greater socio-economic advancement brings less relief and resources to African Americans, risking instead an increased exposure to the 'sedimentation of racial inequality' in US society (Nuru-Jeter et al, 2018: 181).

Differences in social capital between black and white Americans, on the other hand, do not grow with age; if anything they lessen (Ajrouch, Antonucci and Janevic, 2001; Barnes et al, 2004; Peek and O'Neill, 2003). Moreover, there seems to be less impact on older people's health and well-being from unequally resourced neighbourhoods as ageing 'in place' proves less a disadvantage than a source of stability, a compounding of social capital by place, identity and belonging. Where racial differences are evident is in the composition rather than the quantity of social networks, with black Americans having more frequent contact with family, fictive kin and fellow church members, while white Americans have more contact with friends and peer groups (Taylor et al, 2013). Longitudinal research suggests that despite these higher levels of intergenerational contact, older black Americans more often experience loss or breaks in their social relationships, as a result of the greater degree of adversity facing all black lives, suggesting that, though equal in quantity, African Americans experience more precarious social capital (Goldman and Cornwell, 2018).

That the racial divide cutting across life in America seems an inescapable evil, which only becomes a little less unbearable with age, is no doubt one powerful framing of age, race and social division. However, other frameworks are available that avoid the too ready victimisation of the African American community (Appiah, 1998; McDermott and Samson, 2005). As the USA moves from a 'biracial' to a 'multiracial' society, the nature and representation of the country's racialised divisions are being realised in ways other than through the black and white divisions of exclusion, hierarchy, inequality and oppression. We have written elsewhere of the distinction between structural accounts of race and age that frame the black–white divide in terms of advantage and disadvantage, power and oppression and more culturally nuanced accounts that highlight the co-construction and co-development of American culture that continues to take place between and within white and black communities (Gilleard and Higgs, 2013: 53). The transmission of 'typical' American values, concerning autonomy and independence seems as evident within black as in white communities, as do the shared ideals over what constitutes 'successful' ageing' or 'a happy old age' (Laditka et al, 2009; Romo et al, 2013). This is perhaps unsurprising, since 'successful ageing' seems to possess a common framework across many different countries and cultures (Fernández-Balleisteros et al, 2010).

Still, different but equivalent levels of participation in later lifestyles, as well as in social connectedness provide a range of resources for older black and white Americans that help sustain them in and through old age. While the continuation of racially segregated cultures and lifestyles may selectively disadvantage black Americans, not all such 'segregation' effects are necessarily detrimental to health and well-being. At the neighbourhood level, for example, such effects may afford a sense of community and foster more extensive neighbourhood support, especially for those like the retired, whose lives are lived outside the productive economy. Even if ethnic homogeneity tends to sustain inequality and injustice in earlier adult life, later in life it may offer compensatory benefits (Charles, 2003). The problem is in determining what Nancy Fraser has termed 'participatory parity' (Fraser, 2001). What level and what type of segregation promotes a sense of safety and content, and what helps realise social mobility and social interaction? Do black and white communities benefit equally from similar levels of segregation? Addressing this question is not just a matter of empirical inquiry. Recognising that race serves as a source of community, identity and social capital for black and white Americans remains an important consideration in the study of 'race and ageing'. Given the remove that later life has from work and the social relations of production, race may serve as much as a form of community as it does a site of exclusion. Such considerations apply equally when it comes to considering the role of ethnicity in later life, the topic to which we turn next.

Age, ethnicity and cultural distance

If race represents a source of division and inequality while providing a sense of collective identity and community, ethnicity might seem to serve similar ends. Distant from the legacies of chattel slavery and the racialised ideologies that it engendered and maintained, ethnicity in its various social realisations reflects other types of structural difference, one of the more important being that of 'cultural distance'. Differences in values, lifestyles and beliefs vary between different cultural (or national) groups. Such patterns of similarity and difference can be observed and measured along a number of parameters, including difference in culinary habits, dress, gender and inter- and intra-generational relationships, as well as language, religious practices and value systems (Babiker, Cox and Miller, 1980; Mumford and Babiker, 1998; De Santis, Maltagliati and Salvini, 2016). While the subject of some criticism, the concept of cultural distance has a certain heuristic value in distinguishing the divisions between ethnicised compared with racialised social categories. Recognition of cultural difference, for example, was denied those future African Americans who were brought over on the slave ships: denied because they were denied any culture not subsumed by considerations based on a primary racialised divide between those with and those without 'culture'. The increased contribution and co-mingling of African and European American cultures that emerged during the course of twentieth century has added substance to this denial. Indeed, it might be said to have minimised the salience of cultural difference between what otherwise were very unequal communities, with black and white Americans sharing in a common culture, but unequally and with few options to live equally but differently alongside each other.

Cultural distance lies at the heart of ethnic consciousness in ways that categorisation by skin colour and appearance does not.[4] Whether it grows less or more salient with ageing remains open to inquiry. For some, especially perhaps for those with less degree of cultural distance to start with, the experience of ageing and sharing in a common culture may make 'non-ethnic' attributes more central than their ethnicity in shaping their later lifestyles and identity (King et al, 2017). Gender is important in further qualifying ethnicity's effects. Older minority women, for example, seem to prefer a 'flexible migratory pattern' rather than choosing a permanent return, whereas older men seem to prefer the latter (Klok et al, 2017: 34). This enables them to enjoy the 'empowering' aspects of the host culture alongside the nourishment that home represents, in a way that contrasts with men's already existing empowerment (Böcker and Gehring, 2015). For others, faced by the challenge of ageing away from home and the threatened erosion of difference, actively maintaining their cultural distance from the host community, through language, diet, religious practices and clothing, may be one way of retaining their sense of self, of identity in later life and in so doing, holding on to their place in the world (Cool, 1981).

Living longer as a member of an ethnic minority community inevitably means more exposure to the host culture. It might be expected that with increasing age comes a greater familiarisation, even an assimilation and identification with the host culture. Empirical evidence certainly suggests that integration into the host community during working life pays off in material terms. It ensures greater economic parity between minority and host community, irrespective of the closeness of the connection with the culture of origin, or the strength or weakness of ties with the sending community (Zimmermann, 2007; Delaporte, 2018). At the same time, changes in both the host and the sending culture may take place over the course of the immigrant's adult life that lead, in any case, to reductions in the cultural distance between the communities (Storm, Sobolewska and Ford, 2017). Divisions once felt acutely in younger adulthood may grow less salient with time, as a co-product of both age and generational change, leading to a reduction in cultural distance, an increase in social integration and an accumulated resilience borne by experience (Machat-From, 2017: 226). This combination of influences implies that with age comes an easier acceptance of difference and with it a degree of neutralisation against its initially more adverse effects.

Set against this hypothesis of ageing fostering integration and narrowing cultural distance is the other possibility, that longer exposure to cultural divides leads to greater awareness of how great that distance is, thereby accentuating the awareness of differences, even if change in the sending communities is progressively narrowing the gap between sending and host nation. A 'lock-in' to earlier cultural differences may thus lead to a growing alienation from the host culture, compounded by a parallel generational divide that sees second- and third-generation children growing increasingly distant from their ageing parents and/ or grandparents.

As the world of the retired diverges from that of youth and the younger generation, these intergenerational divides may be felt more profoundly, while the divide between host and sending communities only accentuates difference and exclusion. A mix of alienation, integration and separation may well characterise older people from some ethnic minority communities, creating very different patterns of diversity, inequality and division between and within different minority groups, depending upon their differing histories.

Whatever may be the case, not all the consequences of minority status have adverse outcomes in later life (Reus-Pons et al, 2016). The dominance of a structural disadvantage model of ethnicity has diverted attention from more culturally and socially oriented inquiry, making disadvantage all too often the principal parameter when examining ethnic and racial differences, like a kind of inverted orientalism.[5] One consequence is that there has been less exploration of later life as a site of narrating and performing ethnicity and less account made of the balance realised within and between different ethnic communities in their cultural, economic and social assets, capital and resources. Though calls for a change in focus have been made (see, for an earlier example, Blakemore and Boneham, 1995), the demography of disadvantage model continues to pervade the field. It is worth bearing in mind a point Russell King and his colleagues have made, that for older people from ethnic minority backgrounds 'being a migrant in later life can be … a life stage which is fulfilling, enjoyable even liberating' (King et al, 2017: 195). Instead of viewing cultural differences as another stable source of disadvantage, discrimination and inequity, ethnicity can be understood in other ways, as a source of social and cultural distinction, not just division. Ethnicity, in the form of ethnically orientated social capital, may actively sustain a sense of identity and self-worth among older people, forming part of a broader range of culturally inflected options that enable older people to choose how best to age 'in place'.

The notion of 'selective acculturation' (Portes and Rumbaut, 2001: 54) draws attention to the variety of ways that people from minority cultures develop modes of integration alongside modes of difference. Economic integration during working life, for example, may foster greater skills in speaking and reading the host community's language(s), using public and private services and in assimilating consumer preferences, even as other cultural dimensions such as religious practice and moral discourses change little, if at all. Others have drawn attention to the domain specificity of acculturation, especially that between acculturation in public contrasted with private life (Arends-Tòth and van de Vijver, 2004). Whether this results in a closer alignment between ethnic minority and host communities as the workaday experiences of cultural contrasts lessen, or whether the successful preservation of opportunities to continue to age differently helps people age better, remain questions open to empirical inquiry. The point to be stressed is that ethnicity is not always or only a source of exclusion and inequality (Kneale, 2012). That different and not necessarily unequal outcomes are conceivable reinforces the point that treating ethnicity as only ever part of a litany of structural disadvantages and inequalities associated with ageing 'out of place' represents a serious category error. Such framing limits and restricts a fuller understanding of ethnicity and difference in later life. Difference does not have to be overcome; it can be turned to selective advantage. Like ageing itself, ethnicity can be a flexible means of both categorisation and distinction.

This framework of culture, acculturalisation and cultural distance has not, however, dominated most studies of age and ethnicity. Rather, the dominant model in social gerontology has emphasised minority ethnic status as a position of structural disadvantage and actual or potential oppression. Interacting with other disadvantaged statuses, ethnicity has been seen through the various double, triple or quadruple jeopardy hypotheses of ageing badly (Dowd and Bengtson, 1978; Havens and Chappell, 1983; Norman, 1985; Ferraro, 1987; Markides, Liang and Jackson, 1990; Yoo and Sung, 1997; Torres, 2019b).[6] Only a small number of ageing studies have employed a 'contrasting cultures' approach. Even here, the emphasis has been mostly limited to cultural differences in family attitudes toward older relatives, which are then generalised toward broader sets of contrasting beliefs and assumptions about 'care' (Adamson and Donovan, 2005; Dilworth-Anderson, Williams and Gibson, 2002; Gallant, Spitze and Grove, 2010; Lawrence et al, 2008; Miyawaki, 2016; Pyke and Bengtson, 1996). Such 'relational' models neglect wider consideration about the pains and pleasures of later life for those who are living it, and the opportunities ethnicity presents for enjoying 'alternative' ways of living later life, and establishing alternative 'cultures of a third age' through 'doing other' (Wanka et al, 2018).

The experience and social representation of migration impacts upon ethnic differences. While the United States has long framed itself as a society of colonists and immigrants, European countries have experienced these phenomena as a mostly disjunctive experience, threatening rather than reinforcing their sense of national identity. Migration and cultural distance are obviously linked. The further the spatial distance between sending and receiving communities, the greater the cultural difference and consequent disadvantaging. Migration introduces factors other than sheer cultural distance, however. This includes the push and pull factors that induce migration, the circumstances that create opportunities for – or the necessity of – migrating, and the level of disruption that migration induces in the bonds of family prior to migration. For some immigrants, economic reasons dominate the decision and migration is framed around the establishment and accumulation of assets, capital and resources 'in a foreign land' that are expected to be transferred back to an old age safely relocated in the old familial, sending community.

Old age or later life may not be conceived as ending one's life in a foreign country. It may be an anticipated return home, with the prospect of living a richer and more resourceful old age than had the individual never migrated. Such expectations are sometimes, though not always, realised (Baykara-Krumme and Platt, 2018). For others, migration may have involved a more profound, even necessary break, seeking an escape from oppression, injustice and maybe personal unhappiness. Reaching later life in a foreign country may nevertheless remain an experience of alienation and otherness, even for those who were fleeing home. For others, whether they were forced or chose to leave their home community, it may not be nearly so alienating or intimidating. Indeed, as integration develops over the working life, other identities and other concerns may become more prominent (Elrick et al, 2014). Such integration creates the opportunities for choosing how and where to spend one's later life, which aspects of one's adult identity to preserve, which to relinquish and which to develop. For some it means making a home from home, for others living a life of permanent exile and, for yet others, turning cultural distance into a resource rather than a restraint. Research into migrant and minority status consequently offers a more balanced view than that dominating more 'policy' focused ethnic ageing research. Treated as both forms of division and of identity, ethnicity, migration and otherness, like age, should not be fixed as categories of disadvantage and inequality. Like chronological age, they are hard to weigh up mixtures of 'when's, who's and how's', negotiated differently in different settings and at different times (Machat-From, 2017: 273). They add diversity to later life, both in its pains and in its pleasures.

Age and the demography of difference

Although there are clear records of non-European communities living and growing old in European societies well before the modern era, it was not until the 1960s that migration into Europe from non-European destinations reached sufficient numbers to become a 'social issue' within European societies (Ruspini, 2010; Livi-Bacci, 2012; Chin, 2017). Much of that emigration was of people who not only looked different but who dressed differently, spoke differently, and often worshipped differently from the Christian 'host' population. The period of non-European immigration began in the decades of economic expansion and post-war restoration when a diminished Europe struggled to rebuild its economies. Accurate data on the number of non-European migrants entering Europe during the 1950s, 1960s and 1970s are difficult to come by. As pointed out earlier, there are no reliable statistics on the size of ethnic minority communities across most of Europe. Most countries still do not collect statistics on ethnicity: the UK and Ireland are notable as exceptions (Simon, 2017: 2328). Some countries treat not recording ethnicity as a matter of principle, arguing that the only relevant distinction is between 'citizen' and 'non-citizen'. Despite the fact that the public are overwhelmingly supportive of the idea of providing information on ethnic origin, the discomfort most European states have with their own troubled pasts means that there is still a difficulty in confronting ethnic diversity (Escafré-Dublet and Simon, 2012: 232). Hence, empirical evidence of the diversity of later life in many European countries is harder to show. That such ethnic diversity is taking place, however, is clear, as statistics from the UK show.

It was not until 1991 that the UK census introduced a question concerning ethnic origin. In the subsequent two censuses, further developments have made it more specific. However if one takes the broad category of ethnic minority status to refer to all those identifying as 'non-white European' (thus including those identifying as Asian – that is, Bangladeshi, Chinese, Indian, Pakistani or 'other Asian' – and those identifying as black – that is, African or African-Caribbean), this serves as a kind of constant point of reference for the last three UK censuses. What such data indicates is an increasing proportion of the adult population who identify as 'non-white' as well as an increasing, albeit smaller, proportion of 'non-white' older adults. Figure 4.1 illustrates this for the period 1991–2011.

This data shows a rise in the numbers and proportions of people over 65 who identify with a 'non-white' ethnic minority status and a parallel rise within ethnic minority communities in the proportions who are 'old'. In 1991, less than 3 per cent of the minority ethnic population were 'old' (that is, aged 65 or over); by 2011, more than 5 per cent were. Within the different designated non-white ethnicities, those whose age structure is most similar to that of the white British

Figure 4.1: Proportion of census population of England and Wales identifying as 'non-white', by age group, 1991–2011

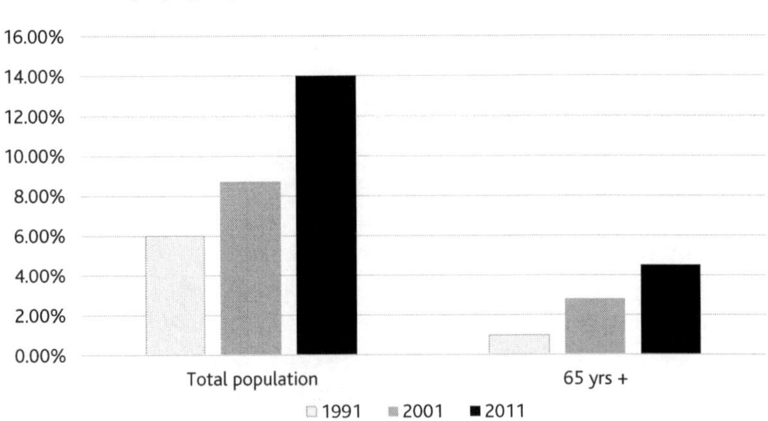

Source: (a) OPCS, 1996: Table 3.1; (b) England and Wales Censuses, 2001 and 2011.

population (approximately 19 per cent aged 65 and over) are people from the Caribbean (14 per cent) followed by those from India (8 per cent); in contrast, people from African or Bangladeshi backgrounds are some of the least aged segments of society (2.5 per cent and 3.5 per cent). While ageing and agedness are matters of more immediate concern to the majority 'host' population, increasingly they are becoming matters of concern to some, though by no means all, ethnic minority communities.

How do the circumstances of the over-65 minority ethnic population differ from the white British majority? Do those similarities and differences vary, in turn, according to the demographic structure of the different ethnic groups, or their cultural distance from the host community, or the extent of the assets and capital they possess? Equally, one might ask about the extent to which 'old age' remains an issue not of assimilation or alienation, but of potential 'return'. Studies exploring differences in the circumstances of the older ethnic majority and their ethnic minority peers are limited, some tentative generalities can be made. First and foremost, older people from ethnic minority backgrounds are, as a whole, structurally worse off. They report worse health, have lower incomes and experience a poorer quality of life compared with older people from the host community (Evandrou, 2000; Ginn and Arber, 2000; Moriarty and Butt, 2004a; Heisig, Lancee and Radl, 2018; Steinbach, 2018). Older people from ethnic minority communities possess fewer assets and are more likely to suffer from limiting long-term illnesses. These differences become even more marked when they are closely matched for age structure, since members of the over-65 minority ethnic community are somewhat younger than over-65's from the host community (Katbamna and Matthews, 2007: 38). Further, experiences and understanding of systems of health and social care are generally more limited among older people from ethnic minority backgrounds and consequently the benefits they can extract from welfare are less (Soom Ammann and van Holten, 2013; Hansen, 2014). On the other hand, evidence concerning the relative social capital that older people from ethnic minority communities can access is mixed. Some studies suggest that contacts with family and living arrangements are more frequent and more robust among minority ethnic communities than they are within the host community (Blakemore and Boneham, 1995; Katbamna et al, 2004; Butt and Moriarty, 2004). The next section considers this question of balance between the potential benefits and costs of ethnic and racial difference in more detail.

The costs and benefits of difference

At various points in this chapter we have drawn attention to the tendency in ageing studies to deploy ethnicity, immigrant status and race primarily as conveyors of selective disadvantage and inequality, with the older, ethnic, racial or immigrant 'other' as the inevitably disadvantaged victim of exclusion, impoverishment and oppression (see Evandrou, 2000; Nazroo, 2006; Dolberg, Sigurðardóttir and Trummer, 2018). There is obviously some truth to this, at least if expressed in financial, material terms (Heisig, Lancee and Radl, 2018; Sullivan and Meschede, 2016). Even so, by narrowing the focus of research on ageing and ethnicity to the perspective of material inequality risks framing 'ethnicity' as no more than another structuring of inequality in the cumulative binaries that constitute the advantaged and the disadvantaged (Zubair and Norris, 2015: 910). The resources that ethnicity and race confer on older people, perhaps more particularly when faced with longstanding disadvantaged circumstances, can easily be ignored or treated as mere 'compensations' (Weibel-Orlando, 1988). Yet there are benefits of difference. Distinct religious practices can and do offer solace in the face of adversity, hardship and loneliness (Ciobanu and Fokkema, 2017). Love for one's family and one's children can help people 'age in place' despite the distance they have travelled from an earlier childhood 'home' (Liversage and Mirdal, 2017). The social capital developed within ethnic minority communities benefits the older generation in part by 'buffering' them against the adverse effects of corporeal age and acculturative stress (Sanders, 2002; Vinokurov andTrickett, 2015). This may deliver a surprising measure of advantage, for example over their age peers who have stayed behind and aged in place (Baykara-Krumme and Platt, 2018).

Older people from ethnic minority backgrounds selectively engage with organisations reflecting (and presumably reinforcing) their 'ethnic-origin' identity, choosing to engage less with the institutions and organisations of the host culture. As a result they draw sustenance from feeling 'at home' even when they are not (Uslaner and Conroy, 2003). As Nee and Sanders (2001: 389–90) have noted, for many 'immigrants who do not possess substantial financial capital, the family (nuclear and extended) constitutes the most important capital asset'. Differences in human and social capital can be as critical in understanding the social divisions associated with ethnic minority status as differences in economic resources. Of course, considerable variation exists between older people from different ethnic minority communities in their access to and experience of such social capital, as well as to financial resources

(Evandrou, 2000; Gierveld, Victor, Burholt and Martin, 2012; van der Pas and Keating, 2015). Hence, it is unwise to treat ethnicity and migrant status as homogenous categories of disadvantage and division just as it is mistaken to treat age as a homogenised category.

Here Putnam's distinction between 'bridging' and 'bonding' social capital, already referred to in Chapter 3 on gender, is relevant (Putnam, 2000). The development of 'bridging capital' can facilitate the 'acculturation' of ethnic minority immigrants and their cultural and economic integration into the host community's educational systems and occupational markets. Such bridging capital is perhaps of most value to young men (and for some, though not all, minority communities, for young women too). In contrast, the accumulation of 'bonding capital' secures a stronger place within one's own community in mid and later adult life. Integration within the networks of kith and kinship may be particularly beneficial to those members of ethnic communities whose lives are lived and shaped outside the labour market. This includes both married women and people of retirement age. Social bonding may also prove useful when there exist within the community 'cross-cultural' entrepreneurs, whose own bridging capital enables them to direct the less well 'bridged' members of their community toward the full range of health and welfare resources of the host community.[7]

Studies of social capital support such assumptions (Cheong et al, 2007). Bonding social capital, linked to the idea of 'ethnic capital' in the form of community integration and participation, has been found to be positively associated with absence of depression among elderly Korean migrants in the USA (Jang et al, 2015). At the same time, differing degrees of 'social capital' can also serve as dimensions of inequality separable from those associated with income or financial capital. This is particularly evident in studies of ageing in ethnic minority communities and their bonding social capital (Platt, 2009; Lancee, 2010). Overall, social capital – viewed as the total size of social networks, intensity of social contacts, and the context of those networks – varies with age, as well as with gender and ethnicity. It can be seen as an asset achieved through individual agency, by the presence of material resources and by the coherence of the community (Moriarty and Butt, 2004: 742). Systematic differences have been observed between ethnic minority groups and in Britain, for example, people from South Asian communities have reported higher levels of social capital compared with people from Caribbean backgrounds, irrespective of age or gender (Blakemore and Boneham, 1995). Although there is a tendency to consider 'bridging' more valuable than 'bonding' social capital, both contribute assets and resources to communities and to individual families and their absence can be detrimental to the quality of later life (Kim, Subramanian and Kawachi, 2006; Muckenhuber, Stronegger and Freidl, 2013).

The social bonds of 'ethnic capital' also help buffer the impact of adversity, even if integration and identification with the host community (that is, bridging capital) offers more long-term material benefits (Niedzwiedz et al, 2016). Research on ethnicity, well-being and social capital is beset with problems and inconsistencies (Goulbourne and Salomos, 2003: 330), however. This reflects the general problem of understanding how social capital affects the distribution of health, material and social well-being within any population (Ferlander, 2007). Studies to date offer equivocal answers although there can be little doubt that the lack of social capital serves a crucial and continuing source of vulnerability for some ethnic minority older people more than it does for others. Whether framed by the concept of social capital, or by ideas of ethnic identity and integration, or a combination of the two, the exploration of ethnicity in later life as a source of social division and difference is likely to grow in importance. This is particularly so as the second generation of non-European Europeans reach into and extend later life. How far such developments enrich later life depends upon a number of factors, not least the differences in the assets, capital and resources that ethnicity and its diversity bring. Here the development of a Bourdieusian approach to multiple capitals offers a more fruitful avenue for research, going beyond the traditional assumption of double or triple jeopardies. Recognising the inherent flexibility in experiencing and expressing race and ethnicity, the intersecting identities they generate and the multiple assets and vulnerabilities that such locations confer seems a good starting point.

Conclusions

In one of the key texts that introduced the study of ethnicity into British gerontology, Ken Blakemore and Margaret Boneham noted how:

> social divisions among older people as a whole are widening. These … cut across and complicate … racial and ethnic differences … Though there never was a common status in old age in industrial society, the uneven spread of occupational pension schemes and other changes are leading to increasing fragmentation and inequality. The frontiers of old age faced by Black and Asian people involve possibilities

> of widening gaps between winners and losers, between affluent and not so well-off communities, and between older people who are sustained by [their] ethnic identity ... and those who are not. (Blakemore and Boneham, 1995: 141)

These points are as apposite now as they were over two decades ago. The divisions in today's multicultural, multi-ethnic societies have arisen through a variety of particular historical processes. Their consequences are being realised in later life as new divisions in the assets, experiences and opportunities of later life. The ageing of minority populations introduces new themes and new understandings of ageing, and of the experience of race, ethnicity and migration. It casts new light on what determines difference, identity and lifestyle in later life while illuminating ethnicity as a social location and a social identity whose meanings differ with age.

Without a theoretical framework, however, the risk is simply an accumulation of empirical findings supporting or failing to support some version of the double/triple jeopardy thesis of cumulative disadvantage. Driven by the concerns of policy makers rather than by attempts to make sense of the new ageing, such studies may gain funding but without furthering understanding. Instead of employing pseudo-stable, essentialised categories such as 'BAME' (black and minority ethnic) communities, it seems preferable to draw upon models of ethnicity 'that emphasise the situational quality of that identity marker' and highlight its relational significance for a particular ethnic group (Elrick, Schneiderhan and Khan, 2014). Like age, ideas of ethnicity are subject to the flux of historical and personal time. The parameters within which that flux manifests itself and the pathways taken towards, and the outcomes of, later life are critical. This includes consideration of the older concepts of class (in the sense of the structural patterning of economic assets, capital and resources by which race and ethnicity are inflected) and gender (in the sense of its cultural co-construction and public and private boundaries) as well as more recent concerns over identity, belonging and cultural distance.

The terms 'ethnicity' and 'race' serve as contextualised and contested collective representations of social difference. Though purporting to reflect stable sources of difference, these terms possess multiple meanings and are expressed in and through multiple structures, not all of which can be reduced to some single hierarchy of disadvantage. The difficult division between 'black' and 'white', for example, goes well beyond the concerns of the communities of North America, just as the points of reference activated in making this distinction differ. The nature, even the acceptance, of the category 'ethnic minority' status is no less complicated. It too varies from place to place in terms of its defining features, the salience given to appearance, compared with differences in dress, language and religion, and in the extent to which its representation is subsumed, at least within North American and European society, under the aegis of the oriental 'other'. Distinctions framed around 'nationality' may have more political than cultural import, while those based upon language and religion may have greater cultural resonance even as their political significance is downplayed. If, following Erikson (and Mannheim), 'identity' is constituted as a key psychological issue in the formation of adulthood, the changing nature of contemporary society and its shifting divisions have made later life yet another site where issues of 'belonging', 'identity' and 'place' are re-enacted. No longer confined to the 'identity conflicts' associated with adolescence and early adulthood, questions of ethnicity, nationality and race are acquiring new significance in shaping the boundaries and the experiences of later life (Gilleard and Higgs, 2016).

While it would be Pollyanna-ish to deny that aspects of ethnic identity are linked to disadvantage and inequity, it would be equally blinkered to restrict social science inquiries to those parameters of disadvantage alone. Ethnicity and race represent more than positions of marginality and oppression. They embody forms of capital and resources that contribute socially, materially and culturally to ageing and ageing well. These statuses of difference and distinction – and the discourse and practices they elicit – contribute to a sense of belonging, of feeling 'at home' in the world. They help make sense of one's life and the direction it takes, no less when people face growing older than when they face growing up. Disturbing some of the complacent assumptions about what constitutes home and belonging, and what is included and what excluded by such definitional boundaries has value in furthering the social science of ageing. Relieved of the relentless work of required assimilation, for some at least, retirement may make old age less a foreign country even as for others the dislocations of age only add to their sense of existing alienation. Failing fully to recognise and explore the costs and benefits of ethnicity, identity and belonging for human flourishing remains a disturbing omission in studies of ageing and ethnicity. We hope this chapter offers possibilities for an alternative perspective, even as it highlights the distances still to be travelled.

Notes

1 Of course it can be argued that the current preoccupation in the US with immigration and managing its southern border has shifted that country's emphasis

on ethnicity and migration a little closer to that articulated by European populist politicians.

2 Statistics based upon country of birth provide the best approximations to the size of the ethnic minority population in countries like France (see, for example, Rallu, 2017).

3 The question of ageing among the ethno-nationalist communities of eastern Europe is seriously under-researched. It involves the history of Ottoman expansion and the conversion of large numbers of peoples of different linguistic heritages to Islam and their subsequent marginalisation in the various wars of independence that were fought during the late nineteenth century. This is further complicated by the mass exchange of populations that followed the collapse of the Ottoman empire and the more recent rise of fundamentalism particularly among the young Muslim communities in Albania, Bosnia, Bulgaria, Kosovo, Macedonia and Montenegro (see Karajkov, 2006).

4 It should be noted that some researchers use the term 'cultural distance' to refer to the subjective sense of distance between one's own culture as a migrant or a member of an ethnic minority and the host culture, rather than as used here to refer to a measurable 'objective' distance (see for example Klok et al, 2017).

5 Here we use the term 'oriental' in the broad sense made of it by Said (1995).

6 The concept of double or triple jeopardy assumes that agedness represents a cultural and material disadvantage in most developed economies, and that the addition of other 'disadvantaged' statuses, associated with ethnicity, gender, race or sexuality 'doubles' or 'triples' the effect of that disadvantaging.

7 The concept of 'cross-cultural entrepreneurship' is taken somewhat loosely from Engelen, Heinemann and Brettel (2009).

5

Disability and later life

Social divisions based upon ethnicity or race, gender or socio-economic position form relatively stable sources of identity across the life course. Other aspects of identity are less fixed, particularly those based on bodily appearance and physical functioning. While gender and race form relatively stable sources of embodied distinction, those categories associated with the corporeal markers of illness, impairment or infirmity decidedly do not. Though capable of serving as sources of identity and implicated in various forms of discrimination and inequality, disability and infirmity form rather more contingent sources of social division in part because of the temporal flux within which they emerge. There is a distinction, for example, between the predictable status of becoming aged and the less predictable status of becoming disabled, ill or infirm. Most people see bodily change as constituting the 'authentic' basis of age and ageing; reminders of the inevitable temporality that is attached to identity, location and status. Those changes that are evidenced by the ageing body, which do not reflect illness or impairment, best signify the universality attributed to growing old. However, the ageing body is also a site and signifier of illness and infirmity, neither of which convey the same message of inevitability, predictability or universality. The statuses of illness, impairment and infirmity embody and reflect the operation of chance and misfortune in a way that ageing does not; and hence they imply an inequality or unfairness that age lacks. And though culture and society may help or hinder the processes of illness and of infirmity, society per se is not considered their originating cause (Mendes de Leon and Rajan, 2014). Although the social provides the context within which people-as-bodies are framed and understood, the body's corporeality serves as the critical reference point for the signs of both ageing and infirmity. Corporeality acts as a common base. Its materiality as age, however, cannot be so easily subcontracted out to the operations of the economy, culture or society: Though in some sense a social division, it is not imbued with the same intimations of unfairness and misfortune.

Bodies, however thoroughly represented by their corporeality, cannot be easily separated from social processes. Ageing, just like impairment and infirmity, occurs within bodies but also within societies; but unlike impairment and infirmity, age does not reflect already existing social divisions nor does it construct new ones. Only in so far as it is fashioned by other, older divisions and inequalities does the corporeality of age foster new sites of difference and disadvantage. Many of these new, age-inflected corporeal divisions reinforce the point that bodies do not change equally; they confer difference as much as, if not more than, they contribute to a common ageing identity. Differences – inequalities – in bodily health, in function and in appearance that arise in mid and later life, do so at different rates and with differing consequences, confounding the universality of age. Some emerge in and through other earlier differences and divisions, some in ways marked by chronology and some in ways that seem to most embody chance or misfortune. Just as any search for a simple, unmediated bodily trajectory, framed as some putative biological process called human ageing will be confounded by considerable corporeal variability, so any search for some underlying social cause accounting for age-associated disabilities will prove equally confounded. Variations, both in ageing and infirmity, are not reducible to or interchangeable with pre-existing socially structured divisions of class, gender, ethnicity or race, even as they often lean upon them. Likewise, the illnesses, infirmities and disabilities accruing in later life are both part of and apart from the biological processes of ageing and the already existing social relations that still differentiate it. They possess, in short, a social determinacy of their own, a power to divide that is, in large part, *sui generis*.

Although at times intimated and sometimes realised earlier in life, most of the infirmities and impairments that ageing bodies acquire have a greater salience, in so far as they reflect ageing and at the same time act as one of its most critical points of difference. Indeed, we would argue, these corporeal realities constitute some of the most salient divisions within ageing societies, particularly when they operate within later life itself. These are evident through the distinctions constructed between the fit and the frail. It is acknowledged that these divisions between the able-bodied and the disabled are not confined to later life, and that they serve as sources of social division at earlier stages of life; however, they take on a particular distinction at older ages since they lean so heavily upon age and agedness. This is not simply a matter of the relative prevalence of disability in later life. The uncertain status of the ageing body and its shades of fitness and functionality make the divisions of corporeal difference more problematic yet potentially more all-encompassing in later life than they do at earlier ages when they appear more distant from the representations of ageing and decline. Unlike those that once situated the divisions of later life within the already established classes of paupers and pensioners, or between old men and old women, the divisions framed by corporeality are riven with uncertainty, with the corresponding inequalities being suffused with a cultural and social mix of chance and inexorability sitting alongside the arbitrariness of social location.

The blurring of corporeal divisions between the fit and the frail, the functional and the infirm, is not itself unique; arguably most of the social divisions in late modernity have become open to a greater degree of inter- and intra-subjective negotiation and repositioning. But by whatever particular combination of chronology and corporeality it is constituted, able-bodiedness – or bodily integrity – forms one pole in this social division which seems to be more important with time. This chapter describes it broadly in terms of 'disability'. In part, this is because disability is already used as a term to describe an important social division running through the life course, and can thus be made comparable with class, ethnicity, gender and sexuality. But herein lies a problem: whether or not to treat disability as a social division in later life in much the same way as it has been treated earlier in life, as a marker of continued distinction, disadvantage and division. If disability is confined to a relatively restricted period of life, especially one that is detached from the main institutions of social reproduction and production, its status as a social identity and as a social position may be questioned. On the other hand, as many before us have noted, the distinction between ageing with, and ageing into, disability is an important one, with material and social consequences. In order to fully address this problem, we need first to review current social theories of disability, theories that have been developed not as part of social gerontology but within the context of the new social movements associated with the long 1960s (Gilleard and Higgs 2013). It is in this context that disability was first delineated as a social division; as a radical part of the subcultures and the countercultures of youth, not as a feature of old age.[1] Hence, we must start with the social theory of disability as it was developed in this period and its aftermath even if it represents a position that is distant from the disabilities that age more often brings.

Disability and social theory

The disability movement and those who became its theorists were at pains to locate the division between people with and without disabilities within the structures of society itself (Oliver 2009, 2013). Physical impairments and illnesses that afflicted individual bodies were construed as individualised representations of a broader category of social exclusion, oppression and restriction. Created and structured by the institutions of society, disability, these theorists argued, was misrepresented as a purely corporeal matter, thereby avoiding recognition of its actual social origins and functions. By acknowledging disability as a social division that was created by the processes of institutionalisation and social power, disability was seen as an identity and a voice fashioned by exclusion and oppression, not by personal tragedy. It was recast within the context of a general politics of liberation, one that extended from gender and race to ethnicity and sexuality (Slorach, 2016). The resolution of such exclusion, oppression and disadvantage was possible not by recourse to individualised rehabilitation and training, but in the context of effecting social change in the various institutions and social structures that had shaped the current division between able-bodied and disabled persons. The location of its inequality was not to be seen in the corporeal, but in the organisation of the education system, the healthcare system, the labour market, and in the restricted access to public spaces and the civic arena (Hahn, 1994; Oliver, 2009, 2013).

Lacking such actively institutionalised structures, the disabilities of later life scarcely figured as potential sites of struggle. It was the young disabled person who was at the centre of this kind of struggle, this movement and this identity. The fight to be heard, to be included, the struggle for rights were active struggles led and directed by younger adults, possessed, or so it seemed, with more authentic disabilities, because they were there 'at the beginning', forming essential aspects of persons-as-adults. The kinds of impairments that were most emblematic of disability were the impairments of young adults, impairments whose bodily origins lay more in biological development than in bodily decay; impairments that affected physical more than mental function, impairments that individuals grew up with, that were capable of articulation, that could be given a voice. Many of those writing and campaigning within the disability movement tradition treated the corporeal as a matter of relative unimportance. More critical to them was the lack of access to education, to work, to housing, to healthcare and to leisure. These restrictions and barriers framed the common experience of all those whose bodies were in some way 'differently' constituted (Hughes and Paterson, 1997).

From this standpoint, it seemed somewhat distracting to insist that bodies matter too, that they mattered as much and with age might well matter more. Ageing into disability was consequently problematic; acknowledging agedness as an authentic archetype for disability risked reversing the gains that had been made by treating society and its dividing practices, not the body, as the site and source of oppression. The disability movement and disability theorising consequently sought a clear separation from age (Jönson and Larsson, 2009). Admittedly, the standard social model of disability has been subject to criticism and has lost some of its former role as an orthodoxy, in part because of its unwavering focus upon social structures and its insistent separation of body from society. The neglect of bodily suffering and corporeal infirmity and the privileging of social disability have begun to be considered too rigid and too simplistic to adequately capture the subjectivities of disabled people (Beaudry, 2016). A personal politics of disability requires more account to be taken of the complexity that exists in the relationship between body, self and society and the difficulties in extricating the effects of one from those of the other (Shakespeare and Watson, 2001: 22). Even so, the authenticity of disability as an identity, its capacity to serve as a cultural, political and social force of change and its persistence as a source of exclusion and marginality mean that disability as division is still located more powerfully in earlier than in later life.

Hence, the argument of this chapter is that the social divisions arising from corporeal difference in later life can only partly be considered through the lens of disability theory and the axioms of the social model. Illness and infirmity arising in mid and later life affect the life chances, the life circumstances and the lifestyles of those in later life, much as they do for younger people, but not because they are made disabling by the institutions of society. Rather, they themselves constitute sources of social distinction and social exclusion. The social divide separating the lives of the fit from the frail, the healthily from the unhealthily aged, is no less real in its social consequences than the divide separating younger disabled people from their able-bodied peers, but it is not identical with it. While many of the advances that have been achieved by the disability movement have undoubtedly benefited older retired people with impairments, many have not touched their lives and many seem if anything to have set them further apart. As with all the new social movements, there is a tendency to equate the disabilities of young adults as the authentic identity in belonging to the community of the disabled, while the agedness of the aged and infirm devalues that currency. Similar points could be made about sexuality, gender, ethnicity or race.

We are critical of the extension of the social disability model to the disabilities arising in later life (Thomas and Milligan, 2015), given that some of the first proponents of the model were keen to exclude the 'frail elderly' from even being considered disabled (Amundson, 1992). On the other hand, those who would deny any division, who would not countenance disability as either a distinction or an identity, miss the significant difficulties, exclusions and hardships that befall those with bodily infirmity. Arguments that claim that all humanity suffers from a collective vulnerability in a fragile world suggest that any further division, especially one based on differences in corporeal integrity, is both oppressive and unwarranted (Turner, 2006). Such denial of difference and the associated refusal to countenance the body as a source, *sui generis*, of material and social difference and inequity renders the category 'disabled' specious as a status. Denied a mark of division, such arguments simply fold disability into the variability of experience, less a category dividing society, more a condition common to all in society (Bickenbach, Rubinelli and Stucki, 2017).

Distinctions exist, however; and they affect the assets and resources, life chances and lifestyles of older people even if those distinctions are less stable, less easily drawn and less easily maintained as sources of identity. A tension exists, of course, in negotiating which side of the divide a person places themself, or is placed by family and friends and by health and social services. The relative size of the two sides of the divide changes with age (and possibly by cohort). While the majority of the older population, judged by both themselves and the wider society they are engaged with, contribute to and participate in the social relations of everyday life without much reference to their relative fitness or frailty, the numbers of people with impairments, infirmities and physical limitations increases exponentially with age, even as the institutional structures that fashion their life chances lose their influence. If later life is now materially and socially secured in most developed economies, much of its security rests on the premise of people in later life 'ageing well'. Negotiating between the statuses of able-bodied or disabled, fit or frail, successfully or unsuccessfully ageing renders disability a key site between a representation as failure (or frailure) and a representation as excluded and oppressed. The disability inherent in many aspects of ageing creates tensions for those who see any attempt to exclude them from the successfully ageing as evidence of socially instituted oppression and culturally inscribed othering (Tesch-Romer and Wahl, 2017), a tension at whose heart lies the problem of authenticity, the authenticity of age and the authenticity of disability.

We recognise the value of the social model of disability and the potential of life-long impairments to frame social divisions whose boundaries and limits are co-created by the social institutions of education, the labour market and public services. However, our point of reference is the emergence of disability and infirmity in later life – what has been called 'ageing into disability' rather than 'ageing with disability' (Monahan and Wolf, 2014: S1). The social model of disability and the disability movement per se are not without relevance to this topic, but arguably they are less pertinent to many of the issues raised by ageing into disability. This is both because of the nature of the underlying impairments impacting on late life disability, the relative instability of the status 'disabled' in such circumstances and the negligible role played by either the educational system or the labour market in delineating between those who have aged into disability and those have aged without disability. The categorisations and social representations of youth and age lean so very differently upon these categories, and their respective representations of disability. We shall return to these issues later. However, before progressing any further, we must address some other, crucial matters of terminology since terminology plays such an important part in reconstructing the social realisation and representation of disability as an experience and as an identity, as a condition and as a division.

What counts as 'disability'?

Definitional issues are not only theoretical. Crucially, they are associated with resource allocation, social policy and welfare entitlements. Their definition provides sites of contestation within the nation state and, increasingly, within global institutions (Palmer and Harley, 2011; Sabariego et al, 2015). While debates over terminology inform and are informed by theoretical models, they also constitute categories that both determine social identities and delineate social divisions and most importantly deliver or fail to deliver material social benefits. The World Bank, the World Health Organisation (WHO) and the United Nations (UN) have each issued statements concerning the definition of disability, with the aim of achieving an international policy consensus (UN, 2006; WHO, 2006: WHO/World Bank, 2011). These definitions blend the demands of the disability movement for an end to exclusion and over-medicalisation with the need for the adequate provision of healthcare, social protection and welfare to those who are often among the most ignored, excluded and disadvantaged in society – people with disabilities.

The WHO's International Classification of Functioning (ICF), categorised 'problems with human functioning' into three interconnected areas:

- impairments, which are problems in body function or alterations in body structure such as paralysis or blindness;

- activity limitations, which are difficulties in executing activities, such as walking or eating;
- participation restrictions, which are problems with involvement in any area of life, such as education, employment and transport.

Disability was used to describe difficulties encountered in any or all three areas of functioning. The ICF sees disability arising from the interaction of health conditions (that is, diseases, injuries and disorders), impairments (that is, specific decrements in body functions and structures) and the physical, personal and social environments in which people live (WHO/World Bank, 2011: 5). How then should these facets of functionality, of underlying health conditions and of the social context best be represented – or understood – as sources of social division in later life?

The term 'impairment' seems to privilege the notion of bodily integrity or normativity implying an already established understanding of what constitutes a normal human body. When coupled with 'activity limitations' it implies that the capacity of a body to serve as a vehicle for human agency is in turn determined by an agreed range of acts, deeds and functions that a human body should be capable of performing. The third term, restrictions, introduces considerations that go beyond the consensual understanding of bodies and bodily functions. Restrictions assume that environments themselves are capable of creating barriers, limitations and obstacles, which prevent individual bodies from realising their personhood by restricting the arena of possible performance, however constituted. While the assumption is often made that these restrictions are fundamentally social in nature, environments may also be physical in nature and their material nature may itself pose restrictions, such as the natural environment being mountainous and rocky or flat and grassy, subject to flooding or subject to drought. Within this framework, each facet, whether in the form of physical and mental impairment, activity limitations or environmental restrictions, alters the possibilities of persons performing as social beings; and each is capable of adding to and further compounding the opportunities and lifestyles that each person can be expected to realise.

Is the dichotomy 'disabled or not' a meaningful source of social categorisation or social division? Should disability be realised in and through the domain of 'limitations' rather than by the presence of impairments or restrictions? If so, would a dimensional or gradational model be preferable to a relational one, using 'activities of daily living' or 'instrumental activities of daily living' indices in ways similar to those composite indices of income and education that are used to assign socio-economic position? As Shakespeare has noted, disability is not simply a matter of access and barriers, any more than it is a matter of underlying impairments or health conditions (Shakespeare, 2012). While some positions might well favour a gradational approach ranking a population in terms of its degrees of fitness and function, others favour a relational one – emphasising the distinctive position of those designated 'infirm' or 'disabled' when set against the assumptions of those designated 'fit' or 'fully functional'. This can seem an unresolvable conundrum (McDermott and Turk, 2011) but ignoring the role of fitness and functionality in realising social divisions in later life risks missing 'the elephant in the room' – the very corporeality of the ageing body (Brayne, 2007). Bodily infirmity and functional limitations are important in marking the social spaces of later life. They affect a person's well-being; they have important consequences for possible lifestyles; and they limit access to resources that enable people to better enjoy later life (Sabariego et al, 2015). Furthermore, they are features by which people in later life themselves seek to draw distinctions, both between themselves at different ages and between themselves and others at the same age (Furman, 1997; Dumas, Laberge and Straka, 2005; Friedman et al, 2015).

There seems no escaping the confounding of disabilities as conditions and disabilities as divisions, or in treating ageing and disability as inextricably aligned phenomena. Agedness – whether represented corporeally or chronologically – and disabledness are each capable of serving as points of distinction, of being represented through a kind of otherness that they each equally possess (that is, people not like me). Both can be understood either as experiences or as statuses, highlighting or underplaying the potential differentiation that exists between ageing as either a chronological or a corporeal process and ageing into disability as a corporeal and temporal transformation of experience and identity. Bickenbach and colleagues argued that the distinction between status and state, between identity and experience is 'deeply theoretical' at the same time as possessing 'far-reaching social consequences' (Bickenbach, Rubinelli and Stucki, 2017). The 'disability as a status' position implicates a binary division between a majority of non-disabled older people who consider themselves in good health but otherwise unmarked and a minority of older people who are set apart by their distinct, identifiable disabilities. The ageing/disability as experience, on the other hand, implies a commonality and continuity among older people, sharing a common chronology, but with a diversity of experience. As a minority status group, older people with disabilities can be represented as the subjects of structural discrimination and disadvantage. In contrast, people who see their disability as an experience or state are more likely to see themselves as part of a continuum of older people, perhaps less fortunate than most, but with no clear point of social division or fraction (Bickenbach, Rubinelli and Stucki, 2017: 545). As 'ageing into disability' is more common than 'ageing with disability', the experiential view of disability might be thought to dominate the subjectivities of later life with relatively few older people choosing to represent themselves as a disabled 'minority', even if they have internalised the ideal of successful ageing as acknowledging no limitations to their ageing. Research tends to suggest this is so (Darling and Heckert, 2010).

Given the policy implications of categorising disability as a status, the division between those with, and those without, disability inevitably serves as a critical point of inflection, determining access and entitlement in the provision of care irrespective of self-ascriptions (Gilleard and Higgs, 2011). Although this becomes somewhat more confounded as agedness and disability lose some of their critical points of distinction, the status of 'disabled' still acts as a boundary, in terms of entitlements to benefits, eligibility for various types of welfare support and access to social care. Such divisions, however, are often represented by other terminology, particularly that of infirmity or, more recently, frailty. Frailty has come to dominate much of the literature concerning impairment and infirmity, with a conflict between those seeking to make a clear distinction between disability and frailty (Fried et al, 2004) and those seeing frailty in terms of cumulative disability (Rockwood, 2005).[2] However, if 'disabled' has become rather less acceptable as a social category, describing someone as 'frail' is even less acceptable. While disability – or even 'Crip' – has acquired a kind of identity for the radical reclaiming of a silenced voice for people with impairments of one sort or another, frailty or infirmity lack such a potential edge. Frailty and infirmity define those without a voice, those who are unable to speak and so must be spoken for; statistics without agency (Higgs and Gilleard, 2014).

Of course, this distinction between the fit and the frail harks back to earlier times, when states created categories of agedness, of disability and of chronic sickness to categorise their pauper populations. If old age was categorised by the economic criteria of impotent to labour, terms like the 'chronic sick', the 'elderly infirm' and the 'aged sick' followed as yet further 'dividing practices' in offering welfare to the aged in need (Grenier, 2007 Gilleard and Higgs, 2013). The conventional distinction between a person occupying a predetermined social category and a person consciously resisting or acquiescing to being assigned to that category retains its significance. The contrast between structures and subjectivities applies as much to disability and infirmity as it does to other social divisions. In the contestations between identity and experience, status and state, distinctions made between those with or without disability, frailty or infirmity lean upon, and are leant upon, by ideas of corporeal agedness, but also by ideas of class, gender and other social divisions. These intersecting locations are further inflected by a distinction between health and illness and between the alternative identities espoused by those with both disabling and non-disabling disease. The next section explores in more detail the basis for thinking of health and disability as 'objective' statuses, as human experiences, and as sources of social division, distinction and identity.

Able-bodiedness as human capital

There is a vast literature within the social sciences that treats disability, frailty and health as outcomes of social division and social inequality. In contrast, the notion that disability is itself a social position has not exercised such a wide purchase. While the disability movement and disability studies were equally prominent in framing disability as a social category, disability within both medical sociology and social gerontology has often been treated as an outcome determined by (other facets of) social location. This is most noticeable in relation to disability in later life (House, Landis and Umberson, 1988; Link and Phelan, 1995; Berkman et al, 2000). Weak social networks, lack of financial resources, limited human capital and chronic hardship have all been seen as the determinants of ill health and disability in later life. By choosing to treat disability as a structural division within later life, we are conscious of moving onto different ground, aligned more with disability studies than ageing studies. At the same time, this kind of positioning of late-life disability as a form of 'health-begets-position' thesis has been explored, but more by economists than by the social sciences (Cornwell, 2009; Schafer, 2013).

Health or the lack of health, able-bodiedness or disability are rarely enumerated within the assets, capital and resources framework that dominates the contemporary approaches to class that were outlined in Chapter 2. Within the social sciences the idea that people possess something similar to 'corporeal capital' has rarely been explored or even easily countenanced. The so-called human capital model that was developed by Gary Becker and others within the framework of classical economic theory has had little purchase within sociology. There have been two notable French exceptions, Pierre Bourdieu and Michel Foucault. Becker's work on human capital influenced Bourdieu's subsequent work on forms of capital (Convert, 2003). Bourdieu, however, rejected Becker's model as too 'individualistic', sidestepping the structuring role played by 'the differential profit rates which different social categories might expect from investments in various markets' (Convert, 2003: 8).

Another exception, remarkable perhaps for being so seemingly dissonant, was Foucault's late engagement with Gary Becker (Foucault, 2008; Becker, Ewald and Harcourt, 2012). Foucault's untimely death prevents our seeing where, if anywhere, that would have led him. Within what is now termed the 'neo-liberal' tradition, Becker treated the individual and collective resources possessed by individuals, such as their abilities, education, knowledge, skills and training, as a stock of human capital (Becker, 1962; Mincer, 1958; Schultz, 1961). The returns from those resources, whether in terms of pay, pensions or profits, he viewed primarily as the consequences of investments made earlier, in education and training. While he acknowledged the corporeal qualities of health and fitness as equally forms of human capital, it was to education and training that he most often turned in formulating tests of his model (Becker, 1962, 1994).

Fundamental to Becker's model of human capital was the differential rate of return on 'wage-labour', that is, the fact that different people in different occupations earned different amounts of money. With more time and investment in education and training, individuals' earnings increased cumulatively during the course of their working lives. Better-educated people gained greater returns from their original investments so that by forgoing income at the start of adult life by continuing in college, they gained a cumulative advantage in the long run, in terms of increasing returns on their capital investment (Schultz, 1961; Becker, 1962). Becker broadened his approach by considering medical care as well as education and training to be investment in human capital, but he made less of the concept of health as a source of human capital (Becker, 1994, 2002). Since the physicality of labour was considered inversely proportional to occupational training and prestige in generating economic returns, it is perhaps unsurprising that human capital theory eschewed the exploration of the 'merely' corporeal in favour of the cerebral as the major source of economic return.

An economist from the same human capital tradition, Martin Grossman, developed the term 'health capital' as a distinct form of human capital. He postulated that individuals inherit an initial stock of health that depreciates over time and at an ever-increasing rate after reaching a certain stage in the lifecycle (Grossman, 1972: 225).

Investing in the stock of health, Grossman saw, offered an economic return by reducing the time lost from market and non-market activities by ill health or disability. The monetary value of this reduction in time lost to sickness he framed as the return on investments in health capital (Grossman, 1972: 225). He further suggested that health was both less valuable as an asset and more costly as an investment in the later years, arguing that investing in health earlier in life yields a greater return, building a greater stock of health capital than can be subsequently achieved later in life. Grossman's model was framed by a productivist model that focused on the operations of a capitalist wage economy when the major source of income differentials were wages. Expressing a 'common sense' approach to ageing that health capital declines as a function of age, Grossman assumed that investment in the last year of life would yield no return, an argument underlying Daniel Callahan's position in favour of curtailing the costs of healthcare after a certain 'stage in the life cycle' because of such diminishing returns (Callahan, 1995).

This type of profit-maximising calculation is unsurprisingly anathema to most gerontologists. Consequently, the concept of health as human capital has remained largely unexplored outside of the field of economics. As a result, the conclusions economists have reached, that the link between social status and health is 'perhaps too complex for any single explanation', for example, have remained largely unexplored.

Within medical sociology, public health and social gerontology, health continues to be seen as an outcome, as the consequence of social structured divisions and inequalities, not itself a factor in structuring divisions and disadvantages. Despite the conclusions of an almost entirely economic evidence that 'much of the link between income and health is a result of the latter causing the former, rather than the reverse' (Cutler, Deaton and Lleras-Muney, 2006: 115), the social determinacy model continues to dominate ageing research and theory. Economists like Becker and Grossman have long acknowledged that there is a 'return' to health derived from education and healthcare, and that health status and education status combine to exercise an interactive effect upon later life earnings which in turn influence the resources available to address ill health and minimise disablement. What such mutual interaction implies, however, is that health itself functions as an asset or resource, conferring status and distinction as much as other social divisions considered being the determinants of health and ill health, disability and frailty in later life. This reciprocity of effects implies that any differential 'decline' in health and consequent 'increase' in disability can itself establish – or cause to emerge – social divisions in later life that are more than the mere accentuation of earlier, older already existing social divisions, such as those of class, ethnicity, gender or race.

Before considering this question further, we should perhaps examine one of Grossman's basic tenets – that health or health capital does indeed show a point of inflection, such that, with increasing age, there is an exponential fall in its rate of return. If such a point can be observed, it then raises the question of whether that point of inflection also serves as the moment when corporeal capital emerges as a new and important source of inequality. In her review of the determinants of cognitive health in later life, Brayne (2007: 238) has pointed out how '[a]ge remains the elephant in the room whose large effects dwarf other risk estimates'. All estimates of the prevalence of disability attest to the increasing association between disability, infirmity and agedness. Data from the 2005 Survey of Income and Program Participation demonstrates a doubling of rates of overall disability in the USA for successive age groups, rising from 11 per cent among those aged 18–44 years, to 24 per cent among those aged 45–64 years, to reach over 50 per cent among those aged 65 years and above (Centers for Disease Control and Prevention, 2009: 422). Although this pattern is pervasive across all social groups and populations, other social divisions do mediate these effects. Thus rates of disablement for women are greater than for men; rates for African Americans are greater than for non-Hispanic white Americans; and rates vary according to the amount of education received, although such effects are all more pronounced in late mid-life, that is, 55–64 years, than they are at later old age, that is, 75 years and above (Minkler, Fuller-Thomson and Guralnik, 2006). A degree of reciprocity exists between disablement and impoverishment, such that rates of poverty are consistently greater among those having a disability than among those without reported disabilities (US Census Bureau, 2016b). These trends are illustrated in Figure 5.1.

Such figures, however, conceal as much as they reveal. Not all disabilities are equal in their impact upon independence, poverty or social position. Several factors mediate the relationship, including differences in the social circumstances of the disabled person, differences in the healthcare consequences of the disability as well as differences in the nature of the impairment or underlying condition (Wilmoth, London and Heflin, 2015). In the American Community Survey, for example, six types of 'limitation' are recorded, ranging from hearing difficulties, difficulties with vision, and cognitive difficulties to difficulties with mobility, self-care and independent living. The

Figure 5.1: Rates of disability and rates of poverty in USA, by age group

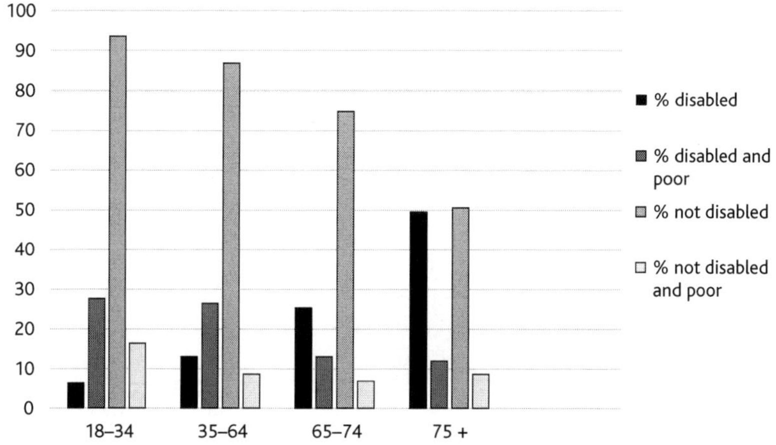

Source: US Census, American Community Survey 2016b: Table B18130.

Figure 5.2: Type of limitation by age group: USA, 2016

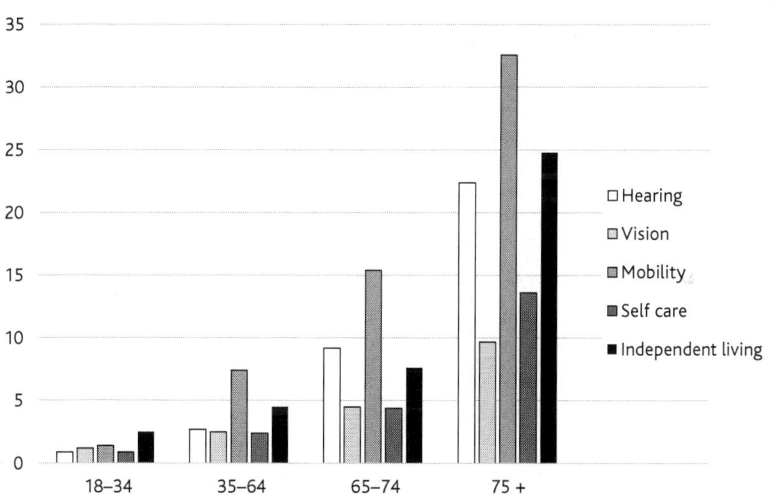

Source: US Census American Community Survey 2016a: Table S1810 Disability characteristics.

association between each of these limitations and chronological age differs, as illustrated Figure 5.2.

How do such variations in health capital impact upon 'successful ageing'? Is there evidence supporting Grossman's model that earlier investments in health/fitness yield greater returns during working life, which progressively diminish with increasing age? How might one demonstrate that disability functions as a structural component determining differences in the opportunities for and obstacles limiting the pursuit of later lifestyles? The next section explores these issues.

The costs and consequences of disablement in later life

While the likelihood of developing impairment and disability before age 65 is strongly linked to socio-economic advantage, impairment and ill health after age 65 show less relationship to indices of socio-economic advantage (Sugisawa et al, 2018). As chronology comes increasingly to determine the presence and extent of disability, so, it can be argued, do the effects of earlier socio-economic advantage lessen. The blunting of earlier disadvantages by age has been termed the 'age-as-leveller' hypothesis, often contrasted with the position that earlier disadvantages become progressively accentuated with age – sometimes known as the cumulative disadvantage hypothesis (Ross and Wu, 1996; Dannefer, 2003; Lynch, 2003). Empirical evidence for such hypotheses is equivocal, though most evidence suggests a degree of 'levelling' growing more marked the longer people live (O'Rand and Lynch, 2018: 76). Thus although the disadvantages arising from disability grow more pervasive with age, disability arguably becomes less disadvantaging as it becomes more prevalent. Hence, the status of disability may be both less reflective of earlier disadvantages and less defining of later life chances than is the case for adults of working age. Does this mean then that disability is actually less a divide in later life?

Disability is undoubtedly disadvantaging at any age. The fact that the relationship between earlier social disadvantage and ageing into disability is less clear-cut than is the case for developing disability during working life does not mean that disability per se is more or less disadvantaging in later life, just that it leans rather less upon earlier divisions. One recent US study illustrates the economic impact of disability, noting how

> [t]en years after disability onset, those with a chronic and severe disability condition have on average experienced a 77 per cent decline in earnings, a 28 per cent decline in after-tax after-transfer income, a 25 per cent decline in food and housing consumption and a 16 per cent decline in consumption of food alone. (Meyer and Mok, 2018: 17)

Numerous other studies attest to the fact that people with disabilities 'are socio-economically disadvantaged and have poorer health than people without disabilities' (Kavanagh et al, 2015: 191). This impact is moderated by age, however, and when rates of poverty in US pensioner and non-pensioner households are compared, more than twice as many households with a disabled person of working age are poor compared with disabled householders who are pensioners (Tinson et al, 2016: 11). A similar pattern has been observed in recent US census data. Householders aged over 65 with severe disabilities were less likely to be in poverty (12 per cent) compared with similarly disabled householders of working age (29 per cent). Both severely disabled pensioner and working age people were much more likely to be poor compared with their non-disabled age peers (Brault, 2012: 22) but the levelling effect of age cannot be ignored.

Various factors contribute to reducing poverty amongst retired people with disabilities, including the effects of redistributed incomes (benefits, pensions, social security payments) and lowered costs of living (greater rates of home ownership, and in the USA, significant Medicare coverage of health bills). Those in more advantaged positions are paradoxically more greatly affected by becoming disabled than those already on the margins, particularly for those in work, compared with those out of work, prior to becoming disabled. Population statistics on the associations of disability, material hardship and age can however fail to reveal the true extent of the differences in everyday living that differentiates between these two age groups (those of working age and those of retirement age). In the US 2015 Compendium of Disability Statistics, for example, a little over one-third of people with a disability aged 21 to 64 had difficulty walking or using stairs, but only 5 per cent used a wheelchair. By comparison, almost two-thirds of people aged over 65 with a disability had such difficulties and twice as many (10 per cent) relied on a wheelchair (Houtenville, Brucker and Lauer, 2016: Tables 3.2 and 3.3).

Thus, while the economic consequences of disability for older people may be less marked, the everyday limitations and restrictions that affect later life are far greater, in no small part because the disabilities of later life are more severe, more intractable and more often progressive. Well-off older people with a disability face less hardship than do their poorer age peers, but even the better off face more isolation and personal distress than do their non-disabled peers, irrespective of their wealth or poverty (Torres et al, 2016). Similar points have been observed in Ireland, where research has shown the greater hardships faced by older people with a severe disability compared with their able-bodied peers and with older Irish households containing someone with only mild or non-limiting disabilities (Cullinan, Gannon and O'Shea, 2013). A recent study in the UK concluded that the 'disability costs faced by older people in Britain are large and increase strongly with severity of disability' (Morciano, Hancock and Pudney, 2015). The 'costs' of disability rise not only with the severity of the disability but also with the status of the household. Older people with a severe disability who live alone, for example, incur greater social and material costs than do older people with a disability living with others (Zaidi and Burchardt, 2005). Since the likelihood of living alone increases with increasing age, even if the relative income of older and younger disabled people favours the former, the costs of living and maintaining one's household are likely to be more onerous and more limiting for the oldest and most severely disabled people since it is they who are most likely to live alone.

Although the costs of disability in later life are difficult to enumerate, they are by no means insignificant. As such, they constitute a materially and socially significant division that is more easily represented as disadvantage than difference. For most older people the identity of disability that has been claimed by many younger people rarely provides the same degree of 'belonging', of 'community'. Identification as 'disabled' possesses less cultural and symbolic value to older people, in large part because it is less stable, more often progressive and more readily framed as experience. This reflects the different social representations that disability has for younger and older people. As Tom Shakespeare pointed out some time ago, positive identification as disabled 'opens up the possibility of subjectification' (Shakespeare, 1996: 96). Such identification is more common among those with early onset disabilities who develop as persons, with disabilities. Those ageing into disability, by contrast, experience disability or infirmity as the disruption of, not an extension of their sense of self (Hahn and Belt, 2004). While older people report the most significant disabilities of any age group, they are nonetheless less likely to identify with disability politics and, perhaps consequently, report lower levels of social participation and satisfaction (Darling and Heckert, 2010: 140). Darling and Heckert found little distinction between those with disability in mid-life and those in later life; the real gap seems to be that between these latter groups and young people with disabilities for whom disability is often a lifelong rather than a life-shortening prospect.

Ageing into disability arguably represents a different kind of division from that characterising people who have developed with a disability, whose 'newness' is of a different nature with different consequences, compared with that conferred upon, and identified with, young adults with disability. Instead of offering additional or alternative sources of identity and community, becoming old and disabled threatens only to lessen and limit such opportunities.

Age, disability and identity

As noted at the start of this chapter, the social model of disability was formulated within the context of the new social movements, when young people with disabilities began to assert their rights as citizens. Full social inclusion and active participation in the institutions of society were their goals, ones that were modelled on the civil rights and women's movements. As those most actively seeking these rights were young people, ageing into disability was either ignored or rendered marginal to their concerns. Considerably more government and non-governmental resources were consequently directed toward younger people with disabilities (Kane, Priester and Neumann, 2007: 271). While the disability movement has overcome some of its earlier disregard for older people, the identity of disability and its location in later life remain problematic (Jönson and Larsson, 2009). Besides the evident fact that older people are not in most cases actively seeking to reinsert themselves into the labour market, factors other than economic status distinguish working age people with disabilities from those of retirement age. These include (a) the nature of the impairment that shapes the disability; (b) the underlying trajectory of the disablement process; (c) the presence of other associated conditions and impairments; (d) the relative tractability of the impairment; (e) its limiting effects; and (f) the capacity afforded for self-management. Should these distinctions be simply subsumed under the more general distinction noted earlier between ageing with disability and ageing into disability, or 'aging with disability' contrasted with 'disability with aging', or should further divisions and distinctions be made (Verbrugge and Yang, 2002)?

Verbrugge and Yang have argued that even this age-based distinction is divisive, setting apart the positions of young and old people with disabilities. Disability and ageing, they argue, 'apply to everyone' (Verbrugge and Yang, 2002: 266). Yet there are very real differences that make the social division associated with disability in later life distinct (or at least make for a distinction between disability arising in mid and later life and early onset disability). People developing disabilities before the age of 21, for example, have better health than people developing disabilities later, even after controlling for age (Verbrugge and Yang, 2002; Jamoom et al, 2008). People with lifelong disabilities are likely to experience continuing personal development alongside their impairment, learning how best to cope with whatever limitations arise. Those developing disabilities in mid and later life, by contrast, are likely to experience a degree of personal diminishment following their disablement that lasts. Of course, all such distinctions involve a degree of over-generalisations; neither early onset nor later life disabilities are of a kind. In the latter case, however, the main distinction seems to be more related to condition-specific trajectories than is the case for disabilities that arise with development. Thus, it is possible to contrast the position of those facing the 'progressive' disablement associated with such chronic conditions as Alzheimer's, cardiovascular disease, diabetes or osteoporosis, with the more 'catastrophic' disablement associated with stroke (Ferrucci et al, 1996). Even so, the patterning of disablement in mid and later life onset disability remains heterogeneous, with considerable variation even when the primary impairment or condition is itself fixed (Nusellder et al, 2006).

Still, it is possible to distinguish between the social location determined by those disabling conditions affecting older people that are generally progressive from those that are characteristic of younger people, whose impairments and associated limitations are more easily integrated as part of a person's sense of self. These typically provide for a degree of predictability that permits both adaption to and identification with the condition. Disabilities with an onset in mid or later life are more difficult to adjust to, and carry the very real prospect of future worsening. The experience of, and anticipated worsening of disability disrupts the possibilities for the kind of accommodation and adaptation available to those with more stable disabilities of early onset. Of course, there are conditions that have an onset earlier in life and which are progressive, but these are relatively uncommon. However severe, disabilities arising early in life still lean upon the idea of difference and development; by contrast, however mild, disabilities arising later in life cannot but lean upon the idea of decay and deterioration.

Progressive disability, however, is more prevalent than disability arising from the catastrophic 'body-drop' associated with stroke or trauma (Yu et al, 2015). This temporal progression presents a paradox in terms of social positioning. While being unable to walk or having great difficulty walking obviously restricts what a person can do, such difficulties can be mitigated by the use of assistive devices such as electric scooters, wheelchairs, walking frames or canes. If the underlying impairment progresses, however, the assistive devices will themselves become unusable – abandoned once they no longer aid the person. Further limitations call for further aids, but each progression renders the former aids less effective as disability becomes disablement. As the experience of disablement dominates, it becomes recast into the more ignominious position of becoming infirm, of frailing. Set apart from the status of disability, the processes of disablement easily slip into an othering whose identity as frailty or infirmity is further and more deeply shaped by the dividing practices of health and social care (Grenier, 2007: 426). No longer open to the negotiations available to those who despite disability report their health as good and their circumstances as happy, those deemed frail have more limited options to become otherwise embodied (Grenier and Hanley, 2007).

In short, disability in later life serves as a social divide, a source of disadvantage, exclusion and inequality that offers more limited purchase for subjectification, resistance or community compared with those who in contrast find themselves ageing almost without noticing, retaining their identity as persons with a difference, a distinction framed by their disability (Gallop, 2015: 325). It is unsurprising, then, that disability, let alone frailty, is rarely acknowledged as an identity by older people themselves (Tarrant, 2016; Warmoth et al, 2016; Shaw et al, 2018). Instead, as Pickard (2014: 549) has noted, the division of old age 'into two ages is no longer concerned so much with delineating normal and pathological aspects in the same individual as in establishing divisions in all individuals aged over 65 between those who are successfully and those who are unsuccessfully ageing'. This bifurcation represents a biomedical reclaiming of the old division between the fit and the frail, rebadged as that between those who are successfully or unsuccessfully ageing. At the same time, it also leans upon an older social division, between those with and without position, those whose old age has been reached by worth, contrasted with those whose frailty encompasses more than mere corporeality. Social position framed as the ownership of health capital forms an implicit point of reference in both. However, unlike the status of disability, frailty offers few possibilities either for community or identity, for status or subjectivity, no tools beyond denial with which age's corporeality can be reclaimed.

An inherent tension exists between the disabilities of later life, with all its instability and otherness and the infirmities of age. While the latter sets persons apart, individualising their circumstances, the capacity of the former to turn disadvantage to advantage, to embrace an identity as disabled is itself compromised. Lacking the virtue of authenticity of being 'truly' disabled, becoming disabled in later life offers at best only a weak defence against the prospect of failing to age well. That such possibilities exist is evident, as can be seen in the growth of self-advocacy movements among people diagnosed with Alzheimer's or Parkinson's disease, who assert 'the value and importance of remaining themselves' (Roger and Medved, 2010: 3; Roger et al, 2014). But such movements remain restricted to a minority of people suffering from these conditions. They are counterbalanced by a much greater number of older people who self-define their success in ageing by reference to their health and fitness and the firmness of their minds (Knight and Riccardielli, 2003; Laditka et al, 2009). Of course, this still leaves other options – beyond mere denial – to assert and represent one's agency and subjectivity. Most notable is the kind of 'gero-transcendence' advocated by Tornstam (1989) that suggests older people escape becoming subject to the social divide of corporeality by expressing and realising their sense of self and belongingness in and through non-corporeal domains. Such disembodiment ('disinvestment in the body'?) is perhaps too costly to achieve, however, or at least to sustain and evidence of its realisation is scanty at best (Jönson and Magnusson, 2001). Instead, we consider another approach, that of enhancing the corporeal self through the effective use of assistive technologies that minimise the divide. It is to this theme that we finally turn.

Disability, technology and critical studies

Reports began emerging in the 1980s that disability rates among older people were declining. This was described as 'one of the most significant advances in the health and well-being of Americans in the past quarter century' (Schoeni et al, 2008: 81). Attempts at accounting for these trends range from advances in medical care, to improved income among those with lower income and rising educational standards. The area showing most improvement was in what are called the 'instrumental activities of daily living' rather than in the basic 'activities of daily living'. One question this patterning of reducing disabilities raised was whether the improvement was the result not of improved function, but of improved access to external resources that helped one function. Such consideration extends from greater access to electric scooters, ICT and online shopping, to more indoor stair lifts in public buildings, improved hearing and visual aids and adaptations of health and fitness regimes to accommodate people with disabilities. Were the divisions (and exclusions) of later life associated with bodily impairment lessening not because of building better bodies but because of improved external resources that minimise the exclusion of people of all ages with disabilities?

Evidence from a number of countries points to the increase in use made of a variety of 'assistive technologies' designed to improve older people's functioning and independence (Löfqvist et al, 2005; Freedman et al, 2006). There is also evidence that gaining access to such resources – whether it be a chair lift, hearing aids, motorised scooters or internet-facilitated services – results in objective and subjective benefits to the persons concerned (Hoenig, Taylor and Sloan, 2003; Fomiatti et al, 2014; Khosravi and Ghapanchi, 2016; Pettersson et al, 2016). There are, however, barriers to the uptake of assistive technologies, in terms of the stigma attached to the aids, the difficulty in using them, and a lack of confidence in trying them out. Evidence of structural inequalities in accessing assistive technologies is ambiguous, but it seems clear that usage is more limited among those developing a disability later, compared with earlier in life and among older people with less education and with greater physical impairments (Gell et al, 2013). A similar relationship exists between the level of complexity of the technology used, age of onset and educational status, with older less educated people from black and ethnic minority backgrounds using mostly low and medium technology devices when compared with the greater use of 'high' technology devices by younger and more educated people (Kaye, Yeager and Reed, 2008; Fang et al, 2019).

While much is now made of a future of 'ambient assistive technologies' enabling older disabled people to live richer and more independent lives, the ambitions for 'an internet of things', for a cybernetics of the future to radically transform the lives of 'frailed' older people remain largely aspirational (Hallewell-Haslwanter and Fitzpatrick, 2018). Given the many barriers to accepting, let alone accessing, 'high' technology devices, one might argue that more effort should be devoted to improving access to the various 'low' and 'medium' level assistive technologies that are of proven value to older people with moderate and severe disabilities. While disability, represented as limitations in carrying out the tasks of daily living, affects an increasing number of older people as they travel deeper into later life, the extent to which disability acts as a source of social division is not just a corporeal matter; it intersects with other socio-economic inequalities. While there is more support for an age-as-leveller model than for the cumulative disadvantage model, particularly when the frame is ageing deeper into disability (Rehnberg, 2019), differences in the adoption and use of technology are also instrumental in maintaining or moderating the inequalities imposed by age and disability (Freedman et al, 2006; Fischer et al, 2014).

Rising levels of education and the expansion of digital technologies will see successive cohorts of people reaching later life who are more familiar with and less averse to technological devices that facilitate access and communication. Even so, a kind of ambivalence exists about what constitutes 'acceptable' or 'virtuous' technologies and their promotion over technologies that seem to support indolence and indulgence. Teaching older people to make use of 'health improving' techniques, such as exercise machines, 'fitbits', brain training and so forth falls into the category of pursuing 'a worthy' old age (Libert, Charlesworth and Higgs, 2019). A considerable research literature exists on the uptake and barriers to such instrumental 'gerontechnologies' (Yusif, Soar and Hafeez-Baig, 2016). By contrast, technological devices designed to deliver more hedonistic pleasures, such as the use of electric scooters, facilitation of internet surfing, online dating, the expansion of in-house entertainment systems or the deployment of 'robotic servants' to work around the house are relatively 'under-researched' gerontological topics because of the implicit indolence they seem to infer. A moral distinction between 'utilitarian' and 'hedonistic' approaches to technology can be discerned and what might be called the relative tolerability of some forms of inequality and exclusion over others.[3]

A further distinction, then, can be made, between more and less acceptable technologies that somehow mirror the acceptable and unacceptable faces of disability. Those 'naturally' disabled by age remain not just less visible but in some way less virtuous, less heroic, less authentic than those who age with disabilities. The true heroes of later life occupy very different positions – the octogenarian mountaineers and marathon runners, mime artists and minstrels who 'despite their age' flaunt their embodied excellence. Meantime, the go-to technologies that enhance agency and subjectivity seem selectively to target younger disabled persons. Those that target older disabled persons remain resolutely less smart and less sophisticated and consequently age more than rejuvenate their users. Only in science fiction, it seems, are fantasies of an unrealised and perhaps unrealisable robotics of 'care' able to excite potential investors, heedless of the possibility that they would, in reality, make of older people actants more than agents (Archibald and Barnard, 2018).

Little research has been conducted to examine the extent to which well-off disabled older men make use of, or access, various forms of 'assistive' technology, in comparison with their poor disabled peers. This is a pity, since the size of that resource-utilisation gap might indicate the scope for minimising at least some of the inequalities associated with later-life disability. Stacked against the hundreds of papers that have explored the role of already existing social divisions in determining health and disability in later life, research into the impact of assets, capital and resources on the quality of life, social inclusion and cultural participation of older people with disability is almost totally absent. Over the course of recent decades, the image of the wheelchair user has been transformed – from being old, female and frail to being young, male and fit. Unlike infirmity, disability has become a much-transformed social and cultural imaginary. It has done so, however, by turning its back on age. The scope for reversing that process exists, no doubt, particularly for those forms of disability that are more or less stable over time and which may well be realised by making later lives more digitally connected. However, as with any attempt to transform a devalued into a valued status, the risk is that such actions only render those older people whose infirmities prove too resistant to such technological fixes, those whose corporeal infirmity is more profoundly progressive or those whose corporeal status is much harder to rebadge, even further excluded. Future technologies no doubt do offer ways to include and enrich the lives of many older people with disabilities, reducing their chances of becoming frailed. But it is important not to let the pursuit of such developments reduce the commitment to better support the frailest, those whose unequal ageing is most deeply embedded in their chronology and corporeality.

Conclusions: corporeality as a *social* divide

Treating the body in later life as a source of social division is undoubtedly problematic. There are many reasons for this – not least the belief that social divisions should be based upon and understood as the distribution of social assets, capital and resources associated with social institutions and structures such as class, gender, race and ethnicity. Social divisions that are presaged upon the corporeal seem harder to represent as social as well as being more problematic in terms of their possibility of social change. If age and ageing, or more especially the bodily processes of ageing, selectively disadvantage those with the most agedness, does that not seem a feature of our species being rather than a product of our social world? The virtue – or wisdom – of attempts to ameliorate the socially deleterious effects of corporeal agedness is more problematic than when what is proposed is the reduction of upstream social injustices, such as poverty, bad housing and transport, poor healthcare or moral turpitude. If these more 'acceptable' inequities are found to be the key to disability, hardship and exclusion, poor health, shorter lives and more suffering, then intervening within these areas seems more realisable and of course much less problematic for critical theorists.

This risks ignoring 'the elephant in the room', those bodily processes of ageing that themselves lead to disability, disease and impairment and which shorten life. The fact that these processes are not randomly distributed across old age but accumulate with increasing age is difficult to come to terms with, without implying a role for social injustice.

Still, if it were the case that fate and the stochastic processes of chance generate such effects, it might not matter so much. But once these factors are recognised by the culture of a society, once they become the site of barriers and distinctions and shape judgements of social worth, such a fatalistic acceptance becomes less satisfying. A search is made for the points of distinction that mark out the differences between the fit and the frail, the successfully and unsuccessfully aged, and the winners and the losers in the race for longevity, where division is turned into difference and disability into identity. Once that search is made, there will be actors and institutions that seek to address such distinctions, offering market or state-mediated options to stay in the race and keep within the boundaries of successfully ageing, which is really not ageing at all, or ageing as little and as lightly as possible (Torres and Hammarström, 2009).

It is unsurprising, then, that the social divisions in later life located in health status and disability are among the least explored areas of social gerontology, even if, as some research implies, this division causes greater marginalisation and social exclusion than other social divisions (Barnes et al, 2006: 27–28; Gilleard and Higgs, 2017; Dahlberg and McKee, 2018). That the research community ignores this distinction is understandable; that it is rejected by older people and those anticipating growing old is no secret. Every jar of anti-ageing cream, every bottle of health-preserving vitamins and minerals sold and every headline promoting dietary and exercise prescriptions to guard against ageing or some age-associated condition from arthritis to Alzheimer's testify to the social significance that health and functionality – corporeal integrity – possess in later life. Some insist that this is mainly the ideological consequence of a neo-liberalism that places the onus for staying well onto the citizen, not the state. However, there has long been a distinction between a 'good' and a 'bad', a 'green' and a 'grey', and a 'fit' and a 'frail' old age which precedes capitalist economies and their recent neo-liberal ideologies.

Framing this division as another example of ideological essentialism masking the truth of human diversity does not seem to fit; nor does treating it as a misplaced materialism that confuses the corporeal with the social. Both positions deflect attention from the difficulties, divisions and inequalities that are inexorably attached to the corporeality of age. The call for society and its institutions 'not to discriminate' or to instead target earlier inequalities of childhood seems virtuous but may overestimate what is possible. While social conditions obtaining during schooling or during working life undoubtedly have an impact upon the onset and extent of later life disability/impairment, the nature and extent of such 'weathering' is unclear. It seems contingent on a range of factors, not least on how disability is reported and whether incidence, prevalence or rate of development is the focus (Gu, Gomez-Redondo and Dupre, 2015).

What is not nearly so contingent is the impact of chronology. The longer later lives extend, the greater our risk of succumbing to impairments and disabilities. How society organises itself to accommodate these emerging divisions demands a wide range of responses – social, cultural, economic, medical and technological. If, however, this division goes unnoticed or is treated as 'merely' ideological, the very real social division between those with and those without infirmities in later life can itself go unacknowledged. Corporeality counts – whether in disability studies or in ageing studies. Attempts to dissolve it within the accumulation of past social disadvantage risk taking the pressure off doing something in the here and now to discount its personal and social impact. Whatever role is played by the inequalities of the past, for those ageing into disability there is only the future in which to engineer the possibilities for greater inclusion. The search to demonstrate the impact of past social inequalities should not overshadow the need to ameliorate the impact that present corporeal inequalities have in the here and now.

Notes

1. Of course the term disability has been widely used in social gerontology, but mostly as a condition or measured outcome and rarely if ever as an articulated, voiced division.
2. Earlier demographic thinking treated frailty as something quite distinct from either disability or infirmity, as a statistical index representing individual differences in the force of mortality – those most frail being those with the greatest propensity to die (Vaupel, Manton and Stallard, 1979). This was later defined by these authors as 'an unobserved nonnegative random variable termed frailty represent[ing] all individual differences in endowment for longevity' (Manton, Stallard and Vaupel, 1986: 635).
3. Research suggests, however, that using hedonistic technologies induces a sense of being 'younger' among older users more than do instrumental devices (Guido, Amatulli and Peluso, 2014).

6

Identity and intersectionality

Previous chapters have explored the 'traditional' social divisions of later life, namely social class, gender, ethnicity/race and disability. It has been argued that each has acquired a greater salience in the study of ageing in large part because of the expansion and diversification of later life itself. Each in their own way has served as both cause and effect in realising the 'new ageing' (Gergen and Gergen, 2000). Unsurprisingly their impact is most noticeable among recently retired cohorts of 'baby boomers' where difference, diversity and inequality are all more notable. Members of the oldest cohorts, by contrast, are less differentiated and less unequal, both in the diversity of their assets and resources and in the cultural habitus that have shaped their later lifestyles.[1] Hence, the later lives of the baby-boomer cohorts define the contours of the new ageing more closely as they are more extensively engaged with the 'cultures of the third age' (Gilleard and Higgs, 2009). No doubt this will become even more evident as the cohort of the 'late' boomers, those born in the 1960s, reach retirement age. For now, however, those cohorts born in the 1940s and 1950s provide the principal arena where the social divisions of later life are most evident and whose consumer habitus continue to expand.

The social divides that we have considered central to this diversification of later life reflect (albeit in a somewhat reified form) many of the social differences, distinctions, identities and inequalities that render contextual the experiences and opportunities that constitute third age culture. This chapter shifts attention away from the sources of such broad social categorisation that have so far been addressed – of able-bodiedness, class, ethnicity, gender and race – towards a more general consideration of how the various social locations of later life are both crossed and realised by the intersections between them. In doing so, the aim is particularly to highlight the role played by the 'new' social movements not least in 'queering' the traditional territory of social divisions with their unmarked and essentialised binary oppositions.[2] Issues of structure and subjectivity that were once central to Marxist approaches to class are now being raised afresh, in the distinction between divisions consciously acknowledged as social identities (or locations) and divisions that are neither acknowledged nor even recognised as identities or locations but which nevertheless serve to structure difference in people's later lives (Moran, 2018). The Marxist contrast between a putative 'class in itself' and 'class for itself' can be extended into the wider debate concerning reflexivity and the social significance of subjectivity in the discursive articulation and practical realisation of difference and division in later life.

Conflict between these two aspects – the structural intersections of divisions within society (of religion, race, gender and class) with the consciousness of individuals occupying multiple social identities makes the notion of social location problematic. The more established social divisions that confer differential access to power, privilege and wealth are qualified and in some cases seem to be overshadowed by the new forms of difference, which focus more on systems of subjective differentiation than on structural advantage. While many of the traditional divisions of class, gender and race can be seen as the products (or realisations) of objective social structures with the latter subjectivities are stimulated and sustained as much by consumerism and the neo-liberal order as by objectively structured sets of interests or oppression. It might be argued that this division between structure and subjectivity itself forms part of the emergence of a second modernity and the continued fracturing of the various 'conscience collectifs' established within its first incarnation. What is 'new' about the social world of this second modernity is how 'new' social movements that privilege different sources of identity and different forms of power confer, reinforce or withhold what Bourdieu (1986) has termed society's cultural and symbolic capital.

In the context of these multiple 'capitals' (social, symbolic, cultural, political, and so on) some have argued that more personalised social identities 'supplant class interest as the chief medium of political mobilization' (Fraser, 1995: 68). This has in turn been accompanied by (or has an elective affinity to) a preference for individual rights as claims for justice, contrasted with earlier collective claims for political and social rights. These latter collective claims were asserted through the rights for the working man; votes for women; religious freedom; racial non-discrimination; and universal social security and health insurance (Ervik and Kildal, 2015). In place of the universalised equalities of first modernity that sought to minimise the material consequences of traditional social divisions, identity politics seeks to ensure individualised forms of 'empowerment' and 'entitlement' on the basis of otherwise unmarked difference and diversity (Franck, 1999: 85–94; Fraser, 2013: 197; Kenny, 2004: 33–34; Sokhi-Bulley, 2016: 34). In the process, a multiplicity of social locations are proclaimed, not necessarily ordered by, or organised within, any single hierarchical framework. This makes it difficult to represent them as projecting onto an underlying 'common' set of interests – the once much vaunted 'rainbow' coalition of the 1960s. Instead, the picture is one of continuing social contestation in the interpretation and organisation of identities and interests. The evolving matrix of such individual 'rights'-based approaches extends from identities framed around the claims of particular ethnic groups to those framed around other forms of exclusion and/or misrecognition arising in the context of previously 'unmarked' differences in sexual preference, in physical appearance, in health status and in the presence of socially disadvantaging physical or mental conditions.[3]

Various new communities, divisions and identities have appeared which have focused upon or in some way privileged the body as a site of distinction, whether in its shape, size, fitness or functionality.[4] These developments have since gone beyond the original concerns of the disability movement, as distinct illnesses and health-related conditions have themselves become sources of social identity, acting as levers for recognition, resources and civic and political change. The AIDS pandemic and its galvanising effect on identity, particularly among members of the homosexual community, was perhaps one of the first manifestations of this explicitly politicised embodiment of identity (Gamson, 1989; Ramirez-Valles and Diaz, 2005). Subsequently, strategies for the prevention of illness, the promotion of health and the preservation of the planet have each in turn formed yet further sources of politicised identity – in the form of veganism, vegetarianism or other related identity communities (Beardsworth and Keil, 1991; Cherry, 2006; Rosenfeld and Burrow, 2017). Like the 'older' new social movements, many of these 'new' new social movements are articulated most powerfully by younger people and are yet to impact upon the 'new' old.[5] Yet signs from the past suggest that they too will divide and differentiate later life much as they are beginning to in earlier adult life. The burgeoning Alzheimer's community is one example of these 'new' new movements infiltrating later life.

Various lines of thought have explored how such claims for identity and community should best be understood. Are they, as some have suggested, reflections of an ever more individualised and individualising society, caught in a regulatory spiral whereby new identities are framed as successive claims on the public commons (Beck, 2002; Carastathis, 2013: 942)? Alternatively, are they, as Bauman has suggested, the outcome of a 'post-socialist' world of consumerism where consumption outperforms production as the source of identity and markets penetrate successive aspects of the life world, including the fashioning of identities and identity claims (Bauman, 2000; Fraser, 2013: 220)? Or do they represent the outcome of an increasingly networked society, where technological innovation has enabled communities of interest to compete with and in many cases overwhelm those communities of propinquity that modernity itself first realised (Bradshaw, 2008)? Yet others see them as outcomes of a neo-liberal form of twenty-first century capitalism (Bohrer, 2018). Whatever their origins (and we would argue that all four elements play their part), collectively they raise the question of whether identity-based lifestyles have now replaced class or other 'structural' divisions as the principal sources of social division and social stratification, not just among the young, but also among those no-longer-young.

This can be considered as two separable questions. The first addresses the creation, maintenance and elaboration of 'social' subjectivities, their consciousness and social realisation of difference and division. Here, in answering such a question, particular consideration can be given to discursive practices and lifestyle. The second addresses the nature of 'objective' social divisions and the social realisation and institutionalisation of differential access to social and material assets and resources. While the former seem to be marked by distinction and by oppression, the latter are objectified as institutionalised strata through which the various forms of capital are circulated (of which income and wealth are but two aspects).

How far has contemporary consumer capitalism diversified power across multiple domains of production, distribution and consumption? Have the old systems of class, gender and race lost much of their salience under the weight of the complexity and contingency thrown up by 'second' modernity? What might such shifting sands imply about the social divisions, past, present and emerging, within later life? Should we conceive of them primarily as the spill-over into retirement of the multiple deprivations and cumulative advantages whose institutional base lies in the productive and reproductive organisation of society? Alternatively, should we consider the multiple sources of difference, distinction and identity woven by past and present patterns of consumption as impelling a reflexive imperative on individuals, to articulate, advance and delineate their social positions that now continues into and through later life? Such questions lead inexorably to the topic of identity, inequality and intersectionality that this chapter now seeks to address.

Identities and intersections

The term 'identity' was rarely employed in the social sciences before the 1960s (Brubaker and Cooper, 2000: 2; Côté, 2006: 4). Through the work of sociologists like Peter Berger and Erving Goffman

(Gleason, 1983: 917), social anthropologists like Fredrik Barth, and social psychologists like Henry Tajfel and John Turner (Eriksen, 2017: 154; Tajfel and Turner, 1979), identity emerged as 'a key issue of the contemporary era' (Côté, 2006: 4). In Côté's view, this proliferation has risked identity 'becom[ing] another Tower of Babel of the social sciences' (Côté, 2006: 6). Positioned somewhere between the individual self and the social collective, identity has been criticised as meaning either 'too much ... too little ... or nothing at all' (Brubaker and Cooper, 2000: 1). In a single concept it represents two rather different phenomena – one being the processes of social identification and the second being the processes of social categorisation. Making such a distinction, however, ignores the similarities in both, while failing to bring out the distinction between structural and processual systems of categorisation. While social divisions are typically construed as the outcomes of structuring influences within society through the relations of production, systems of power, privilege and property and the institutions designed to maintain these systems; social identities are located 'within' individuals even as they are fashioned through processes of social distinction and social division (Craib, 1998; Hall, 1996).

One can argue that social divisions exist whether or not they are realised in individual human consciousness. However, it makes less sense to think of social identities as similar aspects of society or even as social discourses 'spoken' (or 'interpellated') without subjects, in a world that, as Craib (1998: 9) put it, is 'peopled by normotic personalities ... who have no subjective or inner experience'. The process of acquiring, maintaining, revising, or indeed rejecting identities necessarily invokes the realm of subjectivity, even as individuals acquire, maintain, revise or reject their sense of identity in particular cultural contexts. Identity implies both agency and consciousness, however limited the former, and however constrained the latter. It also implies exclusivity and otherness. Such contextual framing of identities has become less stable and yet more extensive in 'second modernity' (Beck, Bonz and Lau, 2003). How far that applies to members of distinct age cohorts remains to be seen. But even this potential variability across age cohorts only adds further to the contestations of identity, introducing 'age cohort' as yet further intersections in the framing (and privileging) of social identities – namely, the use of terms like 'baby boomers', 'X generation', 'millennials', 'generation Z', and so on (Strauss and Howe, 1992, 2000).

Compared with earlier 'modern times', when fewer social divisions were acknowledged and fewer identities available outside the already institutionalised domains of gender, class and religion, the process of articulating and socially realising social identity has become more complex, more effortful and more reflexive in these post-modern times (Giddens, 1991; Bauman, 2000; Archer, 2000, 2007). When Margaret Archer refers to society's reflexive imperative and Ulrich Beck describes the institutionalisation of individuality, they are both drawing attention to the de-standardisation of the life course and the instability of self-narratives or identity talk in locating oneself in the social world (Beck and Beck-Gernsheim, 2001; and Archer, 2012). Part of this process is realised through the amplification and the extension of 'identity work' well beyond the period of youth, where both Erikson and Mannheim saw it firmly sited. Instead, identity is turned into a marketing strategy that can be applied to the consumption of goods and services throughout the whole of the life course (Mannheim, 1936/1998; Erikson, 1961, 1980). It has become work without retirement and, one could add, learning without end.

How might the growth of reflexivity and the individualisation of society be embedded in, or enlightened by, the concept of intersectionality? One answer lies in the genesis of the term itself, whose rapid expansion across the humanities and social sciences has rendered it 'hegemonic' (Mann, 2013), or akin to identity, another all-encompassing 'rubber sheet' covering everything social, from system world to life world (Côté, 2006: 6). There seems to be general agreement that the term originated in a critique of approaches that over-generalised the reach of such binary categories as race and/or gender, concealing the more marginal positions located at critical 'intersections' of the major divisions of class, gender and race.[6] Collins (2015) argues there is a consensus around the general contours defining the term which 'references the critical insight that race, class, gender, sexuality, ethnicity, nation, ability and age operate not as unitary, mutually exclusive entities but as reciprocally constructing phenomena that in turn shape complex social inequalities' (Collins, 2015: 2).

There is less consensus whether this latter aspect – that is, its role in shaping social inequalities' – is or is not central. As a critique, it offers new directions in rethinking identity and social division and new methodologies for studying social division (Cho, Crenshaw and McCall, 2013; Hancock, 2016). Hancock argues that 'intersectionality demands a rearticulation of the relationships between what are traditionally perceived as conceptually distinct analytical categories of difference' (Hancock, 2016: 122). Rather than assuming a hierarchy of differences based upon common sources of power and status, or treating social locations as the summation of multiple positions of advantage and disadvantage, intersectionality places social differences within a more fluid matrix of relations. Where '*ceteris*' are never '*paribus*', particular nodes or intersections become points of privilege or oppression at particular times and under particular contexts.[7] The salience of such points is not fixed however. Intersectionality implies the contingency of each and all social locations: that neither power nor prestige, division nor distinction are fixed in some essential binary network through which society is forever constituted. From an intersectional standpoint, social identities are realised as complex and somewhat fluid phenomena, always only partially realised in and through the experiences of particular groups of people. Neither identity nor location should be reduced to some over-determining, overpowering structure. Age is part of this complexity. A person's place in the life course can no longer be reduced to or determined by any single structure, be it the market or the state, society or nature, no more than can class, gender, or race. People occupy multiple sites of difference, are ascribed multiple identities, and experience their social location through a complex of multiply determined identities; each exercising mutual influence on the articulation and realisation of each other (see Walby, 2009).

This does not mean that identities and structures are irrelevant in determining the experiences and opportunities afforded by later life. Just as the social divisions which identities mirror are not organised independently of each other, so the (potential) 'power to' or the lack of (potential) 'power to' that is located in any particular intersection of social identities is not fixed, even as its limits are constrained by those intersecting categories. If one sees social divisions as 'supra-personal' social facts containing and framing socially constructed identities, then the location of those divisions must be seen as existing in advance of the identities that they confer. Identities, from this perspective, are read-off locations, and locations read off the supra-personal structures that determine how class, gender, race and age are realised. This is the traditional model, whereby advantage and disadvantage are the cumulative product associated with one's position in each social location. If social divisions and identities are co-constructed, with no 'base–superstructure' relationship or 'cause–consequence' system of prioritisation, then each social location represents an intersection of lesser or greater complexity; and of more or less determinacy. Both personal and social identities, those practised and narrated by selves, as well as those ascribed and acted upon by others, are not reducible to any one single source of power, nor are they condemned to impotence by forces operating irrespective of and invisible to people, that keep the dividers from the divided.

The intersectionality of identities and their mutual leaning upon each other serves as a source of stability as well as a point of insecurity. It confers a sense of self that is solidly multidimensional, based upon a number of platforms, whilst also providing innumerable means for othering. Intersectionality makes visible the person as an individual of many selves, while revealing the structures by which their otherness is constituted. Identity exists as the reciprocal of location, in both its subjective and objective sense. It thus helps make sense of social structure and the processes by which structures constitute social location. Arguably, this is brought out most clearly when examining social divisions through the deliberate employment of an 'intersectional lens'. Such a perspective illuminates the multiplicity by which identities are constructed and realised as well as the variability that exists in the power of certain locations to articulate or ignore, enhance or perform particular later lifestyles.

Intersections and the structural division of later life

Several critiques have been made of intersectionality as a fashionably over-extended buzzword in the social sciences (Davis, 2008; McNally 2017). Some have more pointedly criticised the centrality that intersectionality gives to marginality in examining the 'central' structures of society, such as class, gender and race. Others have criticised the hegemony that seems to be exercised by particular groups in controlling its narrative frame, such as the leading role played by race or by women as the fulcrum of intersectionality. Still others have argued that rather than challenging the dichotomised dualities of identity, intersectionality merely reinforces and reifies them, while others argue that, in its ever-expanding reach, intersectionality risks 'covering over' the substantive ontological dilemmas posed by identity, power and social divisions (Knapp, 2005; Carastathis, 2008, 2013; Nash, 2008, 2011; Choo and Ferree, 2010; Wadsworth, 2011; Carbin and Edenheim, 2013). While recognising these potential criticisms, and while eschewing any intention to treat intersectionality as a distinct 'theory', the potential usefulness of using the term to explore the complex of social divisions and social identities arising in later life is considered, addressing the questions this raises, in prioritising structure over subjectivity and in over-determining the role of inequality and power in studying the social divisions of later life.

The complexities of rendering coherent the articulation of identity and the already established structures within which difference and division, identity and belonging are realised seem to require something at least approaching an intersectional standpoint. Rather than restricting this to the exploration of multiple marginalities and oppressions, it is also possible to utilise the argument that 'all … individuals have intersectional identities, produced through the convergence and mutual inflection of relations of oppression and privilege … or through the confluence of "identity determinants"' (Carastathis, 2008: 28). This point has also been made by Yuval-Davis, who notes that everyone's 'concrete social location' is constituted from multiple sites of difference – class, ethnicity, gender, sexuality 'and so on'. While each has its own 'ontological base', none possesses a meaning that can be socially realised (even if it can be semantically defined) without reference to other sources of division – to other identities and to other locations that lean upon, and are in turn leant upon by, each other (Yuval-Davis, 2008: 200). The importance of identity and its inherently relational nature to the other constitute a central aspect of intersectional thinking.

While acknowledging the importance of power in forming and maintaining social divisions, the intersectional perspective acknowledges that power is neither unidirectional nor unidimensional. This does not imply that all divisions are equal; many are not. Nevertheless, social divisions and the social identities and locations they help engineer are not merely reflections of material advantage or disadvantage, of power or powerlessness, or of equality or inequality. Rather than employ terms implying positions of double, triple or quadruple jeopardy, it is possible to realise social locations and social identities as opportunities as well as obstacles, experiences of inclusion as well as of exclusion and as choices as well as constraints.

Writers such as Yuval-Davis have promoted intersectionality as a balance between treating social identities as purely negative phenomena (marked categories of oppression) and recognising their value as sources of belonging and community (Yuval-Davis, 2010). Some advocates of intersectionality might argue that this proposed balancing eliminates the political intent of the originators of the term who sought to challenge those discourses that effectively subordinated some divisions (like ethnicity or able-bodiedness or sexuality) to other supposedly more powerful ones (like class and gender). Inserting age into this matrix of social divisions and identities might be argued to serve a similar function, negating the influence of class, gender and race by claiming that 'oh but it's different when you enter later life'. The response to that statement is, of course, that later life is also different if you are black, disabled, female or gay. It is remarkable how relatively recent such considerations have been, not just as matters of social fact, but also as matters of social salience. From our perspective, the term intersectionality highlights this point, effectively rendering age as an important axis that intersects with, as well as itself being intersected by other social divisions and other social identities.

How might adopting an intersectional approach illuminate the social divisions and differences of later life? Granted the complexity in trying to frame any matrix of social divisions where people are 'concretely' located, complexity can nevertheless be approached through different lenses. On the one hand, one can focus upon identity and the sense of belonging and identification that privileges the work performed by particular communities in articulating and embodying forms of cultural, social and symbolic capital that give meaning and purpose to later life. Being a member of an ethnic or cultural group, with its own distinct traditions, for example, may confer upon age the task of keeping faith with those traditions, in the face of trends toward assimilation to the host culture and the loss of distinction. Alternatively, being identified as an old man may lead some older gay men to feel marginal when judged against the experience and lifestyle promoted within gay culture and gay communities. The common experience of middle class older women and the support they confer upon each other may encourage a more adventurous and outgoing 'extra-familial' approach to the possibilities of later life than that capable of being realised by poorer working class women. On the other hand, it is possible to focus upon the balance of assets, capital and resources that are accrued or lost by people in later life, occupying different social locations, to judge whether the combination of identities and locations add up to or confound the generic position of the cumulative advantage/disadvantage models of later life. How is it possible to compare and contrast white older women who have had poorly paid occupations with no pension entitlement but who are embedded in a wide and intensive network of family, with well-educated older men from ethnic minority backgrounds whose work guaranteed them a defined benefits pension but which attenuated their social ties with family? Even when adopting an explicitly intersectional approach, the question still arises of whether to focus upon structures or subjectivities.

Self-ascribed social identities matter, but do they matter as much as objectively determined social locations in structuring the opportunities and obstacles, advantages and disadvantages experienced in later life? The possibility that they might is raised by the work of the social psychologist, Becca Levy. Her work offers a powerful illustration of how 'agedness' as an identity can affect people's lives, and particularly the degree to which it is identified as a 'devalued' status (Levy, 2009).

In the course of a 38-year follow-up of a sample of 440 people aged between 18 and 44, Levy found those who held primarily negative stereotypes of old age were much more likely, in later life, to suffer from 'cardiovascular events', such as heart attacks, heart disease and stroke.

What Levy's and many other studies show is that subjective representations of 'later life' as a devalued identity or location have a demonstrable impact on life. That impact can be extremely powerful. Similar effects can be observed in research on subjective judgements of socio-economic position, health status and their interaction with age, health, mortality and well-being (Kaplan and Baron-Epel, 2003; Singh-Manoux, Adler and Marmot, 2003; Jylhä, 2009; Präg Mills and Wittek, 2016; Demakakos et al, 2018). An intersectional perspective draws attention to the mediational role played by other, non-age-related identities in identifying one's social location in later life as one of relative power or powerlessness, poverty or richness, opportunity or oppression, independent of 'objective' structural indicators. While not ignoring the structural (or institutional) determinacies that operate in realising any particular intersectional patterning of identities, it is important to recognise that individual subjectivities mediate and modify those objective effects. Different assets and resources, as well as different cultural, social and material capitals are brought into play in these intersectional effects such that the social locations of later life are accentuated, mediated or neutralised as a particularly marked category of advantage or disadvantage through both objective and subjective means.

Structuralist models assume that the institutions of society, represented through the operations of the market, the media, family and the state, provide the major factor in effecting the divisions and the identities of class or gender or ethnicity. Post-structuralist models insist, however, that the 'demi-regularities' these institutions confer upon social identity are both contingent and reciprocal, with markets, media, states and households responding to the narratives and practices that each engenders. The various institutions 'lean on' each other, just as they in turn are 'leant on' by those whose structures they help fashion. While structural models tend to assume an invariance of effects, or an accumulation of invariant effects over time (and hence with age) leading to a progressively 'polarised' pattern of relative advantage against relative and disadvantage, post-structural models are more open. They render the possibility that the flux between objective and subjective divisions, distinctions and identities can change these patterns, including the divisions and distinctions represented by age and by cohort. The result is much greater contingency, leaving space for identities and subjectivities to exercise influence both within and outside the frameworks of class, ethnicity and gender. Agency and identity are, to quote one recent author, realised 'not in freedom from patterned constraint but in our ability to invoke those patterns in non-prescribed ways, enabled in large measure by the very multiplicity of solidarities in which we participate' (Ammerman, 2003: 212).

What determines the relative power of institutional structures to confer identity? It can be argued that the power of institutional structures to determine social roles and social identities is more or less proportional to the power those roles and identities have to overshadow/marginalise other roles and identities. Some identities and some social locations exercise more wide-ranging effects over people's lives than others. In contrast, identities conferred by, or arising within less powerful institutions may be thought to possess more restricted institutional purchase and hence be more easily subsumed beneath those derived from or realised within institutions that are more powerful. Institutional processes, even if only implicitly fashioning social divisions and identities, may thus be of more significance than processes that, though more explicitly ordering such distinctions, are nevertheless realised within less powerful, less all-encompassing settings. At the same time, if such identities are not explicitly ordered by these institutional structures, they might be considered less salient compared with roles, identities and divisions that are more explicitly constructed. In short, it is possible to view the intersection of institutions and identities through systems of power and pervasiveness, on the one hand, and systems that make social divisions and identities more or less explicit on the other.[8]

If age, for example, is in part co-constructed as an unintended consequence of the operations of the economy, the state, markets and/or the media (for example, as retiree or pensioner), it would seem logical that age as an identity co-constructed within such frameworks would be less dominant than the identities of class or gender, which are more directly and deliberately formed by such institutions. In such case, their framings of age would possess a more marginal significance in fashioning 'age' identities, compared with those other identities and their associated divisions. In healthcare settings, where agedness is more deliberately co-constructed, in and through corporeality and chronology, fitness, form and functionality, age as both a chronological and corporeal identity might be thought to exercise a more powerful and potentially more malign influence. Age as an isolated identity may exercise a limited effect, in general, unless and until its effects are mediated through the operations of institutions forming other more explicit identities (and their intersecting operations) which then bring to attention the issues of chronology and corporeality. Hence it is perhaps not so surprising to find that age, in and of itself, does not serve as a major source of identity in most Western societies (Hyde and Jones, 2015).

Intersections and the ordering of age

Age, or as we have framed it, later life, and the meanings and the lifestyles it sustains (or that are sustained in it) have thus far been considered primarily as a social location, or, in more intersectional terms, as a matrix of locations, rather less easily defined or determined by the operations of the economy or the chronological ordering of human capital. While intersectionality helps highlight this point, it does not necessarily move us much further beyond the generality noted above that age is shaped by its intersections with other identity-conferring institutions and structures. Changes in the social nature of later life are undoubtedly taking place but perhaps not because age per se has changed so much as the identities and institutions that increasingly frame it. These now include the burgeoning of new 'minority' identities associated with ethnicity, illness, sexuality, lifestyle and geography. These identities are slowly transforming the social locations of the population in most developed economies, not just in later life but at every point in the life course. While it is important to explore the intersecting influences of other institutions and identities as a means of casting new light on the change in later life and in society, however, we need also not to lose track of the structural 'demi-regularities' that are underpinning much of these changes. These demi-regularities are two-fold. Some can be traced through the institutions that stabilise the accumulation or dis-accumulation of financial, cultural and corporeal assets and resources within and between the generations. Others are realised from the varied positionalities emerging from previously marginal or under-recognised adult identities. The question is: through which vectors are such demi-regularities brought about and how best might they account for how age is both ordered and divided?

Evidence of the multiplication of misery and the densification of disadvantage in later life should not be denied. Inequalities exist in the distribution of assets and capital of people in later life. But are such inequalities defining of age's identities? Do they, in short, order age more powerfully than other sources and structures? The widespread securing of a basic income in retirement, it could be argued, means that frailty and infirmity more than income poverty or lack of wealth 'count' for more in framing the governance of old age. Instead of rich and poor, man and woman, black and white, is age ordered and its social construction fashioned more powerfully by the binary between 'fit' and 'frail' identities. The inevitable directions taken by state funding focus less upon issues of class, ethnicity and gender than they do upon 'burden', 'ill health', 'frailty' and the various parameters of dementia. It is primarily only when the intersectional interstices based upon such corporeal 'object-related' distinctions are activated that the marking of the category of old age as 'different' or even 'unequal' is brought into play. Outside this chronological and corporeal framework, it is not the state but the marketplace and the social relations of reciprocal exchange where counter-narratives are encountered that potentially challenge such reductionist approaches.

In the marketing of services and the courting of consumption, later life is made much more of than its otherwise unidimensional framing as an identity representing a 'cost to society'. Here, within the context of markets, the media, and the personal and social relationships of kith and kin, can more easily be found the opportunities afforded by the intersectionalities of identity, framing age's divisions as difference and diversity, not simply cumulative costs and deepening disadvantage. In contrast, the state (and the various 'NGO' sectors oriented toward the concerns of state) seeks to differentiate its social location primarily through positions of entitlement based upon those same degrees of disadvantage and diminishment, but marked more by differences in corporeality than it is by cultural, financial or social resources.

The relative volume of research conducted on later life reflects these differing structures. Compared with studies examining the adequacy or inadequacy of long-term care, the costs of caregiving, the receipt of welfare benefits and the associations and intersections between 'social', 'economic' and 'corporeal' inequalities, research exploring the market's ordering of age within a diversity of differences has been limited, to say the very least, especially when shorn of any corporeal concerns (for example Norgard and Rodgers, 1997; Tennstedt and Chang, 1998; Dilworth-Anderson, Williams and Gibson, 2002; Concannon, 2007; McIntyre and McDonald, 2012). The task is not, of course, to ignore issues of impoverishment and marginality and the lifelong demi-regularities that pattern inequality, but to widen the scope for exploring how other vectors pattern later lives, in ways other than through the corporeality of fitness versus frailness, health versus disease. The potential of intersectional approaches to extend a broader understanding of the ordering of age, its experiences, lifestyles and the opportunities afforded by 'difference', is underplayed when intersectionality is used simply to pursue the search for multiple oppressions. No doubt many such examples can be found in later life, but bringing intersectionality to bear only on matters of inequality in health and illness is to limits its power radically to revise the way we understand the social divisions and diversity of later life.

As Behrent has noted, the dominance of post-structuralist Foucauldian thought in social science research, especially in the fields of health and welfare, has done as much to sustain the neo-liberal regimes of twenty-first century welfare states as it has to chastise or constrain them (Behrent, 2016: 184–5). Just as the thinnest seams may often contain the richest rewards, we should recognise that exploring later lives through and within so-called marginal identities and locations may offer unexpected riches, both in realising what later life can be and what, for some, it is already becoming. Such explorations will remain constrained, however, if their focus is restricted to resolutely examining the multiplication of misery, the depths of disadvantage and an insistence upon exclusion and oppression as constitutive of later life's differences, distinctions and divisions. These considerations suggest the importance of adopting other methods and techniques beyond the kind of large-scale multivariate quantitative analyses that dominate the field. It might seem preferable, for example, to employ a variety of more qualitative methods that focus upon how particular later lives are lived, how particular later life identities are sustained and how particular later lifestyles are realised, in the context of other identities, other institutions, other locations and interests arising other than from age.

Conclusions

What should be made of the complex of differing cultural and institutional structures that are shaping later life? Is it possible to escape from the inevitable return to the traditional divisions of class, ethnicity and gender by which life at all ages is typically stratified? Can difference be examined other than through the oppressions that limit life's possibilities? These questions, posed at the end of this chapter, underlie much of what we have already written. On a positive note, intersectionality is potentially useful because it problematises overly deterministic standpoints in exploring difference and division in later life. It avoids over-reliance on any one parameter or any one structure demarcating the differentiation of 'successful' or 'unsuccessful', 'well-lived' or 'badly lived' lives. Framed as a political agenda, intersectionality seeks recognition of the marginalisation that may often be missed in the interstices of devalued identities. At the same time, exploring marginality should not mean that difference and diversity are explored primarily as 'lack' or 'less'-ness. The factors enriching or impoverishing later life are not simply reducible to any one ordering. Other positions offer other perspectives, whether represented by different ethnicities or sexualities, or as lived by differently constituted bodies.

This is not a call for an exotic anthropology of ageing; it is a demand to recognise the diversity that already exists in everyday later lives and their social relations. That richness is not fixed by any single set of assets, capital and resources, nor is it determined by any single structure of institutional interest and power. Framed as a critique of mainstream stratification research, intersectionality challenges contemporary forms of reductionism. The dichotomy and polarisation of a society into 'two worlds', such as Disraeli warned about in his nineteenth century novel *Sybil*, and which Titmuss feared faced those in old age given the meanness of the post-war welfare state in the twentieth century and now projected as a future scenario for the twenty-first century, needs to be challenged (Disraeli, 1845; Titmuss, 1955; Crystal, 1980, 2018). Intersectionality offers one way of contesting this kind of binary opposition. We acknowledge that it runs the risk of promoting a degree of diffuseness and dilution in analysis, but it does allow the recognition that age is rarely in and of itself a chosen division, but appears as such primarily through otheridentities and institutional structures that lean and are leaned upon by it.

Notes

1 Evidence of this 'age/cohort' effect is provided by a recent study demonstrating a specific 'age' effect in the relative social exclusion of 'the oldest old', after taking account of other possible mediating factors (Key and Culliney, 2018).

2 Use here of the term 'queering' may need some clarification. We are referring to those approaches, typically associated with 'queer theory', that challenge the incorporation of social divisions into 'essentialised' binaries, originally represented by sex, gender and sexuality, but since extended to question a much wider range of binary identities, such as 'able-bodied/disabled', 'black/white', 'masculine/feminine' or 'straight/gay'. For a more thoroughgoing critique of these assumptions, see Jagose, 1996; Seidman, 1997, 2016.

3 Brekhus has applied the concept of marked and unmarked categories in the social sciences. He uses the concept of 'social markedness' to refer to 'the ways social actors actively perceive one side of a contrast while ignoring the other side as epistemologically unproblematic', with the unmarked category being the assumed unproblematic, socially generic (Brekhus, 1998: 35).

4 This includes, for example, notions of 'fat identity' and 'thin privilege' (see LeBesco, 2004).

5 An exception 'proving the rule' can be found in the Alzheimer's movement, which has gathered strength as a global coalition of interests, extending across continents and generations involving both individuals and families (Beard, 2004).

6 According to Anna Carastathis, intersectionality 'is now used in the literature to refer to the theory or methodology used to identify and study these "real world" phenomena of structural, political, and representational intersectionality' with a specific focus upon 'knowledge generated from and about oppressed groups' (Carastathis, 2014: 307). '[I]ntersectionality', she adds, 'insists that multiple, co-constituting analytic categories are operative and equally salient in constructing institutionalized practices and lived experiences' (Carastathis, 2014: 308). In this perspective, there seems no obvious need to privilege 'oppressed groups', since the metaphor of intersecting divisions can be applied to any variety of marginal or minority groups whose position mediates or modifies the social location associated with more 'mainstream' divisions.

7 The term *ceteris paribus* is used widely in economics to analyse some aspect of the economy while holding other things equal (*ceteris paribus*). The fact that other things are not equal seems of relatively little import for the econometrician, who simply seeks to test a particular thesis concerning a limited set of economic relations (Pietroski and Rey, 1995; Boumans and Morgan, 2001).

8 The labour market is one obvious example. While high-status jobs such as the professions confer power and privilege in the context of the workplace, irrespective of agedness, femaleness or ethnicity, these latter identities might confer a very different pattern of advantages and disadvantages in other contexts – such as in gaining access to a club, public transport or particular cultural arenas.

7

Diversity, difference and division in later life

The central argument of this book is that later life is no longer an unmarked social category, defined and determined by its position at the end of a life already lived. If old age was ever such a straightforwardly structured social category, it is certainly not so now.[1] It occupies a much more interesting social space than that. Not only do most people in the developed economies reach old age, but having reached it, most can reasonably expect to find their journey continue through it. Later life is expanding, in its length and in its diversity, creating a greater variety of ways of being an older person and living a later life. This, it is argued, constitutes a radical change, which is intimately linked with broader social changes associated with what Ulrich Beck called the transition from 'first' to 'second' modernity (Beck and Lau, 2005). The homogeneity of the older population, once taken for granted by policy makers as they legislated to secure old age, has since imploded. It is increasingly difficult to create a unitary set of policies capable of achieving 'a happier old age'.[2] Faced with the diversity and contradictoriness of later life, no singular categorisation of old age is sustainable, whether by markets, states or the service sector. No longer the residue of a life left over after the operations of a society of producers had done its work, later life extends into ever-widening social arenas.[3] Consumerism and its lifestyle distinctions, the growth and multiplicity of social identities, the changing demography of the life course, the competing forms of community and the shift from collective social rights to individual human rights have all combined to transform later life beyond its earlier ordering as the secured end of a modern life.

Later life is not without its boundaries. It is still constrained by the institutions of first modernity as well as by the sheer weight of the body's own ageless ageing. The chapters of this book have tried to capture this duality, of later lives led differently, still shaped by the structures of the past but now fashioning themselves to face the challenges of the future. Many aspects of later life can be understood as the echoes of lives lived within the social divisions and structures laid out by prior experience. At the same time, new divisions and differences are emerging, some beginning in, or just before, old age, others originating at earlier points in the adult life course but refracted differently as people grow older. Some of these can be considered mere elaborations and modifications of already existing divisions; others appear more or less de novo, refreshing the idea of old age as a foreign country. Each social division has its own history and each bears a different relationship to the divisions engendered by social stratification earlier in adult life. What unites them is the diversity they subsume, a diversity shaping the contemporary settings of later life. This is likely to grow more diverse in the future. While such developments are most clearly evident in North America, in Western Europe and in East Asia, they are not restricted to these regions (Hyde and Higgs, 2016; Lamb, Robbins-Ruszkowski and Corwin, 2017: 17). It has not been the intention of this book to explore the global realisation of later-life diversity; no single (or double) authored book could hope to do so. Still we believe that later life is undergoing a global transformation, even if the exact parameters of that change vary considerably from country to country.

The book has focused upon changes already evidenced in Western societies. As the social locations of later life and the inequalities associated with them are becoming subject to an increasingly wide range of sociological analyses, it seems a good time to bring such developments to the fore and to consider how best to make sense of them. No one simple overarching framework can capture all these divisions. Nor can the causal influences shaping them be attributed to one underlying structure within society. Neither structural reductionism, nor cultural essentialism satisfactorily explains the variety of differences and divisions in later life; even the combined structures of ethnicity, gender and class can only go a limited way in accounting for the diversity of locations to be found in later life. The subjectivities that are experienced and realised in later life and the structuring of social relations generated by the productive processes of class or the social reproduction systems of gender are either too distant or diverse to be so determinate.

The intent has been to point out some of the demi-regularities that are still reflected in these divisions while drawing attention to the critical intersections that both locate and problematise their positions, whether as binary divides or cumulative inequalities. In the process of doing so we have tried to highlight the many analytical and methodological issues they present in framing an adequate sociology of age and ageing. This final, concluding chapter will summarise some of the principal ways in which the differences and divisions of later life might best be understood and how any singular mode of understanding must always be recognised as contingent on others. In acknowledging the interconnectedness of the divisions and differences, we hope a fuller understanding can be reached of the diversity and inequalities of later life, the structures that shape them and the various representations and subjectivities that are inflected by them.

Throughout, an attempt has been made to connect the analysis of social divisions and differences as they are realised in later life with questions concerning the use made of terms like social division, difference, identity and inequality more broadly within the social sciences. Revisiting these topics from the perspective of later life, inevitably it seems we return to a central dualism that pervades the social sciences, between 'structures' and 'subjectivities', between the circumstances that position individuals within society and the positioning that people realise in their individual life worlds. Such positioning, in both their agentic and structural form, are subject to contradictory vectors of power, of interest and of advantage. These derive from, and reflect, the various cultural representations and understandings that people have of age and of possible lives that could be lived. The resulting subjectivities are not without structure, no more than the structures themselves can be socially realised without reference to the subjectivities that frame them.

This interplay between structure and subjectivity, once of marginal interest in the sociology of later life because it was considered a period of collective disengagement from work, social reproduction and cultural participation, has become a key concern. Not only is that evidently gendered perspective now outdated, but even the equation between not working and the ascription of a 'role-less role' seems no longer to make much sense.[4] Indeed the concept of role itself seems old-fashioned as roles have been superseded by concepts of identity, habitus and lifestyle, framed by the context of the individualisation and consumer culture of second modernity. The economic standing now enjoyed by many older people and the gravitational pull exercised across the life course by consumption renders this interplay more important than ever.

Structures and subjectivities

Whether founded on cultural, corporeal, financial or social assets, the social divisions of later life have largely been framed in negative terms. An emphasis on the disadvantages, exclusions, inequalities and marginality that accompany the divisions of old age dominates contemporary social gerontology.[5] The argument put forward in this book, however, is that the fragmentation of later life is as much about difference and diversity as it is about exclusion and inequality. This requires recognising the potential richness that arises from the multiplicity of identities and lifestyles of later life as well as acknowledging the inequalities that also exist within it. While social differences can be understood primarily as inequalities, most exist as 'categories of discursive practice' that in turn convey a complex interplay of identities, interests and positionalities. These form part of the organisation of society, its competing practices of distinction, of governance, of production, distribution and consumption as well as the ordering and understandings of its social relationships. Social divisions are an important and necessary part of what Anthias (2012: 8) has called the social landscape, emerging as contestable structures and subjectivities within society. From this perspective, an ontology of each category or division can be proposed, concerning the social nature of gender or race or disability as a product of social structure as well as a collective or social representation of that category. These representations frame the subjective consciousness by which individuals experience and realise their particular location within the social landscape. The organisation of society necessarily implicates a structuring influence upon those representations: the nature of the productive process, for example, in relation to class-consciousness or objective income in relation to financial well-being. At the same time, their social realisation depends upon a plethora of actual, everyday social relations, the iterative discursive constructions that accompany those relations and the cultural, material and societal constraints that facilitate or limit those relations (Hansen, Slagsvold and Moum, 2008).

Concepts of liquidity, reflexivity and institutional individualisation reflect the ways many contemporary sociologists have highlighted the loosening hold of structures and the diversification of their discursive practices in late modern society (see Beck and Beck-Gernsheim, 2001; Giddens, 1991; Archer, 2012; Bauman, 2012). One way of looking at the divisions of society and the ontologically framed positions and socially relational consciousness associated with those positions is, as noted above, to represent them as growing inequalities. But juxtaposing such considerations with the diversity of their subjective realisation as identity or lifestyle is problematic. Such ontologically defined categories seem at best only weakly related to materially realised social locations – as is the case for example in the idea of relational classes in retirement. Their discursive framing outside the context of the labour market demands that other considerations of difference and other discursive contexts be recognised. These need to be capable of being expanded or contracted, elaborated or reformulated as the discursive practices surrounding them change, as alternative representations emerge within people's lives and as society reacts to the cultural and social changes in which later lives are equally if differently embedded. Late life identities, in short, can no longer be read off as the residualised outcomes of pre-framed collective categories, whether from the social relations of past production or the patriarchal structure of past households.

Later life is different now; it is no longer the social sediment left over from earlier adult life. Increasingly, it involves actively shedding old and adopting new identities and responsibilities. While the salience of a person's location in the formal economy and in the processes of social reproduction diminishes, later life (as retirement) offers new spaces where other distinctions can emerge and where other subjectivities can be articulated. These may be located in the economy (as in expanding consumption), or in social locations outside those of earnings and employment, in the corporeality and embodiment of existence. These may be identities and locations framed by different facets of gender, of sexuality, or of ethnicity; or by new forms of community, of interests emerging within or outside the old communities of propinquity). Some of these identities may derive from practices and sources evident before retirement, which undergo a degree of reconfiguration after retirement while others may embody new meanings in retirement, such as those framed by considerations of fitness and frailty. Change in the positionalities between structure and subjectivity may arise from events taking place earlier in the life course, while others may arise only in later (post-working) life. Such changes may render contingent the kinds of discursive practices that once existed around social differences, making the realisation of social division in later life more fluid and more contingent than before.

Positions, polarities and change

Much has been made of the 'hollowing out' of social class-based categories, in terms of their underlying structure as well as their subjectivities (Clark and Lipset, 1991; Pakulski and Waters, 1996b; Kingston, 2000; Beck, 2000, 2007). This debate, however, still centres upon issues framed by work and the relations of production. Bourdieu's shift in the study of class away from a concern with the economic to the cultural dynamics of class has made it easier to integrate the traditional division of class with other, emerging or unmarked, divisions found outside the 'productive economy' (Bottero, 2005: 137; Brubaker, 1985: 772). One consequence is that later life acquires a 'class' salience that previously had been missing or inadequately framed, by distancing it from a position as residuum within the dominant mode of production, framing it instead in terms of consumption and social distinction (Higgs and Gilleard, 2006; Savage, 2015: 176).

Within the world's developed economies, some older people are undoubtedly benefiting more than others as a result of the way the economy is currently engineered (for example, the growth of financialisation, globalisation and marketisation (Lapavitsas, 2011; Hyde and Higgs, 2016). Given that such individuals seem to enjoy more opportunities for consumption and gain access to wider networks from which to draw resources, the question arises is whether such observable distinctions constitute discrete categories by which a conscious identification with one's socio-economic location arises. Outside the framework of work and labour markets, how do such socio-economic considerations operate as sources of identity or positions of distinction? Does such identification of interests operate to an equal degree among the 'better' off, the 'middling' sort or the 'worse' off in retirement? Empirical research on social identities suggests that neither 'class' nor 'age' serve a prominent role among older people in fashioning their sense of identity or social self (Hyde and Jones, 2015). Rather than providing the positive elements of identity, in the UK at least 'class labels proliferate ... only to prompt negative reactions to them' (Savage, 2015: 367).

Conscious of their own personal ageing, are older people equally conscious of other differences between their own and others' later lives. Do older people construct an imaginary other against which they assure their own place in the world and might this be with reference to another's old age rather than another's ethnicity, gender, income or sexuality? Less aware of the various ways that the inequalities engendered by culture, economics and society 'get under the skin' (Ferraro and Shippee, 2009), might people in later life consciously forge their lifestyles through the contrasts with their own past contextualised by their present circumstances. Of course, such engagements may be most consciously encountered in the social relations of family and home more than they are in the context of markets and the media. Arguably, as more time is spent in the former settings than in the latter, the framing of a present by a historical sense of identity may overlay the subjectivity of later life. How much then does a generational consciousness of class impact upon individual subjectivities in later life compared with other structural positions by which their later lifestyles are constructed? At an empiricist level, subjective appraisals of people's socio-economic location seem generally more salient in affecting their health and well-being, compared with the impact of their 'objective' location (Cummins, 2000; Veenhoven, 2002; Singh-Manoux, Adler and Marmot, 2003; Arber, Fenn and Meadows, 2014). The indeterminacy between subjective and objective locations may be even more evident in later life, since the former subjectivities are linked to settings where many of the distinctions afforded by employment, income and occupational status are missing.[6]

The point is that these two processes of social location – those understood as structuring inequalities and those understood as fashioning identities – never fully 'mirror' each other at any point in life and they do so less now and in retirement. Structures and subjectivities alike contribute to realising social divisions and social differences, both in how they are experienced and how they shape later life. The 'new' social movements have accentuated the contingency in structural and subjective positions that characterises second modernity. Identity now serves as both a source of stability and a structure of difference. The shift that age institutes from employment to leisure, from a life organised outside the household to a life organised within the context of the household, from work-organised social relations to self-organised social relations represents a position of both enhanced choice and vulnerability. The 'cultural turn' within the social sciences can be seen as an attempt to integrate the subjectivities of life-worlds with the structures of 'system-worlds', making sociological sense, as it were, of the invocation that the personal is inseparable from the political. Whether this change 'really' changes anything is debateable. Any interpretation of social difference, whether as distinction or division, identity or inequality, demands an acknowledgement of both material interests and cultural power. The point is that more so now than in the past, the nature of power and the nature of interests change over time and, increasingly, over the life course.

Structuring difference: identities and interests

Understanding social divisions primarily as consciously created social identities is as mistaken as is viewing them as constituted solely as structured sources of inequality. Both perspectives have a degree of purchase: but neither alone can serve as the primary base from which to constitute, let alone explore, social division in later life. Most of the social divisions examined in this book are those that have been organised, lived and experienced by older people whose own later lives are being fashioned within the socio-economic structures and cultural imaginaries of the twenty-first century. Other divisions, structured at other times and within other settings, may have been as or more important and may well have exercised much greater influence over later lives lived in earlier times. In the context of the greater 'reflexivity' of contemporary advanced economies, however, with their emphasis on choice, distinction and the 'individualisation' of experience, the social divisions we have focused upon are realised through a complex of conjunctions of objective conditions that render persons 'subject' to, but not 'subservient' to, their social and cultural influence. While the conjunctions of objective power, social location and sense of self may foster a subjective identification with particular social locations that most reflect or represent the interests of those so identified; changes in culture, economy and society are such as to ensure sufficient space around any such identifications as to guarantee some scope at least to perform one's identity otherwise.

The discourses and practices that are embedded within and realised through the various institutionalised positions available in contemporary life have become more flexible, contingent and intersectional. 'Co-constructed' by the activities of the market, the state, the media and the family, they evolve over the course of individuals' own lifetimes and the priorities set by chance and circumstance. Successive cohorts of retirees are arguably becoming exposed and rendered subject to the increasing space between the objective circumstances of their past collective working lives and their individually realised retirement lifestyles.[7] People now in their eighties or older, those most separated in time from their working life, may yet experience a later life that is ironically more closely tied to the social relations of their past working lives. By contrast, those now in their sixties, who are closest in time to working life, may have experienced a wider variety of more diversely constituted objective circumstances, resulting in a greater variety of differing and diverse interests.

Despite the 'already existing' presence of the institutionalising processes of past work and social reproduction that still weigh upon those once subject to them, the relative lack of determinacy operating between structure and identity in contemporary society means that the organisational power and representational influence of social locations are perhaps more subject to revision and reconstitution now, both before and after retirement, than was the case in the past. Social time appears to move faster in second modernity; the past passes more quickly into history, and different forms and sources of power rise and fall, spread and coalesce in unpredictable ways. The systems of production and exchange that now dominate the economy have diversified in ways that seem more complex and contradictory than was the case in 'slow capitalism' (Agger, 2015). In the face of such 'speed' and 'liquidity', the structures that still hold between working life and retirement, the subjectivities they define and the interests they define are less easily read and the inequalities they create are less easily determined (Cummins, 2000).

This does not mean that there are no objective divisions of interest or inequalities of power within the arena of later life; nor does it imply that such objectively structured differences no longer matter. The increasing dominance exercised by the market, however, compared with that once exercised by the state, has accelerated the processes of individualisation (Giddens, 1991; Beck and Beck-Gernsheim, 2001; Bauman, 2009). The 'downsizing' of the state has been taking place for several decades, even if it is not taking place at the same rate across all the developed economies (Lee and Strang, 2006). Still, the consequence is that consumer power exercises wider effects across the life course, and its various realisations in shaping social divisions as social identities maintains and magnifies the impact of individuals' social locations within the economy. For most prosperous societies, the social location of later life is governed as much by the cultural and social capital residing in individuals' personal belongings than it is by the communities that were once created by work and the workplace. The old communities of propinquity are challenged or confounded by new communities of interest where 'social relations are built around profession (scientific community), religion (Jewish community), sexual preference (gay community), or interest (stamp collecting, railroads, science fiction, music, art, environmentalism, or health)' (Bradshaw, 2008: 6).

The institutionalisation of individualisation operates through mechanisms that combine elements of what Bourdieu (1977) termed 'habitus' and what Butler (1993) has called 'performativity'. Each division of society, 'be it social, sexual, ethnic, or otherwise, exists when there are agents capable of imposing themselves as authorised to speak … in its place and in its name' (Bourdieu, 1989a: 15). The social realisation of social divisions increasingly demands their articulation as identities, which in turn requires the necessary discourse, habits, lifestyles and performances to frame such 'identity work' (Snow and Anderson, 1987). For many retired people the discourses and habits realised by current consumption rather than their previous employment serves as the template, if not of their identity, at least of their chosen lifestyle.

Once seen as processes that operated largely through the contexts of youth and the 'entry' positions into adult life, identity 'work' now encompasses the whole of the life course (Gilleard and Higgs, 2016). No longer solidified in the consciousness of early adulthood, and the social divisions predetermined by education, community and occupation, identity work now extends over the whole of life. Changes in education, in family structure, in leisure, neighbourhoods and work seem to demand continuing reflection and reconstruction, in what Margaret Archer (2012) has called society's reflexive imperative. 'Identity work' is forever demanded, by the market, by the media and by the state itself, at all times and at every point in the life course. As a process, identity has no resolution, no ultimate self-realisation, either at the beginning or at the end of adult life, as once envisioned by Erikson (1959, 1980). At most, there are periods of settling down into what seem 'semi-permanent' social locations but the conditions of life, whether early, middle or late, have become party to what Bauman has called the contingencies of 'liquid life' (Bauman, 2000, 2005). Subject to the ubiquitous tyranny of choice, markets and the media contribute in equal measure to articulating and rearticulating ways of living life more contingently than ever demanded by the old, solid institutions of industry and the nation state, that once dominated first modernity (Salecl, 2011).

Making sense of this process of change requires consideration of what we once, after Esping-Andersen, termed 'fog lamps' and 'leitmotifs' (Gilleard and Higgs, 2005: 149). At that time, we focused upon class, community and cohort (or generation) as the principal leitmotifs used by earlier social thinkers to understand social change. Since then, we have widened our angle of vision, including social locations and structuring influences less closely aligned to time, place and the economy. Competing with those traditional categorisations are the social locations that are more closely defined by and oriented toward the body and the unmarked categories of ethnicity and race, fitness and functionality, gender and sexuality (Gilleard and Higgs, 2013; Higgs and Gilleard, 2015). While later life still reflects, at least in part, lifestyles that are selected or shaped by the individual's history, retirement lifestyles are now inextricably connected with, as well as constrained by, the structuring influence of social categories outside the social relations of production and their implicit divisions. The determining influences of these categories may wax and wane at different points in the life course, and in consequence of the changing directions individuals' later lives may take. Changes in health, personal relationships and residence in particular may render more salient the emergent categories of later life which, though never entirely absent earlier in life, may come increasingly to define it –as sources of identity, forms of capital or through the 'dividing practices' associated with health and social care.[8] The divisions arising from age's corporeality, and the categorical dichotomies constructed by judgements of fitness against frailty, able-bodiedness against disability, capacity against incapacity are, we believe, important if still neglected sources of difference, distinction and division. As work and education end and the network of family and friends frays, ageing takes on an increasingly 'do-it-yourself' quality, demanding agency just when agency is harder to come by and as the power to do and the power over our doings weakens. As the influence of past structures ceases to determine present status, the location of interests and power shifts from society toward the individual, from social to human capital, and arguably from the symbolic order of society to the corporeal imaginary.

Divisions, interests and power

This brings us back to the issue of power and its significance in establishing identities and structuring social locations. Power has been the subject of a considerable body of writing in the social sciences (for example Dahl, 1957; Bachrach and Baratz, 1962; Wrong, 1968; Foucault, 1982, 2000; Giddens, 1982; Dowding, 1996; Poggi, 2001; Morriss, 2002; Lukes, 2005). One feature of this writing has been the importance given to the power to resist the oppressive influences of attributions of devalued statuses, and instead to assert and perform other than as one's position expects (Archer, 2007; Clegg, 1989; Giddens, 1982). Approaching social divisions in terms of positions of relative power both to assert and to resist – whether or not these are framed as positions of advantage – requires an understanding of power as 'the ability to make ... a difference' (Poggi, 2001: 3) and the arenas in which such differences are claimed and made. As we consider the question of power, we should again recall how, in first modernity, agedness was framed largely as powerlessness – represented by the category of the impotent aged unable to labour, rather than by their chronology (Gilleard, 2017; Roebuck, 1979).

Conceived in such relational terms, power has been represented most often as the capacity of an individual or group to assert or impose their interests over others (the power over) as well as the degree of freedom an individual or group possesses to choose to act, whether or not in the face of opposing interests (the power to). In emphasising the former, Poggi defined power (or 'social power' as he terms it) as the ability to control resources and thereby deprive others of 'salient human values' (Poggi, 2001: 14). Foucault, in contrast, conceptualised power as an endemic, pervasive feature of all relationships, a 'power to' as much as a 'power over', which, though based upon unequal 'assets, capitals and resources', has at its heart a struggle between what he called 'the games of power' and 'the states of domination' (Foucault, 1982: 791–2, 1988: 19). Power, in such circumstances, includes the power to assert a position or identity as well as the power to resist the ascribing positions of others.

In contrast to many other statuses, agedness (and frailty) serves as an identity that is more often ascribed by and upon others. Age as identity – and the identity ascribed to age – places those so identified at risk of disadvantage. Those possessing alternative interests, capital and identities have varying degrees of power to resist such ascriptions, depending in part upon the size and extent of the assets, capital and resources associated with those alternative identities. Those more easily rendered 'subject' to the ascriptions of age and agedness are likely also to be identified with other sources of lack, of lacking more generally, cultural, financial, human and social capital. The fact that many older people do occupy social locations with power to assert an identity other than that of their age indicates how age might be thought of less as the product of identity work than as an arena – a social location – whose power resides in the extent to which it can bring other identities and statuses into play. In those 'games of power' that Foucault came to believe operated in all social relations, richer and more resourceful identities may successfully be asserted other than being aged and these may be critical in resisting the social categorisation of impotence and 'frailure'.[9]

Lacking obvious exchange value, those attributed primarily with frailty and infirmity are denied agency and instead assigned a position from which it is progressively more difficult to escape – a position of intractable decline and irremediable disablement. Where once the state assigned the majority of the aged to the category of 'those impotent through age' and later to the category of 'old age pensioner' (in Britain, shortened to being an 'OAP'), there now exists confusion and contradiction in attempts to recategorise or recalibrate 'age'. Despite the widespread charges of ageism that academics deploy to berate these processes, those most able to distance themselves from such categorisation possess, or have previously accumulated and maintained a wider and more extensive set of assets and resources to be successfully other than 'old'[10]

This raises the related question of how if at all the interests of age groups are served. Are there any unitary interests served by age per se? Alternatively, is it more reasonable to assume that within the heterogeneous locations that now constitute later life, a diversity of assets, capital and identities exist through which age is articulated?

Putting it this way takes us back to reconsider how terms like 'interests' connect both with identity and with social division. Where the classical Marxist position sees the conflict of objective material interests as being at the heart of class society, with the interests of labour set in contradiction to those of capital, Bourdieusian sociology makes such conflicts more complex and covert, subject to the search for distinction. As society becomes more engaged with consumer culture, there is less clarity in what constitutes class divisions and what constitutes a conflict of interests. Arguably, the most powerful divisions in later life are those that can marshal the greatest amount of assets, capital and associated identities by which to resist the ascriptions of agedness and the corporeal delineations of frailty and infirmity.

In challenging the analytical purchase of 'identity', Brubaker and Cooper have pointed out how 'identity' is often opposed to 'interest' in an effort to highlight and conceptualise non-instrumental modes of social and political action. With a slightly different analytical emphasis, identity is used to underscore the manner in which individual or collective action may be governed by particularistic self-understandings rather than by 'putatively universal self-interest' (Brubaker and Cooper, 2000: 6). These authors contrast identity based upon a sense of self and belonging as a source of social action with interests, which derive from the material advantages accruing from one's social location. Actions based upon increasing or advancing one's material interests, they suggest, differ from those based upon strengthening or shoring up one's social identity. If social divisions are equally framed around interests and identities, then social actions derived from one's position within a social category or division may be deemed as 'interest serving' or as 'identity preserving'. The power to act may reflect the material and symbolic capital that confers the power to act. In so far as age contributes to the accumulation of wealth – in the form of assets such as pension holding or property owning – it might well serve the material interests of older people to act in such a way as to increase or maintain the value of those assets. In which case, might those interests not represent the interests of all those holding significant assets, irrespective of their age?

Age and property relations might coincide in circumstances where asset holding is strongly correlated with age, but in such cases it is the accumulation of assets, not age qua chronology or corporeality, that counts. By contrast, in so far as age contributes to impairment and physical limitations, those disadvantages might well lead older people to support policies and practices that decrease the social exclusion and disablement of people on low incomes. Allying one's interests with the asset-holding minority in society may prove incompatible with the interests of those experiencing physical and material limitations and low pay. What then constitutes the most salient aspect of an older person's identity, and hence their perceived interests, may of course have shifted over their life course, in part because of decisions and circumstances made without full recognition at the time. Identities and interests may not be neatly and consistently aligned, but structurally determined categories and divisions originating earlier in life may provide sources of stability when set against a background of growing chance and insecurity such as is met with in later life. At the same time, as change and instability extend over the life course, and all of life becomes less subject to the processes of institutionalisation and standardisation, even the social locations once secured and stabilised under welfare capitalism no longer seem so self-evident. Decisions over social action are less clearly reducible to past or present social positions and social interests no longer so evidently running through them like the letters through sticks of rock. In second modernity, most identities, interests and social locations are relatively less stable and determinate. This potential indeterminacy highlights the vexed problem of 'intersectionality' and the difficult search to find the stable interstices in society where common interests lie.

Ageing outside of division: the inherent intersectionality of later lives?

As already noted, attempts to take account of the diversification of identity, interests and position have brought the contested notion of 'intersectionality' to centre stage (Choo and Ferree, 2010). In utilising intersectionality as a tool to consider the social divisions of later life, we have tried to make sense of the multiplicity of forms, styles and cultures that individual later lives embody. This draws attention to the ways by which differing social identities and social locations are aligned with differing patterns of cultural, financial and social assets, capital and resources. Bourdieu's notion of different forms of capital can serve as a further critical element in this matrix of power, difference, division and diversity (Bourdieu, 1986). The simple social categorisation of old age, whether based on class, corporeality or chronology, is unsustainable. The use of any totalising social representation of the social divisions marking later life fails fully to capture the complexities that are now realised within the collective representations brought about by the institutions of the media, the market and the state. No single structure, or its associated identities, can fully capture the different lifestyles and life circumstances with which people in later life make sense of and navigate their way in the world. Set in train by circumstances from the past and the contingencies of the present, social differences continue diversifying later life through a multiplicity of influences and modes of representation, dominated by consumption, consumerism and choice. As we wrote some 20 years ago, 'the shift toward the ... new cultures of ageing has by no means sorted out many of the contradictions associated with consumer society' (Gilleard and Higgs, 2000: 210). Those contradictions have remained and multiplied.

The use of the term 'intersectionality' is, as pointed out, problematic. It risks confounding two elements of division that should be more usefully separated. On the one hand, intersectionality is framed by the contingency of all social structures and identities and the ontological diversity underlying their social categorisation or division. On the other hand, the contestation surrounding the presumed centrality and importance attached to these various divisions, identities and stratifications seems to depend less upon their power than on their powerlessness, their oppression by the unmarked categories by which society judges and rewards its members. While much of the debate over intersectionality in the USA has focused upon the relative salience of race in adjudicating between positions of advantage and disadvantage, subsequent developments in Europe have led to a widening lens whereby a host of other divisions and distinctions are introduced, serving as equally important mediating influences, including the categorisations associated with age and chronology, both with and without connotations of advantage and oppression, power and powerlessness.

The shift from social categories and classes to social identities and locations illustrated by the new social movements may reflect a more general social change that has occurred from first to second modernity; however, the material circumstances of later lives are still the necessary background that enables or constrains the opportunities that people in later life have to realise a preferred lifestyle. At the same time, ethnicity, race and sexuality are important influences on what those preferences might be. Just as every division seems to draw attention to still further divisions and every distinction calls forth further distinctions, these competing and intersecting claims for place and position require that individuals at all ages and stages of life draw upon, articulate and realise not just one master identity, one master location, one self-same life story, but many. In this era of the 'reflexive imperative' (Archer, 2012), age may struggle to be heard. Whether as a category or an identity, age or agedness arguably performs a limited set of functions and interests, even as they are clearly implicated in the realisation of many other social locations, including those of race, class, sexuality, gender and/or able-bodiedness. Rather than being a central form of categorisation or identity, however, age, or later life, can be seen as a social arena whose salience is determined more by its intersections with other social divisions and identities than by its standing alone. Age may be a factor in promoting or demoting, advantaging or disadvantaging the position of an individual and the interests attached to those occupying their position – as a homeowner, a member of a minority ethnic community, a disabled person or a homosexual – without age itself having much of a determining role outside of these social contexts.

While class, ethnicity, gender, health status, race and religion all matter as potential categories, identities and sources of division at each stage of life, many of the social heritages that were once central to the older person have been gradually revised. This is particularly the case as the ageing person becomes subject to the corporeal processes of illness, impairment and infirmity. Battling for social position in such circumstances may be less about asserting the value or resisting the devaluation of chronological age than upon negotiating a position of wellness in illness, of functionality despite disablement (Greenhalgh, 2018: 69). The 'agonisms' of freedom, to use Foucault's borrowed term, may be less focused upon agedness per se, than in striving to retain as much as possible evidence of corporeal competency (or integrity) and personal and social visibility. The actions and discourses expressed in such circumstances are no doubt made harder, or easier, by the legacy of a person's previous position in the formal economy, by their ethnic heritage and by the various resources acquired by gendered existence. However, as the corporeality of an individual's social location grows in salience, the cultural, economic and social assets and capital concealing the corporeality of age largely fade – though they do not disappear altogether. If the passage of time serves as an asset for much of the life span, leading to the accumulation of human and material capital and resources by which individuals can pursue their interests and fashion their lifestyles – much as Laslett (1989) saw might be most fully realised in the 'third age' – there comes a time when chronology and corporeality may take away more than they contribute.[11] At this point, the limits of individualisation risk being overtaken by the necessities of collective support, when a time for divisions, distinctions and their various intersections can be replaced by a need for care and comfort. Such circumstances should serve as a reminder that the 'liquid' nature of life, though never fixed, is nevertheless finite.

Corporeality and the social in later life

In reaching such a conclusion, it might seem that we are advocating a position that puts the body at the heart of age's identity and bodily interests at the heart of age's interests. This is not our position. We do not consider that age is 'at bottom' a corporeal affair. Rather we believe that age's social realisation and the social divisions and differences that shape its social location as age do so in large part through its intersection with a variety of institutionalised social structures that are oriented around and toward the body. This is not to say that later lifestyles are not shaped by and intersect with other divides and interests. Nor do we believe that later lifestyles are unaffected by considerations other than those of the body, such as those concerning family and family relationships. The point is that so many of the social divisions that intersect in later life derive much of their meaning from their leaning upon some combination of chronology and corporeality.

Understanding social division is critical in understanding the nature of society, social change and the dispositions and distinctions of social life. This is so at all stages of the life course. The articulation, categorisations, identities and interests associated with social division are not realised in the same ways or to the same extent, however, and age matters. The study of the structuring influences by which later lives are distinguished from each other and from other periods in the life course serves to illuminate the changing nature of later life at the same time as it shines a light on the changing nature of society itself. The interconnections between age and other social divisions and the extent to which each leans upon the other render any simple account of ageing and society inadequate. Treating later life as simply the outcome of cumulative advantage and disadvantage, whether through arithmetical formulations such as double, triple or quadruple jeopardy, or by reference to some other zero-sum analysis, is not only limited but is misleading. Corporeality and chronology should not be treated as mere social products. Old age, or rather later life, is an important and growing social arena. It is an arena where society's divisions and different social positions are illuminated and realised. But they are realised in ways that differ from other times in people's lives. It is not that social divisions disappear or are somehow levelled out or neutralised by age. Equally, age is not some kind of superordinate identity or source of division that overshadows other structures and other identities. Quite the opposite. Later life is no longer a major source of division or identity in the way that it was in first modernity when the body generally only mattered as a source of labour power.

Less a source than a site of division, later life has become a series of social locations where many of the social divisions of earlier in life are rearranged, redefined and recalibrated, but always to some greater or lesser degree in relation to the body marked as ageing.

In short, later life is a site where the corporeal confronts the social (Gilleard and Higgs 1998). Gender, ethnicity and sexuality are important social markers of identity, irrespective of the age of the person or the economic or other material differences and inequalities they may possess. But the distinctions of age's able-bodiedness and corporeal integrity create new inequalities, realise new exclusions and establish new distinctions, more so in later life than at any other stage of life. These corporeal inequalities can potentially override the traditional inequalities associated with 'class' or 'race', and with increasing agedness they often do. But while class and race can also make for forms of solidarity, can express and exercise interests and engender forms of social capital, the corporeality of ageing seems to dominate as a form of capital incapable of establishing alternative sites of resistance or community or indeed of allying itself in opposition to the dominant interests of the day.

As we have argued, the salience of age and the body as corporeal identity is not invariant. In health and social care settings, for example, the division between fitness and frailty, between health and disease, between dependency and independency often seems to fill the social location of old age as old age. Outside these settings, other divisions and distinctions can serve to delineate a social space that is common across the generations, where inequality and diversity jostle to define lifestyles and identities whose realisation in later life may be more muted but still capable of distinct articulation. Even when age leads to a general diminishment of 'power over' others through the distancing that later life entails from the relations of production and from social reproduction this does not necessarily lead to a consequent loss of 'power to' articulate other relational identities and fashion other relational lifestyles. Some notion of class or status is needed to recognise that older people are not all equally positioned to exercise the 'power to' maintain one's status as a social agent, to articulate and assert identities other than sheer agedness and to realise chosen lifestyles that mediate or modify the social location of later life. Even then, there are limits in the exercise of such power, determined as much by chronology and corporeality as by the connections of capital.

The reflexive imperative of second modernity ensures that at every stage of life, people confront challenges and choices in realising their sense of self, their place in the world and their goals and aspirations for their future. Such subjectivities are not necessarily directed toward realising any particular location for later life as in continuing to secure a sense of self, place and direction for their life. The diversity of such selves, places and plans inevitably leans upon the cultural, economic and social contexts in which people have lived, but enabling and ensuring a continuing diversity of interests and identities in later life is arguably as difficult for the individual as it is for the state, no matter what assets and resources each may command. By contrast, the political response to the division of later life into the fit and the frail, the healthy and the sick, the functional and the impaired is much less difficult to determine and much easier to administer. Whatever critique may be advanced of the social model of disability, one thing seems clear, namely the insistence of its demands on the need of the state and other public bodies to minimise the social exclusion consequent upon corporeal impairment. While an ever-expanding body of research has sought to establish the individual ecological and social determinants of disease and frailty in later life, much less has addressed the most effective ways of minimising the social consequences of such corporeal inequalities. It is here where ageism needs to be combatted, here where collective resources need to be invested and here where the power of the individual can least be exercised. It is also here where social divisions cut deepest into the well-being of people in later life. Research should be directed toward enriching our understanding of later life, including all the parameters, corporeal, cultural and economic, that over-determine its social ordering and social realisation. It should also be directed at examining the relative contribution that these social divisions and differences make in creating diversity and identity as well as in determining exclusion and inequality in later life. We hope this book may lead gerontology toward such goals.

Conclusions

As later life has extended its reach in society and become common to people's experiences and expectations, it has become a progressively larger social and cultural space. It has also become harder to define or delineate as a distinct social category. Instead of later life forming a division, it has become itself a site of other divisions. These diversifying later lives are realised in and can be represented by a variety of social locations that contribute to the broader social landscape. They can be examined and understood in different ways, as inequalities or identities; as diversity or division; as opportunity or oppression. They can be treated as the outcomes or the reflections of social structures, as well as the subjectivities and inter-subjectivities fashioned within the collective consciousnesses of an expanding multicultural world. These different ways of approaching social division and difference in later life are as intriguing as they are problematic. This is in large part the consequence of the complexity and interconnections that exist in all social locations between structure and experience and between the intersecting impacts of distinct social locations.

While class, ethnicity and gender function as sources of social division throughout the life course, in later life other divisions emerge, not least those derived from the corporeality of the body. This includes not only the emergence of identities based upon the presence or absence of impairments and physical limitations, but also the identities framed more narrowly around illness and disease. Some of these identities seem at present mostly confined to earlier adult life, while others have already become realised in later life. Some, but by no means all, are becoming increasingly powerful sources of division and inequality. While it is possible that sexuality in later life will in the future become more a source of diversity than a site of oppression, it is more difficult to be so optimistic about the division between the fit and the frail, the healthy and the sick. Despite the work performed by organisations such as the Alzheimer's Society in different countries in promoting a positive identity for people with Alzheimer's disease and other forms of dementia, the trend toward multiple morbidity with increasing age renders such identities difficult to sustain as sources of an unproblematic 'neurodiversity'. They risk merging into a less identifiable location that is perhaps too easily reduced to that between the fit and the frail, the successfully and the unsuccessfully aged.

The more ageing there is, the more this division is realised – a division often amplified by health and social care systems operating in the context of ever-tightening restrictions in service provision and an individualisation of health promotion. To date, the social and personal consequences of this division have been explored less often than the many attempts at discovering its origins. While human capital theory might suggest that investing in education and health early in life should prove the 'best' strategy to secure health, wealth and well-being in old age, the other side of that model implies a decreasing return from investments made late in life. Reframed as the cumulative disadvantage model still implies that late-life disability and ill health are the effects of inequalities compounded throughout life, with each successive inequality building upon earlier ones. In whatever different ways the research into the causes of ageing-into-disability is viewed, it is also clear that much less research has been devoted to identifying the adverse social consequences of that division, let alone investigating how to ameliorate them. The importance of corporeality and chronology as sources of inequality has been overlooked in comparison with gerontology's focus upon the impact of the inequalities of class, gender and ethnicity. We hope this book goes some way to rebalancing the concerns of social gerontology; not by rejecting the role of these latter categories in shaping the inequalities of later life, but in acknowledging that ageing also brings other considerations into play, not least those associated with the body. The body divides as much as does society. Whatever their origin, making social divides less disadvantageous remains the challenge, without sacrificing, one might add, the diversity they also bring.

Notes

1. Greenhalgh (2018) has noted how the post-war cohort of medical and social researchers of old age tended to picture it as 'slow moving and monotonous' even if the narratives of older people were not (Greenhalgh, 2018: 38).
2. This was the title of a discussion paper outlining the British government's vision of a future old age, beyond that already legislated for by the hard-pressed welfare state of the immediate post-war years (DHSS, 1978).
3. Examples of what we mean by 'ever-widening' social arenas include expanding engagement by the over-sixties with cruise holidays, green politics, master athletics and, of course, the new social media.
4. Applying the term 'role-less role' to describe the social position of older people was common practice in post-war social gerontology (see Burgess, 1960; Cumming et al, 1960; Tunstall, 1966; Hiltz, 1979).
5. The number of books, papers and reports addressing 'ageing and inequality', 'unequal ageing' or 'inequalities in later life' that has been published since 2010 is vast. There is little evidence for a more positive spin being placed upon the diversification of later life – beyond the gradual transformation of the earlier term 'old age' into 'later life' (Cann and Dean, 2009; Goudswaard et al, 2012; Patsios et al, 2012; Betti et al, 2015; Centre for Ageing Better, 2017; OECD, 2017).
6. The relationship between 'objective' and 'subjective' class and status positions has been subject to much study, presaged in part on the repeated finding that 'the relationship between objective and subjective class remains weak' (Kluegel, Singleton and Starnes, 1977: 610). Multiple factors have been used to explain this, not least the trends toward increasingly individualised notions of what determines 'class' (Davis and Robinson, 1988: 110–11) and of what constitutes 'inequality' (Ricci, 2016). Savage's recent work on class and class consciousness in the twenty-first century shows that this disparity every bit as evident in Britain now as it was in late twentieth century America (Savage, 2015). In the academy the Marxist idea of 'class consciousness' has been replaced with the idea that discourses about class and status are multi-determined by cultural processes operating both within and outside the social relations of production (see Fantasia, 1995; Bottero, 2004; Shildrick and Macdonald, 2013). It seems reasonable to assume such processes are more pronounced in post-working life as subjective appraisals of socio-economic

position in later life bear a weaker relationship to objective financial status (Hansen, Slagsvold and Moum, 2008; Plagnol, 2011).

7 For example, irrespective of past occupation, recent cohorts of retirees in the UK are more likely to be homeowners, own more liquid and non-liquid assets, including pension fund wealth, are likely to spend more on consumer durables and are more likely to have inherited wealth than past cohorts. For historical data on pensioner income and assets, see Lydall (1955) and Shorrocks (1975); for rising consumer trends among UK pensioner households, see Higgs et al (2009); Hyde et al (2011); Jones et al (2008); for recent consumer trends, see ONS 2018b: Table A11, 'Detailed household expenditure by age of household reference person'; for trends in pensioner assets and income, see *ONS Wealth & Assets Survey*, 2018a: Tables 5.19, 'Distribution of net household financial wealth, by household type', and 5.21, 'Individuals by age, by household net financial wealth'.

8 The term 'dividing practices' comes from Foucault's writings on governance and the methods by which structures of governance create divisions both within and between persons (see Foucault, 1982).

9 This neologism refers to the elision between frailty and failure that acts as the imagined antithesis to the thesis of 'healthy', 'normal' or 'successful' ageing.

10 Many people aged 65 or more who maintain positions of authority, influence and power on the world stage can consider their aged status a mere appendage to their status as celebrities, as politically powerful or as simply rich. The struggle with the paradoxes raised by terms such as 'successfully aged' illustrates the dilemmas posed by seeking such recalibration. Where age can serve as a positive identity lies at the extremes of distinction – such as the world's oldest man or woman, or as the oldest paraglider or weightlifter. Without the identity of achievement that is associated with those qualifying roles, 'the oldest' would be a hollowed out term, with scarcely any additional value. For a further discussion of the issue of ageism and interests, see Higgs and Gilleard (2019).

11 After a certain point, agedness itself seems to serve as a determinant of social exclusion, over and above any effects of class, education, gender or even relative healthfulness (Key and Culliney, 2018).

References

Abbott, P., Tyler, M., and Wallace, C. (2006). *An Introduction to Sociology: Feminist perspectives.* London: Routledge.

Adamson, J., and Donovan, J. (2005). 'Normal disruption': South Asian and African/Caribbean relatives caring for an older family member in the UK. *Social Science and Medicine*, 60, 1, 37–48.

Addis, E., and Joxhe, M. (2017). Gender gaps in social capital: A theoretical interpretation of evidence from Italy, *Feminist Economics*, 23, 2, 146–171.

Agger, B. (2015). *Speeding Up Fast Capitalism: Cultures, Jobs, Families, Schools, Bodies.* London: Routledge.

Ajrouch, K.J., Antonucci, T.C., and Janevic, M.R. (2001). Social networks among blacks and whites: the interaction between race and age, *The Journals of Gerontology: Series B*, 56, 2, 1, S112–S118.

Ammerman, N.T. (2003). Religious identities and religious institutions. In M. Dillon (ed), *Handbook of the Sociology of Religion.* Cambridge: Cambridge University Press, pp 207–224.

Amundson, R. (1992). Disability, handicap, and the environment. *Journal of Social Philosophy*, 23, 1, 105–119.

Anthias, F. (1998). Rethinking social divisions: some notes towards a theoretical framework. *The Sociological Review*, 46, 3, 505–535.

Anthias, F. (2001). The concept of 'social division' and theorising social stratification: looking at ethnicity and class. *Sociology*, 35, 4, 835–854.

Anthias, F. (2012). Intersectional what? Social divisions, intersectionality and levels of analysis. *Ethnicities*, 13, 1, 3–19.

Anttonen, A. and Meagher, G. (2013) Mapping marketisation: concepts and goals, in G. Meagher and M. Szebehely, (eds), *Marketisation in Nordic Eldercare: A research report on legislation, oversight, extent and consequences*, Stockholm Studies in Social Work, 30. Stockholm: Stockholm University, pp 13–22.

Antonovsky, A. (1967). Social class, life expectancy and overall mortality. *The Milbank Memorial Fund Quarterly*, 45, 2, 31–73.

Appiah, K.A. (1998). Race, culture, identity: misunderstood connections. In K.A. Appiah and A. Gutmann (eds), *Color Conscious: The Political Morality of Race.* Princeton, NJ: Princeton University Press, pp 30–105.

Arber, S. and Cooper, H. (1999). Gender differences in health in later life: the new paradox? *Social Science & Medicine*, 48, 1, 61–76.

Arber, S., Fenn, K., and Meadows, R. (2014). Subjective financial well-being, income and health inequalities in mid and later life in Britain. *Social Science and Medicine*, 100, 12–20.

Archer, M.S. (2000). *Being Human: The Problem of Agency*. Cambridge: Cambridge University Press.

Archer, M.S. (2007). *Making Our Way through the World*. Cambridge: Polity Press.

Archer, M.S. (2012). *The Reflexive Imperative in Late Modernity*. Cambridge: Cambridge University Press.

Archibald, M.M., and Barnard, A. (2018). Futurism in nursing: technology, robotics and the fundamentals of care. *Journal of Clinical Nursing*, 27, 11–12, 2473–2480.

Arends-Tóth, J., and van de Vijver, F.J. (2004). Domains and dimensions in acculturation: implicit theories of Turkish–Dutch. *International Journal of Intercultural Relations*, 28, 1, 19–35.

Assari, S. (2018). Unequal gain of equal resources across racial groups. *International Journal of Health Policy and Management*, 7, 1, 1–9.

Atkinson, A. (1995). What is happening to the distribution of income in the UK? *Proceedings of the British Academy*, 82, 317–351.

Atkinson, D. (2004). *Counseling American Minorities* (6th edition). New York: McGraw-Hill.

Atkinson, W (2010). *Class, Individualization and Late Modernity: In Search of the Reflexive Worker*. Basingstoke: Palgrave.

Atkinson, W. (2015). *Class*. Cambridge: Polity Press.

Atkinson, W. (2017). *Class in the New Millennium: The Structure, Homologies and Experience of the British Social Space*. London: Routledge.

Babiker, I.E., Cox, J.L., and Miller, P.M. (1980). The measurement of cultural distance and its relationship to medical consultations, symptomatology and examination performance of overseas students at Edinburgh University. *Social Psychiatry*, 15, 109–116.

Bachrach, P., and Baratz, M.S. (1962). Two faces of power. *American Political Science Review*, 56, 947–952.

Bajekal, M., Blane, D., Grewal, I.N.I., Karlsen, S., and Nazroo, J. (2004). Ethnic differences in influences on quality of life at older ages: A quantitative analysis. *Ageing and Society*, 24, 5, 709–728.

Bambra, C., Smith, K.E., Garthwaite, K., Joyce, K.E., and Hunter, D.J. (2011). A labour of Sisyphus? Public policy and health inequalities research from the Black and Acheson Reports to the Marmot Review. *Journal of Epidemiology and Community Health*, 65, 5, 399–406.

Bandeen-Roche, K., Seplaki, C.L., Huang, J., Buta, B., Kalyani, R.R., Varadhan, R., Xue, Q-L., Walston, J.D., and Kasper, J.D. (2015). Frailty in older adults: a nationally representative profile in the United States. *The Journals of Gerontology: Series A* 70, 11, 1427–1434.

Barker, D.K. (2015). Unstable feminisms: a new Marxian class analysis of domestic labor. *Rethinking Marxism*, 27, 3, 431–439.

Barnes, C., Mercer, G., and Shakespeare, T. (1999). *Exploring Disability: a Sociological Reader.* Cambridge: Polity Press.

Barnes, L.L., Mendes de Leon, C.F., Bienias, J.L., and Evans, D.A. (2004). A longitudinal study of black–white differences in social resources. *The Journals of Gerontology Series B: Psychological Sciences and Social Sciences*, 59, 3, S146–S153.

Barnes, M., Blom, A., Cox, K., and Lessof, C. (2006). *The Social Exclusion of older People: Evidence from the First Wave of the English Longitudinal Study of Ageing (ELSA)*. Final Report. Office of the Deputy Prime Minister, Social Exclusion Unit, London.

Barnes, L.L., De Leon, C.F.M., Lewis, T.T., Bienias, J.L., Wilson, R.S., and Evans, D.A. (2008). Perceived discrimination and mortality in a population-based study of older adults. *American Journal of Public Health*, 98, 7, 1241–1247.

Barrett, A.E. and Toothman, E.L. (2017). Multiple "old ages": The influence of social context on women's aging anxiety. *The Journals of Gerontology: Series B*, 73(8), e154–e164.

Bartley, M. (2004). *Health Inequality: An Introduction to Theories, Concepts and Methods*. Cambridge, Polity Press.

Bauman, Z. (2005). *Liquid Life*. Cambridge: Polity Press.

Bauman, Z. (2009). *Contemporary Social Evils*. Cambridge: Polity Press.

Bauman, Z. (2012). *Liquid Modernity* (2nd edition). Cambridge: Polity Press.

Baykara-Krumme, H., and Platt, L. (2018). Life satisfaction of migrants, stayers and returnees: reaping the fruits of migration in old age? *Ageing and Society*, 38, 8, 721–745.

Beard, R. (2004). Advocating voice: organisational, historical and social milieux of the Alzheimer's disease movement. *Sociology of Health and Illness*, 26, 6, 797–819.

Beardsworth, A.D., and Keil, E.T. (1991). Vegetarianism, veganism, and meat avoidance: recent trends and findings. *British Food Journal*, 93, 4, 19–24.

Beaudry, J.-S. (2016). Beyond (models of) disability? *Journal of Medicine and Philosophy*, 41, 210–228.

Beck, U. (2002). *Individualization: Institutionalized individualism and its social and political consequences.* London: Sage Publications.

Beck, U. (2007). Beyond class and nation: reframing social inequalities in a globalizing world 1. *British Journal of Sociology*, 58, 4, 679–705.

Beck, U., and Beck-Gernsheim, E. (2001) *Individualization: Institutionalized Individualism and Its Social and Political Consequences*. London: Sage.

Beck, U., and Lau, C. (2005). Second modernity as a research agenda: 'theoretical and empirical explorations in the 'meta-change' of modern society. *British Journal of Sociology*, 56, 4, 525–557.

Beck, U., Bonz, W., and Lau, C. (2003). The theory of reflexive modernisation: problematic, hypotheses and research programme. *Theory Culture and Society*, 20, 2, 1–33.

Becker, G.S. (1962). Investment in human capital: a theoretical analysis. *Journal of Political Economy*, 70, 5, 2, 9–49.

Becker, G.S. (1993). Nobel lecture: the economic way of looking at behaviour. *Journal of Political Economy*, 101, 3, 385–409.

Becker, G.S. (1994). Human capital revisited. In G.S. Becker (ed), *Human Capital: A Theoretical and Empirical Analysis with Special Reference to Education* (3rd edition). Chicago: University of Chicago Press, pp 15–28.

Becker, G.S. (2002). The age of human capital. In E.P. Lazear (ed), *Education in the Twenty-First Century*. Palo Alto, CA: Hoover Institution Press, pp 3–8. http://media.hoover.org/sites/default/files/documents/0817928928_3.pdf

Beckett, M. (2000). Converging health inequalities in later life – an artefact of mortality selection? *Journal of Health and Social Behavior*, 41, 1, 106–119.

Beechey, V. (1979). On patriarchy. *Feminist Review*, 3, 1, 66–82.

Behrent, M.C. (2016). Conclusion: the strange failure (and peculiar success) of Foucault's project. In D. Zamora and M.C. Behrent (eds), *Foucault and Neoliberalism*. Cambridge: Polity Press, pp 176–186.

Bell, D. (2000). *The End of Ideology: On the Exhaustion of Political Ideas in the Fifties: With 'The Resumption of History in the New Century'*. Cambridge, MA: Harvard University Press.

Bennett, K.M. (2007). "No sissy stuff": Towards a theory of masculinity and emotional expression in older widowed men. *Journal of Aging Studies*, 21, 4, 347–356.

Bergman, M.M., and Joye, D. (2001). *Comparing Social Stratification Schemas: CAMSIS, CSP-CH, Goldthorpe, ISCO-88, Treiman, and Wright*. Cambridge: Cambridge Studies in Social Research.

Bergman, M.M., Lambert, P., Prandy, K., and Joye, D. (2002). Theorizing, construction and validation of a social stratification scale: Cambridge Social Interaction and Stratification Scale (CAMSIS) for Switzerland. *Swiss Journal of Sociology*, 28, 7–25.

Berkman, L.F., Glass, T., Brissette, I., and Seeman, T.E. (2000). From social integration to health: Durkheim in the New Millennium. *Social Science and Medicine*, 51, 843–857.

Berlin, I. (2010). *The Making of African America: The Four Great Migrations*. New York: Penguin Books.

Best, S. (2005). *Understanding Social Divisions*. London: Sage Publications.

Betti, G., Bettio, F., Georgiadis, T., and Tinios, F. (2015). *Unequal Ageing in Europe: Women's Independence and Pensions*. Basingstoke: Palgrave Macmillan.

Bhabha, H. (1994). *The Location of Culture*. London: Routledge.

Bickenbach, J., Rubinelli, S., and Stucki, G. (2017). Being a person with disabilities or experiencing disability: Two perspectives on the social response to disability. *Journal of Rehabilitation Medicine*, 49, 7, 543–549.

Blakemore, K., and Boneham, M. (1995). *Age, Race and Ethnicity: A Comparative Approach*. London: Sage.

Böcker, A.G.M., and Gehring, A.J. (2015). Returning 'home' after retirement? The role of gender in return migration decisions of Spanish and Turkish migrants. *Review of Social Studies*, 2, 1, 77–97.

Bohrer, A. (2018). Intersectionality and Marxism: a critical historiography. *Historical Materialism*, 26, 2, 46–74.

Bois, J. P. (1994). *Histoire de la Vieillesse*. Paris: Presses Universitaires de France.

Bonoli, G. (2007). Time matters: post industrialization, new social risks, and welfare state adaptation in advanced industrial democracies. *Comparative Political Studies*, 40, 5, 495–520.

Bottero, W. (2004). Class identities and the identity of class. *Sociology*, 38, 5, 985–1003.

Bottero, W. (2005). *Stratification: Social Division and Inequality*. London: Routledge.

Bottero, W. (2015). Social class structures and social mobility: the background context. In M. Formosa and P. Higgs (eds), *Social Class in Later Life: Power, Identity and Lifestyle*. Bristol: Policy Press, pp 15–32.

Bouchard, L., Albertini, M., Batista, R., and de Montigny, J. (2015). Research on health inequalities: a bibliometric analysis (1966–2014). *Social Science and Medicine*, 141, 100–108.

Boumans, M., and Morgan, M.S. (2001). Ceteris paribus conditions: materiality and the application of economic theories. *Journal of Economic Methodology*, 8, 1, 11–26.

Bourdieu, P. (1977). *Outline of a Theory of Practice*. Cambridge: Polity Press.

Bourdieu, P. (1984). *Distinction: A Social Critique of the Judgement of Taste*. London: Routledge.

Bourdieu, P. (1985). The forms of capital. In J.G. Richardson (ed.) *Handbook of Theory and Research for the Sociology of Education*. Westport, CT: Greenwood Press, pp 241–250.

Bourdieu, P. (1986). Forms of capital. In J.G. Richardson (ed), *Handbook of Theory and Research for the Sociology of Education*. New York: Greenwood Press, pp 241–258.

Bourdieu, P. (1989a). What makes a social class? On the theoretical and practical existence of groups. *Berkeley Journal of Sociology*, 32, 1–17.

Bourdieu, P. (1989b). Social space and symbolic power. *Sociological Theory*, 7, 1, 14–25.

Bourdieu, P., and Accardo, A. (2002). *The Weight of the World: Social Suffering in Contemporary Society*. Cambridge: Polity Press.

Bradley, H. (2014). Class descriptors or class relations? Thoughts towards a critique of Savage et al. *Sociology*, 48, 3, 429–436.

Bradshaw, T.K. (2008). The post-place community: contributions to the debate about the definition of community. *Community Development*, 39, 1, 5–16.

Brault, M.W. (2012). Americans with disabilities: 2010. *Current Population Reports.* Pub no P70–131. www.includevt.org/wp-content/uploads/2016/07/2010_Census_Disability_Data.pdf

Brayne, C. (2007). The elephant in the room – healthy brains in later life, epidemiology and public health. *Nature Reviews Neuroscience*, 8, 3, 233–239.

Breen, R. (2005). Foundations of a neo-Weberian class analysis. In E.O. Wright (ed), *Approaches to Class Analysis*. Cambridge: Cambridge University Press, pp 31–50.

Brekhus, W. (1998). A sociology of the unmarked: redirecting our focus. *Sociological Theory*, 16, 1, 34–51.

Bristow, J. (2015). *Baby Boomers and Generational Conflict*. London: Springer.

Brown, L. (2016). Vertical and horizontal approaches to the making of racial statistics in Britain. *Ethnic and Racial Studies*, 39, 10, 1812–1830.

Brown, T.H., and Hargrove, T.W. (2017). Psychosocial mechanisms underlying older black men's health. *The Journals of Gerontology: Series B*, 73, 2, 188–197.

Brown, T.H., O'Rand, A.M., and Adkins, D.E. (2012). Race-ethnicity and health trajectories: tests of three hypotheses across multiple groups and health outcomes. *Journal of Health and Social Behavior*, 53, 3, 359–377.

Brown, W. (1995). *States of Injury: Power and Freedom in Late Modernity*. Princeton, NJ: Princeton University Press.

Brubaker, R. (1985). Rethinking classical theory: the sociological vision of Pierre Bourdieu. *Theory and Society*, 14, 6, 745–775.

Brubaker, R., and Cooper, F. (2000) Beyond 'identity'. *Theory and Society*, 29, 1–47.

Burgess, E.W. (1960). Aging in Western culture. In E.W. Burgess (ed), *Aging in Western Societies.* Chicago: University of Chicago Press, pp 3–28.

Butler, J. (1993). *Bodies That Matter: On the Discursive Limits of 'Sex'*. New York: Routledge.

Butt, J. and Moriarty, J. (2004). Social support and ethnicity in old age. In C. Hennessy and A. Walker (eds), *Research Highlights from the Growing Older Programme*. Buckingham: Open University Press, pp 167–187.

Buttery, A.K., Du, Y., Busch, M.A., Fuchs, J., Gaertner, B., Knopf, H., and Scheidt-Nave, C. (2016). Changes in physical functioning among men and women aged 50–79 years in Germany: an analysis of National Health Interview and Examination Surveys, 1997–1999 and 2008–2011. *BMC Geriatrics*, 16, 1, 205, 1–11.

Calasanti, T.M. and Zajicek, A.M. (1993). A socialist-feminist approach to aging: Embracing diversity. *Journal of Aging Studies,* 7, 2, 117–131.

Calasanti, T.M. (1996). Incorporating diversity: Meaning, levels of research, and implications for theory, *The Gerontologist*, 36, 2, 147–156.

Calhoun, C. (1995). *Critical Social Theory: Culture, history, and the challenge of difference.* Cambridge: Wiley-Blackwell.

Callahan, D. (1995). *Setting Limits: Medical Goals in an Aging Society*. Washington, DC: Georgetown University Press.

Cann, P., and Dean, M. (eds) (2009). *Unequal Ageing: The Untold Story of Exclusion in Old Age.* Bristol: Policy Press.

Carastathis, A. (2008). The invisibility of privilege: a critique of intersectional models of identity. *Les Ateliers de l'Éthique*, 3, 2, 23–38.

Carastathis, A. (2013). Identity categories as potential coalitions. *Signs: Journal of Women in Culture and Society*, 38, 4, 941–965.

Carastathis, A. (2014). The concept of intersectionality in feminist theory. *Philosophy Compass*, 9, 5, 304–314.

Carbin, M., and Edenheim, S. (2013). The intersectional turn in feminist theory: a dream of a common language? *European Journal of Women's Studies*, 20, 3, 233–248.

Carling, A. H. (1991). *Social Division*. London: Verso.

Cartwright, A., and O'Brien, M. (1974). Social class variations in health care and in the nature of general practitioner consultations. *The Sociological Review*, 22, 1 (Suppl), 77–98.

Causa, O., and Hermansen, M. (2018). Income redistribution through taxes and transfers across OECD Countries. *LIS Working Paper Series*, No 729, *LIS Cross National Data Center.* www.lisdatacenter.org/wps/liswps/729.pdf

Centre for Ageing Better (2017). *Inequalities in Later Life.* London: Centre for Ageing Better.

Centers for Disease Control and Prevention (2009). Prevalence and most common causes of disability among adults – United States, 2005. *Morbidity and Mortality Weekly Report*, 58, 421–426.

Chakravarty, S.R., and D'Ambrosio, C. (2010). Polarization orderings of income distributions. *Review of Income and Wealth*, 56, 1, 47–64.

Chamberlain, A.M., St. Sauver, J.L., Gerber, Y., Manemann, S.M., Boyd, C.M., Dunlay, S.M., Rocca W.A., Finney Rutten, L.F., Jiang, R., Weston, S.A. and Roger, V.L. (2015). Multimorbidity in heart failure: a community perspective. *The American Journal of Medicine,* 128, 1, 38–45.

Chamberlain, J. (1892). Old-age pensions. *The National Review*, 18, 108, 723–739.

Chan, T.-W., and Goldthorpe, J.W. (2007). Class and status: the conceptual distinction and its empirical relevance. *American Sociological Review*, 72, 512–532.

Charles, C.Z. (2003). The dynamics of racial residential segregation. *Annual Review of Sociology*, 29, 1, 167–207.

Chau, R.C., Foster, L., & Yu, S.W. (2017). The effects of defamilization and familization measures on the accumulation of retirement income for women in the UK. *Journal of Women & Aging*, 29, 6, 551–561.

Cheong, P.H., Edwards, R., Goulbourne, H., and Solomos, J. (2007). Immigration, social cohesion and social capital: a critical review. *Critical Social Policy*, 27, 1, 24–49.

Cherry, E. (2006). Veganism as a cultural movement: a relational approach. *Social Movement Studies*, 5, 2, 155–170.

Chin, R. (2017). *The Crisis of Multiculturalism in Europe: A History*. Princeton, NJ: Princeton University Press.

Cho, S., Crenshaw, K.W., and McCall, L. (2013). Toward a field of intersectionality studies: theory, applications, and praxis. *Signs: Journal of Women in Culture and Society*, 38, 4, 785–810.

Choo, H.Y., and Ferree, M.M. (2010). Practicing intersectionality in sociological research: A critical analysis of inclusions, interactions, and institutions in the study of inequalities. *Sociological Theory*, 28, 2, 129–149.

Ciobanu, R.O., and Fokkema, T. (2017). The role of religion in protecting older Romanian migrants from loneliness, *Journal of Ethnic and Migration Studies*, 43, 2, 199–217.

Clark, T.N., and Lipset, S.M. (1991). Are social classes dying? *International Sociology*, 6, 4, 397–410.

Clegg, S. (1989). *Frameworks of Power*. London: Sage Publications.

Cokley, K. (2007). Critical issues in the measurement of ethnic and racial identity: a referendum on the state of the field. *Journal of Counseling Psychology*, 54, 3, 24–234.

Cole, M. (2016). *Racism: A Critical Analysis*. London: Pluto Press.

Collins, P.H. (1990). *Black Feminist Thought: Knowledge, Consciousness and the Politics of Empowerment*. London: HarperCollins.

Collins, P.H. (2015). Intersectionality's definitional dilemmas. *Annual Review of Sociology*, 41, 1–20.

Concannon, L. (2007). Developing inclusive health and social care policies for older LGBT citizens. *British Journal of Social Work*, 39, 3, 403–417.

Convert, B. (2003) Bourdieu: Gary Becker's critic. *Economic Sociology: European Electronic Newsletter*, 4, 2, 6–9. Max Planck Institute for the Study of Societies (MPIfG), Cologne.

Cool, L.E. (1981). Ethnic identity: a source of community esteem for the elderly. *Anthropological Quarterly*, 54, 4,179–189.

Cooper, R., Hardy, R., Aihie Sayer, A., Ben-Shlomo, Y., Birnie, K., Cooper, C., Craig, L., Deary, I.J., Demakakos, P., Gallacher, J., McNeill, G., Martin, R.M., Starr, J.M., Steptoe, A. and Kuh, D. (2011). Age and gender differences in physical capability levels from mid-life onwards: the harmonisation and meta-analysis of data from eight UK cohort studies. *PLOS One*, 6, 11, Article e27899.

Cornwell, B. (2009). Good health and the bridging of structural holes. *Social Networks*, 31, 92–103.

Cornwell, B. (2011a). Age trends in daily social contact patterns. *Research on Aging*, 33, 5, 598–631.

Cornwell, B. (2011b). Independence through social networks: Bridging potential among older women and men. *Journals of Gerontology Series B: Psychological Sciences and Social Sciences,* 66, 6, 782–794.

Côté, J. (2006). Identity studies: How close are we to developing a social science of identity? An appraisal of the field. *Identity*, 6, 1, 3–25.

Craib, I. (1998). *Experiencing Identity*. London: Sage Publications.

Crenshaw, K. (1991). Mapping the margins: Intersectionality, identity politics, and violence against women of color. *Stanford Law Review*, 43, 6, 1241–1299.

Crenshaw, K. (2016) Postscript. In H. Lutz, M.T. Herrera-Vivar, and L. Supik (eds), *Framing Intersectionality: Debates on a Multi-Faceted Concept in Gender Studies*. London: Routledge, pp 221–233.

Cribb, J., Keiller, A.N., and Waters, T. (2018). *Living Standards, Poverty and Inequality in the UK: 2018*. London: Institute of Fiscal Studies.

Crompton, R. (2008). *Class and Stratification* (3rd edition). Cambridge: Polity Press.

Cronin, A. (2004). Sexuality in gerontology: A heteronormative presence, a queer absence'. In S.O. Daatland and S. Biggs (eds), *Ageing and Diversity: Multiple Pathways and Cultural Migrations.* Bristol: Policy Press, pp 107–22.

Crystal, S. (1980). *America's Old Age Crisis: Public Policy and the Two Worlds of Aging.* New York: Basic Books.

Crystal, S. (2018). Cumulative advantage and the retirement prospects of the hollowed-out generation: a tale of two cohorts. *Public Policy and Aging Report*, 28, 1, 14–18.

Crystal, S., and Shea, D. (1990). Cumulative advantage, cumulative disadvantage, and inequality among elderly people. *The Gerontologist*, 30, 4, 437–443.

Crystal, S., and Shea, D. (2002). Introduction: cumulative advantage, public policy, and late-life inequality. *Annual Review of Gerontology and Geriatrics*, 22, 1, 1–13.

Cullinan, J., Gannon, B., and O'Shea, E. (2013). The welfare implications of disability for older people in Ireland. *The European Journal of Health Economics*, 14, 2, 171–183.

Cumming, E., and Henry, W.E. (1961). *Growing Old: The process of disengagement.* New York: Basic Books.

Cumming, E., Dean, L.R., Newell, D.S., and McCaffrey, I. (1960). Disengagement – a tentative theory of aging. *Sociometry*, 23, 1, 23–35.

Cummings, J.L., and Jackson, P.B. (2008). Race, gender, and SES disparities in self-assessed health, 1974-2004. *Research on Aging*, 30, 2, 137–167.

Cummins, R.A. (2000). Objective and subjective quality of life: an interactive model. *Social Indicators Research*, 52, 1, 55–72.

Cutler, D., Deaton, A., and Lleras-Muney, A. (2006). The determinants of mortality. *Journal of Economic Perspectives*, 20, 3, 97–120.

Dahl, R.A. (1957). The concept of power. *Behavioral Science*, 2, 201–215.

Dahlberg, L., and McKee, K. (2018). Living on the edge: social exclusion and the receipt of informal care in older people. *Journal of Aging Research*, Article ID 6373101. http://dx.doi.org/10.1155/2016/6373101

Dahrendorf, R. (1959). *Class and Class Conflict in Industrial Society* (Vol 15). Stanford, CA: Stanford University Press.

Dannefer, D. (1987). Aging as intracohort differentiation: accentuation, the Matthew effect, and the life course. *Sociological Forum*, 2, 2, 211–236.

Dannefer, D. (1988). Differential gerontology and the stratified life course: conceptual and methodological issues. *Annual Review of Gerontology and Geriatrics*, 8, 3–36.

Dannefer, D. (2003). Cumulative advantage/disadvantage and the life course: cross-fertilizing age and social science theory. *The Journals of Gerontology Series B: Psychological Sciences and Social Sciences*, 58, 6, S327–S337.

Danziger, S.H., and Weinberg, D.H. (1994). The historical record: Trends in family income, inequality, and poverty. In S.H. Danziger, G.D. Sandifer and D.H. Weinberg (eds), *Confronting Poverty: Prescriptions for Change*. Cambridge, MA: Harvard University Press, pp 18–50.

Daric, J. (1951). Mortality, occupation and socio-economic status. *Vital Statistics-Special Reports, Selected Studies*, 33, 10, 175–187.

Darling, R.B., and Heckert, D.A. (2010). Orientations toward disability: differences over the life course. *International Journal of Disability, Development and Education*, 57, 2, 131–143.

Davis, K. (2008). Intersectionality as buzzword. *Feminist Theory*, 9, 1, 67–85.

Davis, N.J., and Robinson, R.V. (1988). Class identification of men and women in the 1970s and 1980s. *American Sociological Review*, 53, 1, 103–112.

Deaton, A., and Paxton, C. (1998). Aging and inequality in health and income. *American Economic Review*, 88, 248–253.

De Beauvoir, S. (1977). *Old Age*. Harmondsworth, Middlesex: Penguin Books.

Delaporte, I. (2018). *Ethnic Identity and the Employment Outcomes of Immigrants in France*. CesiFo Junior Economist Workshop, CesiFo Group, Munich.

Demakakos, P., Biddulph, J.P., de Oliveira, C., Tsakos, G., and Marmot, M.G. (2018). Subjective social status and mortality: the English longitudinal study of ageing. *European Journal of Epidemiology*, 33, 729–739.

Depp, C.A., and Jeste, D.V. (2006). Definitions and predictors of successful aging: a comprehensive review of larger quantitative studies. *The American Journal of Geriatric Psychiatry,* 14, 1, 6–20.

Dermott, E., and Pantazis, C. (2014). Gender and poverty in Britain: Changes and continuities between 1999 and 2012. *Journal of Poverty and Social Justice*, 22, 3, 253–269.

Dermott, E., and Pantazis, C. (2016) *Gender, Poverty and Exclusion: Final report 2012 PSE Study*. Bristol: Bristol University Press.

DeSA, UN (2018). *World population prospects: the 2017 revision. Key findings and advanced tables.* Population Division of the Department of Economic and Social Affairs of the United Nations Secretariat, New York. https://esa.un.org/unpd/wpp/Publications/Files/WPP2017_KeyFindings.pdf

De Santis, G., Maltagliati, M., and Salvini, S. (2016) A measure of the cultural distance between countries. *Social Indicators Research*, 126, 3, 1065–1087.

De Souto-Barreto, P., Ferrandez, A.M., and Guihard-Costa, A.M. (2011). Predictors of body satisfaction: differences between older men and women's perceptions of their body functioning and appearance. *Journal of Aging and Health*, 23, 3, 505–528.

Devi, S. (2012). Getting to the root of America's racial health inequalities. *The Lancet*, 380, 9847, 1043–1044.

DeWilde, C. (2004).The multidimensional measurement of poverty in Belgium and Britain: A categorical approach. *Social Indicators Research*, 68, 3, 331–369.

DeWilde, C., and Raeymaeckers, P. (2008). The trade-off between home-ownership and pensions: individual and institutional determinants of old-age poverty. *Ageing and Society*, 28, 6, 805–830.

DHSS (Department of Health and Social Security) (1978). *A Happier Old Age: A Discussion Paper on Elderly People in Society.* London: HMSO.

DICE (2016), At risk of poverty rate, by sex and age groups, 1995 - 2015, Ifo Institute, Munich. http://www.cesifo-group.de/DICE/fb/jfQeGk8F

Dionigi, R.A. (2015). Stereotypes of aging: their effects on the health of older adults. *Journal of Geriatrics*, Article ID 954027. http://dx.doi.org/10.1155/2015/954027

Dilworth-Anderson, P., Williams, I.C., and Gibson, B.E. (2002). Issues of race, ethnicity, and culture in caregiving research: a 20-year review (1980–2000). *Gerontologist*, 42, 2, 237–272.

Disraeli, B. (1845). *Sybil or the Two Nations*. London: Henry Colburn.

Dolberg, P., Sigurðardóttir, S.H., and Trummer, U. (2018). Ageism and older immigrants. In L. Ayalon and C. Tesch-Römeer (eds), *Contemporary Perspectives on Ageism*. Champagne, IL: Springer, pp 177–191.

Dowd, J.J., and Bengtson, V.L. (1978). Aging in minority populations an examination of the double jeopardy hypothesis. *Journal of Gerontology*, 33, 3, 427–436.

Dowding, K. (1996). *Power*. Buckingham: Open University Press.

Dumas, A., & Laberge, S. (2005). Social class and ageing bodies: Understanding physical activity in later life. *Social Theory & Health*, 3, 3, 183–205.

Dumas, A., Laberge, S., and Straka, S.M. (2005). Older women's relations to bodily appearance: the embodiment of social and biological conditions of existence. *Ageing and Society*, 25, 6, 883–902.

Durkheim, E. (1982). *The Rules of Sociological Method*. New York: The Free Press.

Düvell, F., and Jordan, B. (2003). *Migration: The Boundaries of Equality and Justice*. Cambridge: Polity Press.

Elrick, J., Schneiderhan, E. and Khan, S. (2014). Talking like a generation: the 'documentary' meaning of ethnicity for aging minority Britons. *Sociology*, 48, 6, 1173–1189.

Engelen, A., Heinemann, F., and Brettel, M. (2009). Cross-cultural entrepreneurship research: Current status and framework for future studies. *Journal of International Entrepreneurship*, 7, 3, 163–189.

Erikson, E.H. (1959). *Childhood and Society*. New York: W.W. Norton.

Erikson, E.H. (1961). *Childhood and Society* (2nd edition). New York: W.W. Norton.

Erikson, E.H. (1980). *Identity and the Life Cycle*. New York: W.W. Norton.

Eriksen, T.H. (2017). *What is Anthropology?* London: Pluto Press.

Erk, J. (2017). Is age the new class? Economic crisis and demographics in European politics. *Critical Sociology*, 43, 1, 59–71.

Ervik, R., and Kildal, N. (2015). From collective to individual responsibility? Changing problem definitions of the welfare state. In R. Ervik, N. Kildal and E. Nilssen (eds), *New Contractualism in European Welfare State Policies*. London: Routledge, pp 93–119.

Escafré-Dublet, A., and Simon, P. (2012). Ethnic statistics in Europe: the paradox of colour blindness. In A. Triandafyllidou, T. Modood and N. Meer (eds), *European Multiculturalisms: Cultural, Religious and Ethnic Challenges*. Edinburgh: Edinburgh University Press, pp 213–237.

Estes, C.L., Swan, J.H., and Gerard, L.E. (1982). Dominant and competing paradigms in gerontology: towards a political economy of ageing. *Ageing and Society*, 2, 2, 151–164.

Eurostat (2014). *Eurostat statistics explained: Glossary of terms: Purchasing Power Parities.* http://ec.europa.eu/eurostat/statistics-explained/index.php/Glossary:Purchasing_power_parities_ (PPPs)

Eurostat (2016). *People at risk of poverty or social exclusion.* http://ec.europa.eu/eurostat/statisticsexplained/index.php/People_at_risk_of_poverty_or_social_exclusion

Evandrou, M. (2000). Social inequalities in later life: the socio-economic position of older people from ethnic minority groups in Britain. *Population Trends*, 101, 11–18.

Fantasia, R. (1995). From class consciousness to culture, action, and social organization. *Annual Review of Sociology*, 21, 1, 269–287.

Fang, M.L., Canham, S.L., Battersby, L., Sixsmith, J., Wada, M., and Sixsmith, A. (2019). Exploring privilege in the digital divide: implications for theory, policy, and practice. *The Gerontologist*, 59, 1, Special Issue, e1–e15.

Featherstone, M. (1990). Perspectives on consumer culture. *Sociology*, 24, 1, 5–22.

Featherstone, M. and Turner, B.S. (1995) Body and Society: An introduction. *Body & Society,* 1, 1, 1–12.

Featherstone, M., Hepworth, M., and Turner, B. S. (eds) (1991). *The Body: Social process and cultural theory.* London: Sage Publications.

Ferlander, S. (2007). The importance of different forms of social capital for health. *Acta Sociologica*, 50, 2, 115–128.

Fernández-Ballesteros, R., Garcia, L.F., Abarca, D., and Blanc, E. (2010). The concept of 'ageing well' in ten Latin American and European countries. *Ageing and Society*, 30, 1, 41–56.

Ferraro, K.F. (1987). Double jeopardy to health for black older adults? *Journal of Gerontology*, 42, 5, 528–533.

Ferraro, K.F. (2007). Afterword: The gerontological imagination. In K.F. Ferraro and J.M. Wilmoth (eds) *Gerontology: Perspectives and Issues, Third Edition.* New York: Springer Publishing, pp 325–342.

Ferraro, K.F., and Shippee, T.P. (2009). Aging and cumulative inequality: how does inequality get under the skin? *The Gerontologist*, 49, 3, 333–343.

Ferraro, K.F., Shippee, T.P., and Shafer, M.H. (2009). Cumulative inequality theory for research on aging and the life course. In V.L. Bengtson, M. Silverstein, N.M. Putney and D. Gans (eds), *Handbook of Theories of Aging*. New York: Springer, pp 413–433.

Ferrucci, L., Guralnik J.M., Simonsick, E., Salive, M.E., Corti, C., and Langlois, J. (1996). Progressive versus catastrophic disability: a longitudinal view of the disablement process. *The Journals of Gerontology Series A: Medical Sciences*, 51A, 3, M123–130.

Fessler, P., and Schürz, M. (2018). Private wealth across European countries: the role of income, inheritance and the welfare state, *Journal of Human Development and Capabilities*, 19, 4, 521–549.

Fine, B. (2010) *Theories of Social Capital : Researchers Behaving Badly*. London: Pluto Press.

Fischer, S.H., David, D., Crotty, B.H., Dierks, M., and Safran, C. (2014). Acceptance and use of health information technology by community-dwelling elders. *International Journal of Medical Informatics*, 83, 9, 624–635.

Fleischer, D.Z. and Zames, F. (2001). *The Disability Rights Movement: From Charity to Confrontation*. Philadelphia: Temple University Press.

Flemmen, M. (2013) Putting Bourdieu to work for class analysis: reflections on some recent contributions. *British Journal of Sociology*, 64, 2, 325–343.

Flemmen, M., Jarness, V., and Rosenlund, L. (2018). Social space and cultural class divisions: the forms of capital and contemporary lifestyle differentiation. *The British Journal of Sociology*, 69, 1, 124–153.

Fomiatti, R., Moir, L., Richmond, J., and Millsteed, J. (2014). The experience of being a motorised mobility scooter user. *Disability and Rehabilitation: Assistive Technology*, 9, 3, 183–187.

Formosa, M., and Higgs, P. (eds) (2013). *Social Class in Later Life: Power, Identity and Lifestyle*. Bristol: Policy Press.

Forrest, R. (2018). Housing and asset based stratification in the enrichment economy. *Critical Housing Analysis*, 5, 2, 4–13.

Forrest, R., and Hirayama, Y. (2018). Late home ownership and social restratification. *Economy and Society*, 47, 2, 257–279.

Foster, L., Tomlinson, M. and Walker, A. (2019). Older people and Social Quality–what difference does income make? *Ageing & Society*, 39, 11, 2351–2376.

Foucault, M. (1982). The subject and power. *Critical Inquiry*, 8, 4, 777–795.

Foucault, M. (1988). The ethic of care for the self as a practice of freedom. In J. Bernauer and D. Rasmussen (eds), *The Final Foucault*. Cambridge, MA: MIT Press, pp 1–20.

Foucault, M. (2000). Governmentality. In J.D. Faubion (ed), *Power: Essential Works of Foucault, 1954–1984*. London: Penguin Books, pp 201–222.

Foucault, M. (2008). *The Birth of Biopolitics: Lectures at the College de France, 1978-1979,* trans. G. Burchell. London: Palgrave Macmillan.

Fox, L., and Pacus, J. (2018). Deconstructing poverty rates among the 65 and older population: why has poverty increased since 2015? *US Census, SEHSD Working Paper*, 13.

Franceschi, C., Motta, L., Valensin, S., Rapisarda, R., Franzone, A., Berardelli, M., Motta, M., Monti, D., Bonafe, M., Ferrucci, L. and Deiana, L (2000). Do men and women follow different trajectories to reach extreme longevity? *Aging Clinical and Experimental Research*, 12, 2, 77–84.

Franck, T.M. (1999). *The Empowered Self: Law and Society in the Age of Individualism.* Oxford: Oxford University Press.

Frank, A. W. (1990). Bringing bodies back in: A decade review. *Theory, Culture & Society,* 7, 1, 131–162.

Fraser, N. (1995). From redistribution to recognition? Dilemmas of justice in a 'post-socialist' age. *New Left Review*, 112, 68–68.

Fraser, N. (1997). *Justice Interruptus: Critical reflections on the 'Postsocialist' condition.* Abingdon: Routledge.

Fraser, N. (2000). Rethinking recognition. *New Left Review*, 3 (NS), 107–121.

Fraser N. (2001). Recognition without ethics? *Theory, Culture and Society*, 18, 21–42.

Fraser, N. (2008). *Adding Insult to Injury: Nancy Fraser debates her critics.* London: Verso.

Fraser, N. (2013). *Fortunes of Feminism: From State Managed Capitalism to Neoliberal Crisis.* London: Verso.

Freedman, V.A., Agree, E.M., Martin, L.G., and Cornman, J.C. (2006). Trends in the use of assistive technology and personal care for late-life disability, 1992–2001. *The Gerontologist*, 46, 1, 124–127.

Freedman, V.A., Wolf, D.A. and Spillman, B.C. (2016). Disability-free life expectancy over 30 years: a growing female disadvantage in the US population. *American Journal of Public Health*, 106, 6, 1079–1085.

Freeman, G.P. (2004). Immigrant incorporation in Western democracies 1. *International Migration Review*, 38, 3, 945–969.

Freixas A., Luque, B. and Reina, A. (2012). Critical feminist gerontology: in the back room of research. *Journal of Women and Aging*, 24, 1, 44–58.

Fried, L.P., Ferrucci, L., Darer, J., Williamson, J.D. and Anderson, G. (2004). Untangling the concepts of disability, frailty, and comorbidity: implications for improved targeting and care. *The Journals of Gerontology Series A: Biological Sciences and Medical Sciences*, 59, 3, M255–M263.

Friedman, S., Savage, M., Hanquinet, L., and Miles, A. (2015). Cultural sociology and new forms of distinction. *Poetics*, 53, 1–8.

Furman, F. (1997). *Facing the Mirror: Older Women and Beauty Shop Culture.* London: Routledge.

Galobardes, B., Shaw, M., Lawlor, D.A., Lynch, J.W., and Smith, G.D. (2006a). Indicators of socioeconomic position (part 1). *Journal of Epidemiology and Community Health*, 60, 1, 7–12.

Galobardes, B., Shaw, M., Lawlor, D.A., Lynch, J.W., and Smith, G.D. (2006b). Indicators of socioeconomic position (part 2). *Journal of Epidemiology and Community*, 60, 1, 95–101.

Ganzeboom, H.B., and Treiman, D.J. (1996). Internationally comparable measures of occupational status for the 1988 International Standard Classification of Occupations. *Social Science Research*, 25, 3, 201–239.

Gallant, M.P., Spitze, G., and Grove, J.G. (2010). Chronic illness self-care and the family lives of older adults: a synthetic review across four ethnic groups. *Journal of Cross-Cultural Gerontology*, 25, 1, 21–43.

Gallop, J. (2015). The view from queer theory. *Age, Culture, Humanities*, 2, 323–328.

Gamson, J. (1989). Silence, death, and the invisible enemy: AIDS activism and social movement 'newness'. *Social Problems*, 36, 4, 351–367.

Garland-Thomson, R. (2013). Disability studies: A field emerged. *American Quarterly*, 65, 4, 915–926.

Garland-Thomson, R. (2014). The story of my work: how I became disabled. *Disability Studies Quarterly*, 34, 2, 1–16.

Gatrell, P. (2019). *The Unsettling of Europe: The Great Migration to Europe 1945 to the Present.* London: Allen Lane.

Gee, G.C., Walsemann, K.M., and Brondolo, E. (2012). A life course perspective on how racism may be related to health inequities. *American Journal of Public Health*, 102, 5, 967–974.

Gell, N.M., Rosenberg, D.E., Demiris, G., LaCroix, A.Z., and Patel, K.V. (2013). Patterns of technology use among older adults with and without disabilities. *The Gerontologist*, 55, 3, 412–421.

Gergen, K.J., and Gergen, M.M. (2000). The new aging: self-construction and social values. In R.W. Schaie and J. Hendricks (eds), *The Evolution of the Aging Self: The Societal Impact on the Aging Process.* New York: Springer, pp 281–306.

Geronimus, A.T. (1992). The weathering hypothesis and the health of African-American women and infants: evidence and speculations. *Ethnicity and Disease*, 2, 207–221.

Geronimus, A.T., Hicken, M., Keene, D., and Bound, J. (2006). 'Weathering' and age patterns of allostatic load scores among blacks and whites in the United States. *American Journal of Public Health*, 96, 5, 826–833.

Gibson, D. (1996). Broken down by age and gender: "The problem of old women" redefined. *Gender & Society*, 10, 4, 433–448.

Giddens, A. (1982). Power, the dialectic of control and class structuration. In *Profiles and Critiques in Social Theory*. London: Palgrave, pp 197–214.

Giddens, A. (1991). *Modernity and Self-Identity: Self and Society in the Late Modern Age*. Cambridge: Polity Press.

Gierveld, J.D.J., van der Pas, S., and Keating, N. (2015). Loneliness of older immigrant groups in Canada: effects of ethnic-cultural background. *Journal of Cross-Cultural Gerontology*, 30, 3, 251–268.

Gilleard, C. (2002). Aging and old age in medieval society and the transition of modernity. *Journal of Aging & Identity*, 7, 1, 25–41.

Gilleard, C. (2017). *Old Age in Nineteenth-century Ireland: Ageing under the Union*. London: Springer.

Gilleard, C., and Higgs, P. (1998). Ageing and the limiting conditions of the body. *Sociological Research Online*, 3, 4, 1–11.

Gilleard, C., and Higgs, P. (2000). *Cultures of Ageing: Self, Citizen and the Body*. London: Pearson.

Gilleard, C., and Higgs, P. (2005). *Contexts of Ageing: Class, Cohort and Community*. Cambridge: Polity Press.

Gilleard, C., and Higgs, P. (2009). The power of silver: age and identity politics in the 21st century. *Journal of Aging & Social Policy*, 21, 3, 277–295.

Gilleard, C., and Higgs, P. (2011). Frailty, disability and old age: a re-appraisal. *Health*, 15, 5, 475–490.

Gilleard, C., and Higgs, P. (2013). *Ageing, Corporeality and Embodiment*. London: Anthem Press.

Gilleard, C., and Higgs, P. (2016). Connecting life span development with the sociology of the life course: a new direction. *Sociology*, 50, 2, 301–315.

Gilleard, C., and Higgs, P. (2017). Ageing, corporeality and social divisions in later life. *Ageing and Society*, 37, 1681–1702.

Gilleard, C., and Higgs, P. (2018). Unacknowledged distinctions: corporeality versus embodiment in later life. *Journal of Aging Studies*, 45, 5–10.

Gimpelson, V., and Treisman, D. (2018). Misperceiving inequality. *Economics and Politics*, 30, 1, 27–54.

Ginn, J., and Arber, S. (2000). Ethnic inequality in later life: variation in financial circumstances by gender and ethnic group. *Education and Ageing*, 15, 1, 65–84.

Gleason, P. (1983). Identifying identity: a semantic history. *Journal of American History*, 69, 4, 910–931.

Goldman, A.W., and Cornwell, B. (2018). Social disadvantage and instability in older adults' ties to their adult children. *Journal of Marriage and the Family*, 80, 5, 1314–1332.

Goldthorpe, J.H. (1997). The 'Goldthorpe' class schema: some observations on conceptual and operational issues in relation to the ESRC review of government social classifications. In *Constructing Classes: Towards a New Social Classification for the UK*. Swindon: ESRC/ONS.

Goldthorpe, J.H. (2000a). Rent, class conflict, and class structure: a commentary on Sørensen. *American Journal of Sociology*, 105, 6, 1572–1582.

Goldthorpe, J.H. (2000b). Analysing social inequality: a critique of two recent contributions from economics and epidemiology. *European Sociological Review*, 26, 6, 731–744.

Goldthorpe, J.H. (2010). Class analysis and the reorientation of class theory: the case of persisting differentials in educational attainment. *The British Journal of Sociology*, 61, 311–335.

Goudswaard, K., van Vliet, O. Been, J., and Caminada, K. (2012). *Pensions and Income Inequality in Old Age.* CESifo DICE Report 10, no 4.

Goulborne, H., and Salomos, J. (2003). Families, ethnicity and social capital. *Social Policy and Society*, 2, 4, 329–338.

Greenhalgh, C. (2018). *Ageing in Twentieth-Century Britain.* Oakland: University of California Press.

Grenier, A. (2007). Constructions of frailty in the English language, care practice and the lived experience. *Ageing and Society*, 27, 425–445.

Grenier, A., and Hanley, J. (2007). Older women and 'frailty': aged, gendered and embodied resistance. *Current Sociology*, 55, 2, 211–228.

Grossman, M. (1972). On the concept of health capital and the demand for health. *Journal of Political Economy*, 80, 2, 223–255.

Grundy, E., and Holt, G. (2001). The socioeconomic status of older adults: how should we measure it in studies of health inequalities? *Journal of Epidemiology and Community Health*, 55, 12, 895–904.

Gu, J., Gomez-Redondo, R., and Dupre, M.E. (2015). Studying disability trends in aging populations. *Journal of Cross Cultural Gerontology*, 30, 21–49.

Guido, G., Amatulli, C., and Peluso, A.M. (2014). Context effects on older consumers' cognitive age: the role of hedonic versus utilitarian goals. *Psychology and Marketing*, 31, 2, 103–114.

Guillemard, A.-M. (1975). Gerontology, a relatively new area of social science in France. *The Gerontologist*, 15, 3, 212–218.

Guillemard, A.-M. (1982). Old age, retirement, and the social class structure: toward an analysis of the structural dynamics of the later stage of life. In T.K. Hareven and K. Adams (eds), *Aging and the Life Course Transition: An Interdisciplinary Perspective*. New York: Guildford Press, pp 221–243.

Hahn, H. (1994). The minority group model of disability: implications for medical sociology. *Research in Sociology of Health Care*, 11, 3–24.

Hahn, H. (2002). Academic debates and political advocacy: The US disability movement. In C. Barnes, M. Oliver and L. Barton (eds), *Disability Studies Today*. Cambridge: Polity Press, pp 162–189.

Hahn, H.D., and Belt, T.L. (2004). Disability identity and attitudes toward cure in a sample of disabled activists. *Journal of Health and Social Behavior*, 45, 453–464.

Haitz, N. (2015). *Old-Age Poverty in OECD Countries and the Issue of Gender Pension Gaps.* DICE Report, 13, 2, 73–75. https://search.proquest.com/docview/1707067058?accountid=14511

Hald, A. (1987). On the early history of life insurance mathematics. *Scandinavian Actuarial Journal,* 1/2, 4–18.

Hall, S. (1996). Who needs identity? In S. Hall and P. du Gay (eds), *Questions of Cultural Identity*. London: Sage Publications, pp 1–17).

Halleröd, B. (2009). Ill, worried or worried sick? Inter-relationships among indicators of wellbeing among older people in Sweden. *Ageing & Society*, 29, 6, 563–584.

Hallewell-Haslwanter, J., and Fitzpatrick, G. (2018). The development of assistive systems to support older people: issues that affect success in practice. *Technologies*, 6, 1, 2–21.

Hammer, B., Prskawetz, A. and Freund, I. (2015). Production activities and economic dependency by age and gender in Europe: A cross-country comparison. *The Journal of the Economics of Ageing*, 5, 86–97.

Hancock, A.-M. (2016). *Intersectionality: An Intellectual History*. Oxford: Oxford University Press.

Hansen, E.B. (2014). Older immigrants' use of public home care and residential care. *European Journal of Ageing*, 11, 1, 41–53.

Hansen, T., Slagsvold, B., and Moum, T. (2008). Financial satisfaction in old age: a satisfaction paradox or a result of accumulated wealth? *Social Indicators Research*, 89, 2, 323–338.

Haselton, M. (2018). *Hormonal: How hormones drive desire, shape relationships and make us wiser.* London: Oneworld Publications.

Havens, B., and Chappell, N.L. (1983). Triple jeopardy: age, sex and ethnicity. *Canadian Ethnic Studies/Etudes Ethniques au Canada*, 15, 3, 119–132.

Hazan, H. (2015). *Against Hybridity: Social Impasses in a Globalizing World*. Cambridge: Polity Press.

Heap, J. and Fors, S. (2015). Duration and accumulation of disadvantages in old age. *Social Indicators Research* 123, 2, 411–29.

Hearn, J. (2016). Neglected intersectionalities in studying men: Age/ing, virtuality, transnationality. In H. Lutz, M.T. Herrera-Vivar and L. Supik (eds), *Framing Intersectionality: Debates on a Multi-Faceted Concept in Gender Studies*. London: Routledge, pp 89–104.

Heinrich, G. (2000). *Affluence and poverty in old age: New evidence from the European Community Household Panel.* IRISS. http://iriss.ceps.lu/documents/irisswp11.pdf

Heisig, J.P., Lancee, B., and Radl, J. (2018). Ethnic inequality in retirement income: a comparative analysis of immigrant–native gaps in Western Europe. *Ageing and Society*, 38, 10, 1963–1994.

Herd, P. (2006). Do functional health inequalities decrease in old age? Educational status and functional decline among the 1931–1941 birth cohort. *Research on Aging*, 28, 3, 375–392.

Higgs, P. (1995). Citizenship and old age: the end of the road? *Ageing & Society*, 15, 4, 535–550.

Higgs, P., and Formosa, M. (2015). The changing significance of social class in later life. In M. Formosa and P. Higgs (eds), *Social Class in Later Life: Power, Identity and Lifestyle.* Bristol: Policy Press, pp 169–181.

Higgs, P., and Gilleard, C. (2006). Departing the margins: social class and later life in a second modernity. *Journal of Sociology*, 42, 3, 219–241.

Higgs, P., and Gilleard, C. (2014). Frailty, abjection and the 'othering' of the fourth age. *Health Sociology Review*, 23, 1, 10–19.

Higgs, P., and Gilleard, C. (2015). Fitness and consumerism in later life. In E. Tulle and C. Phoenix (eds), *Physical Activity and Sport in Later Life*. London: Palgrave Macmillan, pp 32–42.

Higgs, P., and Gilleard, C. (2019). The ideology of ageism versus the social imaginary of the fourth age: two differing approaches to the negative contexts of old age. *Ageing & Society*, (2019), 1–14, online first, doi:10.1017/S0144686X19000096

Higgs, P., Hyde, M., Gilleard, C., Victor, C., Wiggins, R., and Jones, I.R. (2009). From passive to active consumers? Later life consumption in the UK from 1968–2005. *The Sociological Review*, 57, 1, 102–124.

Higgs, P. and Jones, I.R. (2009). *Medical Sociology and Old Age: Toward a sociology of health in later life*. London: Routledge.

Hiltz, S.R. (1979). Widowhood: a roleless role. *Marriage and Family Review*, 1, 6, 1–11.

Hodgson, V. (2018). Stereotypical representations of women and ageing: a review of literature and photographic practice. *Postgraduate Journal of Women, Ageing and Media* (PGWAM), 4, 64–74.

Hoenig, H., Taylor Jr, D.H., and Sloan, F.A. (2003). Does assistive technology substitute for personal assistance among the disabled elderly? *American Journal of Public Health*, 93, 2, 330–337.

Hoffmann, R., Kröger, H., and Pakpahan, E. (2018). Pathways between socioeconomic status and health: does health selection or social causation dominate in Europe? *Advances in Life Course Research*, 36, 23–36.

Hooyman, N.R. (1999). Research on older women: Where is feminism? *The Gerontologist*, 39, 1, 115–118.

House, J.S., Landis, K.R. and Umberson, D. (1988). Social relationships and health. *Science*, 241, 540–545.

House, J.S., Lantz, P.M., and Herd, P. (2005). Continuity and change in the social stratification of aging and health over the life course: evidence from a nationally representative longitudinal study from 1986 to 2001/2002 (Americans' Changing Lives Study). *The Journals of Gerontology: Series B*, 60, S2, S15–S26.

Houtenville, A., Brucker, D., and Lauer, E. (2016). *Annual Compendium of Disability Statistics: 2015*. Institute on Disability, University of New Hampshire, Durham, NH. https://scholars.unh.edu/iod_chhs/21/

Hudson, R.B., and Gonyea, J.G. (2012). Baby Boomers and the shifting political construction of old age. *The Gerontologist*, 52, 2, 272–282.

Hughes, B., and Paterson, K. (1997). The social model of disability and the disappearing body: towards a sociology of impairment. *Disability and Society*, 12, 3, 325–340.

Huisman, M., Kunst, A.E., and Mackenbach, J.P. (2003). Socioeconomic inequalities in morbidity among the elderly: a European overview. *Social Science and Medicine*, 57, 861–873.

Hunter, A. (2019) Older migrants: inequalities of ageing from a transnational perspective. In S. Westwood (ed), *Ageing, Diversity and Equality: Social Justice Perspectives*. Abingdon: Routledge, pp 194–208.

Hurd Clarke, L. (2019) Gender, (in)equality and the body in later life. In S. Westwood (ed), *Ageing, Diversity and Equality: Social justice perspectives*. Abingdon: Routledge, pp 36–47.

Hurd Clarke, L. and Korotchenko, A. (2016). 'I know it exists... but I haven't experienced it personally':older Canadian men's perceptions of ageism as a distant social problem. *Ageing & Society*, 36, 8, 1757–1773.

Hyde, M., and Higgs, P. (2016). *Ageing and Globalisation*. Bristol: Policy Press.

Hyde, M., and Jones, I.R. (2015). Social class, age and identity in later life. In M. Formosa and P. Higgs (eds), *Social Class in Later Life: Power, Identity and Lifestyle*. Bristol: Policy Press, pp 73–94.

Hyde, M., Higgs, P., Gilleard, C., Victor, C., Wiggins, D., and Jones, I.R. (2011). Ageing, cohorts and consumption: the British experience, 1968–2005. In I.R. Jones, P. Higgs and D.J. Ekerdt (eds), *Consumption and Generational Change: The Rise of Consumer Lifestyles*. New Brunswick, NJ: Transaction Publishers, pp 107–140.

Iacovou, M. (2018). Household structure and risk of poverty or social exclusion. In A.B. Atkinson, A.-C. Guio and E. Marlier (eds), *Monitoring Social Inclusion in Europe, 2017 Edition*. Luxembourg: Publications Office of the European Union, pp 333–351.

Idler, E. and Benyamini, Y. (1997). Self-rated health and mortality: A review of twenty-seven community studies. *Journal of Health and Social Behavior*, 38, 1, 21–37.

Jagose, A. (1996). *Queer Theory: An Introduction*. New York: NYU Press.

Jamoom, E.W., Horner-Johnson, W., Suzuki, R., Andresen, E.M., & Campbell, V.A. (2008). Age at disability onset and self-reported health status. *BMC Public Health*, 8, 1, 10.

Jang, Y., Park, N.S., Chiriboga, D.A., Yoon, H., An, S., and Kim, M.T. (2015). Social capital in ethnic communities and mental health: a study of older Korean immigrants. *Journal of Cross Cultural Gerontology*, 30, 2, 131–141.

Jarvis, B.F., and Song, X. (2017). Rising intragenerational occupational mobility in the United States, 1969 to 2011. *American Sociological Review*, 82, 3, 568–599.

Jones, I.R., Hyde, M., Victor, C.R., Wiggins, R.D., Gilleard, C., and Higgs, P. (2008). *Ageing in a Consumer Society: From Passive to Active Consumption in Britain*. Bristol: Policy Press.

Jönson, H., and Larsson, A.T. (2009). The exclusion of older people in disability activism and policies – a case of inadvertent ageism? *Journal of Aging Studies*, 23, 1, 69–77.

Jönson, H., and Magnusson, J.A. (2001). A new age of old age? Gerotranscendence and the re-enchantment of aging. *Journal of Aging Studies*, 15, 4, 317–331.

Jylhä, M. (2009). What is self-rated health and why does it predict mortality? Towards a unified conceptual model. *Social Science and Medicine*, 69, 3, 307–316.

Kane, R.L., Priester, R., and Neumann, D. (2007). Does disparity in the way disabled older adults are treated imply ageism? *The Gerontologist*, 47, 3, 271–279.

Kaplan, G., and Baron-Epel, O. (2003). What lies behind the subjective evaluation of health status? *Social Science and Medicine*, 56, 8, 1669–1676.

Karajkov, R. (2006). *The Young and the Old: Radical Islam Takes Root in the Balkans*. https://www.worldpress.org/Europe/2335.cfm

Katbamna, S., and Matthews, R. (2007). *Ageing and Ethnicity in England: A Demographic Profile of BME Older People in England*. London: Age Concern.

Katbamna, S., Ahmad, W., Bhakta, P., Baker, R., and Parker, G. (2004). Do they look after their own? Informal support for South Asian carers. *Health and Social Care in the Community*, 12, 5, 398–406.

Kavanagh, A.M., Krnjacki, L., Aitken, Z., LaMontagne, A.D., Beer, A., Baker, E., and Bentley, R. (2015). Intersections between disability, type of impairment, gender and socio-economic disadvantage in a nationally representative sample of 33,101 working-aged Australians. *Disability and Health Journal*, 8, 2, 191–199.

Kawachi, I., Subramanian, S.V. and Almeida-Filho, N. (2002). A glossary for health inequalities. *Journal of Epidemiology & Community Health*, 56, 9, 647–652.

Kaye, H.S., Yeager, P., and Reed, M. (2008). Disparities in usage of assistive technology among people with disabilities. *Assistive Technology*, 20, 4, 194–203.

Kelley-Moore, J.A., and Ferraro, K.F. (2004). The black/white disability gap: persistent inequality in later life? *The Journals of Gerontology: Series B*, 59, 1, S34–S43.

Kenny, M. (2004). *The Politics of Identity*. Cambridge: Polity Press.

Key, W., and Culliney, M. (2018). The oldest old and the risk of social exclusion. *Social Policy and Society*, 17, 1, 47–63.

Khosravi, P., and Ghapanchi, A.H. (2016). Investigating the effectiveness of technologies applied to assist seniors: a systematic literature review. *International Journal of Medical Informatics*, 85, 1, 17–26.

Kim, J., and Miech, R. (2009). The black–white difference in age trajectories of functional health over the life course. *Social Science and Medicine*, 68, 4, 717–725.

Kim, D., Subramanian, S.V., and Kawachi, I. (2006). Bonding versus bridging social capital and their associations with self rated health: a multilevel analysis of 40 US communities. *Journal of Epidemiology and Community Health*, 60, 2, 116–122.

King, N., and Calasanti, T. (2013). Men's aging amidst intersecting relations of inequality. *Sociology Compass*, 7, 9, 699–710.

King, R. (2000). Generalisations from the history of return migration. In B. Ghosh (ed), *Return Migration: Journey of Hope or Despair?* Geneva: United Nations Publications, pp 7–55.

King, R., Lulle, A., Sampaio, D., and Vullnetari, J. (2017). Unpacking the ageing–migration nexus and challenging the vulnerability trope. *Journal of Ethnic and Migration Studies*, 43, 2, 182–198.

Kingston, P.W. (2000). *The Classless Society*. Stanford, CA: Stanford University Press.

Kingston, A., Davies, K., Collerton, J., Robinson, L., Duncan, R., Kirkwood, T.B., and Jagger, C. (2015). The enduring effect of education – socioeconomic differences in disability trajectories from age 85 years in the Newcastle 85+ Study. *Archives of Gerontology and Geriatrics*, 60, 3, 405–411.

Klok, J., van Tilburg, T.G., Suanet, B., and Fokkema, T. (2017). Transnational aging among older Turkish and Moroccan migrants in the Netherlands: determinants of transnational behavior and transnational belonging. *Transnational Social Review*, 7, 1, 25–40.

Kluegel, J.R., Singleton, R., and Starnes, C.E. (1977). Subjective class identification: A multiple indicator approach. *American Sociological Review*, 42, 4, 599–611.

Knapp, G.-A. (2005). Race, class, gender, reclaiming baggage in fast travelling theories. *European Journal of Women's Studies*, 12, 3, 249–265.

Kneale, D. (2012). *Is Social Exclusion Still Important for Older People?* London: The International Longevity Centre – UK.

Knight, T., and Ricciardelli, L.A. (2003). Successful aging: perceptions of adults aged between 70 and 101 years. *International Journal of Aging and Human Development*, 56, 3, 223–245.

Kohli, M. (2015). Generations in aging societies: inequalities, cleavages, conflicts. In C. Torp (ed), *Challenges of Aging: Retirement, Pensions, and Intergenerational Justice*. London: Palgrave Macmillan, pp 265–288.

Kohn, M. (1995). *The Race Gallery: The Return of Racial Science*. London: Vintage.

Korpi, W. (1975). Poverty, social assistance and social policy in post-war Sweden. *Acta Sociologica*, 18, 2-3, 120–141.

Kosnick, K. (2016). Sexuality and migration studies: The invisible, the oxymoronic and heteronormative othering, in H. Lutz, M.T. Herrera-Vivar and L. Supik (eds), *Framing Intersectionality: Debates on a Multi-Faceted Concept in Gender Studies*. London: Routledge, pp 121–136.

Krekula, C. (2007). The intersection of age and gender: reworking gender theory and social gerontology, *Current Sociology* 55, 2, 155–171.

Kreuter M.W., and Lezin, N. (2002). Social capital theory: Implications for community-based health promotion. In R.J. DiClemente, R.A. Crosby and M.C. Kegler (eds), *Emerging Theories in Health Promotion Practice and Research: Strategies for improving public health*, San Francisco, CA: Jossey-Bass, pp 228–254.

Krieger, N. (2012). Methods for the scientific study of discrimination and health: an eco-social approach. *American Journal of Public Health*, 102, 5, 936–944.

Krippner, G. (2005). The financialization of the American economy. *Socio-Economic Review,* 3, 173–208.

Laditka, S.B., Corwin, S.J., Laditka, J.N., Liu, R., Tseng, W., Wu, B., Beard, R.L., Sharkey, J.R., and Ivey, S.L. (2009). Attitudes about aging well among a diverse group of older Americans: implications for promoting cognitive health. *The Gerontologist*, 49, S1, S30–S39.

Lamb, S., Robbins-Ruszkowski, J., Corwin, A., Calasanti, T. and King, N. (2017). *Successful Aging as a Contemporary Obsession: Global perspectives*. New York: Rutgers University Press.

Lambert, P.S., and Bihagen, E. (2014). Using occupation-based social classifications. *Work, Employment and Society*, 28, 3, 481–494.

Lancee, B. (2010). The economic returns of immigrants' bonding and bridging social capital: the case of the Netherlands. *International Migration Review*, 44, 1, 202–226.

Lapavitsas, C. (2011). Theorizing financialization. *Work, Employment and Society*. 25, 4, 611–626.

Laslett, P. (1989). *A Fresh Map of Life: The Emergence of the Third Age*. London: Weidenfeld and Nicolson.

Lawrence, V., Murray, J., Samsi, K., and Banerjee, S. (2008). Attitudes and support needs of black Caribbean, South Asian and white British carers of people with dementia in the UK. *British Journal of Psychiatry*, 193, 3, 240–246.

Layte, R. and Whelan, C. (2003). Moving in and out of poverty. *European Societies* 5, 2, 167–191.

LeBesco, K. (2004). *Revolting Bodies: The Struggle to Redefine Fat Identity*. Amherst: University of Massachusetts Press.

Lee, C.K., and Strang, D. (2006). The international diffusion of public-sector downsizing: network emulation and theory-driven learning. *International Organization*, 60, 4, 883–909.

Leisering, L. and Leibfried, S. (2001). *Time and Poverty in Western Welfare States: United Germany in Perspective.* New York: Cambridge University Press.

Levinas, E. (1994). Une éthique de la souffrance. In J.-M. von Kaenel (ed.) Souffrance: Corps et Ame, Epreuves Partages. *Autrement. Série Mutations*, 142, 127–137 (Paris, France).

Levine, M., and Crimmins, E. (2014). Evidence of accelerated aging among African Americans and its implications for mortality. *Social Science and Medicine*, 118, C, 27–32.

Levy, B.R. (2003). Mind matters: Cognitive and physical effects of aging self-stereotypes. *The Journals of Gerontology Series B: Psychological Sciences and Social Sciences,* 58, 4, 203–211.

Levy, B. (2009). Stereotype embodiment: a psychosocial approach to aging. *Current Directions in Psychological Science*, 18, 6, 332–336.

Levy, R., and Bühlmann, F. (2016). Towards a socio-structural framework for life course analysis. *Advances in Life Course Research*, 30, 30–42.

Lewin, C.G. (2003). *Pensions and Insurance before 1800: A social history.* East. Linton: Tuckwell Press.

Libert, S., Charlesworth, G., and Higgs, P. (2019). Cognitive decline and distinction: a new line of fracture in later life? *Ageing and Society*, (2019), 1–19, online first, doi:10.1017/S0144686X19000734

Lin, N. (2000). Inequality in social capital. *Contemporary Sociology* 29, 6, 785–795.

Link, B., and Phelan, J. (1995). Social conditions as fundamental causes of disease. *Journal of Health and Social Behavior*, 36, 80–94.

Liversage, A., and Mirdal, G.M. (2017). Growing old in exile – a longitudinal study of migrant women from Turkey. *Journal of Ethnic and Migration Studies*, 43, 2, 287–302.

Livi-Bacci, M. (2012). *A Short History of Migration.* Cambridge: Polity Press.

Löfqvist, C., Nygren, C., Iwarsson, S., and Szeman, Z. (2005). Assistive devices among very old persons in five European countries. *Scandinavian Journal of Occupational Therapy*, 12, 181–192.

Lopes, A. (2015). Measuring social class in later life. In M. Formosa and P. Higgs (eds), *Social Class in Later Life: Power, Identity and Lifestyle.* Bristol: Policy Press, pp 53–71.

Lucal, B. (1994). Class stratification in introductory textbooks: relational or distributional models? *Teaching Sociology*, 22, 2, 139–150.

Lukes, S. (2005) *Power: A Radical View* (2nd edition). London: Palgrave Macmillan.

Lutz, H., Vivar, M.T.H., & Supik, L. (eds) (2016). *Framing Intersectionality: Debates on a multi-faceted concept in gender studies.* London: Routledge.

Luo, Y., Xu, J., Granberg, E., and Wentworth, W.M. (2011). A longitudinal study of social status, perceived discrimination, and physical and emotional health among older adults. *Research on Aging*, 34, 3, 275–301.

Lydall, H. (1955). The life cycle in income, saving, and asset ownership. *Econometrica: Journal of the Econometric Society*, 23, 2, 131–150.

Lynch, S.M. (2003). Cohort and life-course patterns in the relationship between education and health: a hierarchical approach. *Demography*, 40, 2, 309–331.

MacDonald, B., and Rich, C. (1983). *Look Me in the Eye: Old women, aging and ageism.* San Francisco, CA: Spinsters Ink.

Machat-From, L. (2017). Identity, old(er) age and migrancy: a social constructionist lens. *Linköping Studies in Arts and Science No 716.* Faculty of Arts and Sciences. Norrköping: Linköping University Electronic Press.

Macintyre, S. (1997). The Black Report and beyond: what are the issues? *Social Science and Medicine*, 44, 6, 723–745.

Malik, K. (1996). *The Meaning of Race: Race, History and Culture in Western Society*. London: Macmillan.

Mann, M. (1973). *Consciousness and Action among the Western Working Class*. London: MacMillan Publishing Company.

Mann, S.A. (2013). Third wave feminism's unhappy marriage of post-structuralism and intersectionality theory. *Journal of Feminist Scholarship*, 4, 4, 54–73.

Mannheim, K. ([1936] 1998). The problem of generations. In P. Kecskemeti (ed), *Essays on the Sociology of Knowledge: Collected Works of Karl Mannheim* (Volume 5). Abingdon: Routledge, pp 276–321.

Manton, K.G., Stallard, E., and Vaupel, J.W. (1986). Alternative models for the heterogeneity of mortality risks among the aged. *Journal of the American Statistical Association*, 81, 395, 635–644.

Markides, K.S., Liang, J., and Jackson, J.S. (1990). Race, ethnicity, and aging: conceptual and methodological issues. In R. Binstock and L. George (eds), *Handbook of Aging and the Social Sciences*. San Diego, CA: Academic Press, pp 112–129.

Marmot, M.G. (2006). Status Syndrome: A challenge to medicine. *JAMA*, 295, 11, 1304–1307.

Marshall, B. (1994). *Engendering Modernity: Feminism, social theory and social change.* Cambridge: Polity Press.

Marshall, G., Newby, H., Rose, D., and Vogler, C. (2005). *Social Class in Modern Britain.* London: Routledge.

McDaniel, S.A. (2003). Hidden in the household: Now it's men in mid-life. *Ageing International,* 28, 4, 326–344.

McDermott, M., and Samson, F.L. (2005). White racial and ethnic identity in the United States. *Annual Review of Sociology*, 31, 245–261.

McDermott, S., and Turk, M.A. (2011). The myth and reality of disability prevalence: measuring disability for research and service. *Disability and Health Journal,* 4, 1, 1-5.

McGann, M., Ong, R., Bowman, D., Duncan, A., Kimberley, H. and Biggs, S. (2016). Gendered ageism in Australia: Changing perceptions of age discrimination among older men and women. *Economic Papers: A Journal of Applied Economics and Policy*, 35, 4, 375–388.

McIntyre, M., and McDonald, C. (2012). The limitations of partial citizenship: health care institutions underpinned with heteronormative ideals. *Advances in Nursing Science*, 35, 2, 127–134.

McKinnon, C. (1982). Feminism, Marxism, method and the state: An agenda for theory.*Signs*, 7, 1, 515–541.

McLanahan, S.S., Sørensen, A. and Watson, D. (1989). Sex differences in poverty, 1950-1980. *Signs*, 15, 1, 102–122.

McLaughlin, S.J., Connell, C.M., Heeringa, S.G., Li, L.W., and Roberts, J.R. (2010). Successful aging in the United States: prevalence estimates from a national sample of older adults. *The Journals of Gerontology: Series B*, 65B, 2, 216–226.

McNally, D. (2017). Intersections and dialectics: critical reconstructions in social reproduction theory. In T. Bhattacharya (ed), *Social Reproduction Theory: Remapping Class, Recentering Oppression.* London: Pluto, pp 94–111.

McNay, L. (2004). Agency and experience: Gender as a lived relation. The Sociological Review, 52, 173–190.

Meagher, M. (2014). Against the invisibility of old age: Cindy Sherman, Suzy Lake, and Martha Wilson. *Feminist Studies*, 40, 1, 101–143.

Mendes de Leon, C.F., and Rajan, K.B. (2014). Psychosocial influences in onset and progression of late life disability. *Journals of Gerontology B: Psychological Sciences and Social Sciences*, 69, 2, 287–302.

Merton, R.K. (1968). The Matthew effect in science: the reward and communication systems of science are considered. *Science*, 159, 3810, 56–63.

Meyer, T., and Bridgen, P. (2008). Class, gender and chance: The social division of welfare and occupational pensions in the United Kingdom. *Ageing and Society*, 28, 3, 353–381.

Meyer, B.D., and Mok, W.K.C. (2018). Disability, earnings, income and consumption, *Journal of Public Economics*, 171, 51–69. https://doi.org/10.1016/j.jpubeco.2018.06.011

Miller, P. (2017). *Patriarchy*. London: Routledge.

Mincer, J. (1958). Investment in human capital and personal income distribution. *Journal of Political Economy*, 66, 4, 281–302.

Minkler, M., Fuller-Thomson, E., and Guralnik, J.M. (2006). Gradient of disability across the socioeconomic spectrum in the United States. *New England Journal of Medicine*, 355, 7, 695–703.

Miyawaki, C.E. (2016). Caregiving practice patterns of Asian, Hispanic, and non-Hispanic white American family caregivers of older adults across generations. *Journal of Cross-Cultural Gerontology*, 31, 1, 35–55.

Möhring, K. (2017). Is there a motherhood penalty in retirement income in Europe? The role of lifecourse and institutional characteristics. *Ageing & Society*, 38, 12, 2560–2589.

Molyneux, M. (2002). Gender and the silences of social capital: Lessons from Latin America. *Development and Change*, 33, 2, 167–188.

Monahan, D.J., and Wolf, D.A. (2014). The continuum of disability over the lifespan: the convergence of aging with disability and aging into disability. *Disability and Health Journal*, 7, 1, S1–S3.

Moonesinghe, R., Zhu, J., and Truman, B.I. (2011). Health insurance coverage – United States, 2004 and 2008. *Morbidity and Mortality Weekly Report*, 60 (suppl), 35–37.

Moriarty, J., and Butt, J. (2004). Inequalities in quality of life among older people from different ethnic groups. *Ageing and Society*, 24, 5, 729–753.

Moran, M. (2018). Identity and identity politics: a cultural-materialist history. *Historical Materialism*, 26, 2, 21–45.

Morciano, M., Hancock, R.M., and Pudney, S.E. (2015). Disability costs and equivalence scales in the older population in Great Britain. *Review of Income and Wealth*, 61, 3, 494–514.

Morris, L. (2014). *Social Divisions*. London: Routledge.

Morriss, P. (2002). *Power: A Philosophical Analysis*. Manchester: Manchester University Press.

Moya, M., and Fiske, S.T. (2017). The social psychology of the great recession and social class divides. *Journal of Social Issues*, 73, 1, 8–22.

Muckenhuber, J., Stronegger, W.J., and Freidl, W. (2013). Social capital affects the health of older people more strongly than that of younger people. *Ageing and Society*, 33, 5, 853–870.

Mumford, D.B., and Babiker, I.E. (1998). Validation of a self-administered version of the Cultural Distance Questionnaire among young British volunteers working overseas. *European Journal of Psychiatry*, 12, 244–253.

Myles, J. (1989). *Old Age in the Welfare State: The Political Economy of Public Pensions.* Lawrence, KA: University Press of Kansas,

Nash, J. (2008). Re-thinking intersectionality. *Feminist Review*, 89, 1–15.

Nash, J. (2011). Home truths on intersectionality. *Yale Journal of Law and Feminism*, 23, 2, 445–470.

Nazroo, J. (2006) Ethnicity and Old Age. In J.A. Vincent, C. Phillipson and M. Downs (eds), *The Futures of Old Age.* London: Sage Publications, pp 62–78.

Nee, V., and Sanders, J. (2001). Understanding the diversity of immigrant incorporation: a forms-of-capital model. *Ethnic and Racial Studies*, 24, 3, 386–411.

Nef, T., Ganea, R.L., Müri, R.M., and Mosimann, U.P. (2013). Social networking sites and older users–a systematic review. *International Psychogeriatrics*, 25, 7, 1041–1053.

Nelson, E.A., and Dannefer, D. (1992). Aged heterogeneity: fact or fiction? The fate of diversity in gerontological research. *The Gerontologist*, 32, 1, 17–23.

Neugschwender, J. (2016). *Pension Systems and Income Inequality among the Elderly in Europe.* PhD thesis, Faculty of Social Sciences at the University of Mannheim. https://ub-madoc.bib.uni-mannheim.de/41262/1/Neugschwender%20Dissertation%202016-09-16.pdf

Newman, A.B., and Brach J.S. (2001). Gender gap in longevity and disability in older persons. *Epidemiologic Reviews*, 23, 2, 343–50.

Newman, K.S. (2003). *A Different Shade of Gray: Midlife and Beyond in the Inner City.* New York: New Press.

Niedzwiedz, C.L., Richardson, E.A., Tunstall, H., Shortt, N.K., Mitchell, R.J., and Pearce, J.R. (2016). The relationship between wealth and loneliness among older people across Europe: is social participation protective? *Preventive Medicine*, 91, 24–31.

Norman, A. (1985). *Triple Jeopardy: Growing Old in a Second Homeland* (No 3). London: Centre for Policy on Ageing.

Norgard, T.M., and Rodgers, W.L. (1997). Patterns of in-home care among elderly black and white Americans. *Journals of Gerontology Series B*, 52, 93–101.

Norris, P. and Inglehart, R. (2005). Gendering social capital: Bowling in women's leagues?" In (eds.) B. O'Neill and E. Gidengil, *Gender and Social Capital.* London: Routledge, pp 73–98.

Nuru-Jeter, A.M., Michaels, E.K., Thomas, M.D., Reeves, A.N., Thorpe Jr, R.J., and LaVeist, T.A. (2018). Relative roles of race versus socioeconomic position in studies of health inequalities: a matter of interpretation. *Annual Review of Public Health*, 39, 169–188.

Nusselder, W.J., Looman, C.W.N., and Mackenbach, J.P. (2006). The level and time course of disability: trajectories of disability in adults and young elderly. *Disability and Rehabilitation*, 28, 16, 1015–1026.

Öberg, P. (1996). The absent body–a social gerontological paradox. *Ageing & Society*, 16, 6, 701–719.

O'Brien, M. (2010). Older male labour force participation in OECD countries: Pension reform and "the reserve army of labour". *International Labour Review*, 149, 3, 239–259.

OECD (2017) *Preventing Ageing Unequally*. Paris: OECD Publishing. https://read.oecd-ilibrary.org/employment/preventing-ageing-unequally_9789264279087-en

Office of Population Censuses and Surveys (1996). *Ethnicity in the 1991 Census. Vol One. Demographic Characteristics of the Ethnic Minority Populations*. London: HMSO.

Ojala, H., Pietilä, I., and Nikander, P. (2016). Immune to ageism? Men's perceptions of age-based discrimination in everyday contexts. *Journal of Aging Studies*, 39, 44–53.

Oliver, M. (2009). *Understanding Disability: From Theory to Practice* (2nd edition). London: Palgrave MacMillan.

Oliver, M. (2013). The social model of disability: thirty years on. *Disability and Society*, 28, 7, 1024–1026.

ONS (Office for National Statistics) (2017). Household disposable income and inequality in the UK: financial year ending 2016. www.ons.gov.uk/peoplepopulationandcommunity/personalandhouseholdfinances/incomeandwealth/bulletins/householddisposableincomeandinequality/financialyearending2016#gradual-decline-in-income-inequality-over-the-last-decade

ONS (Office for National Statistics) (2018a). *Financial Wealth: Wealth in Great Britain*. www.ons.gov.uk/peoplepopulationandcommunity/personalandhouseholdfinances/incomeandwealth/datasets/financialwealthwealthingreatbritain

ONS (Office for National Statistics) (2018b) *Family Spending in the UK: April 2017 to March*. www.ons.gov.uk/peoplepopulationandcommunity/personalandhouseholdfinances/expenditure/bulletins/familyspendingintheuk/financialyearending2018

O'Rand, A.M. (1996). The precious and the precocious: understanding cumulative disadvantage and cumulative advantage over the life course. *The Gerontologist*, 36, 2, 230–238.

O'Rand, A.M. (2006). Stratification and the life course: Life course capital, life course risks, and social inequality. In R.H. Binstock, L.K. George, S.J. Cutler, J. Hendricks and J.H. Schulz (eds), *The Handbook of Aging and the Social Sciences* , 6th edition. New York: Academic Press, pp 145–162.

O'Rand, A., and Lynch, S. (2018). Socioeconomic status, health and mortality in aging populations. In M.D. Hayward and M.K. Majmundar (eds), *Future Directions for the Demography of Aging: Proceedings of a Workshop*. Washington, DC: The National Academies Press, pp 67–95.

Pakulski, J., and Waters, M. (1996a). The reshaping and dissolution of social class in advanced society. *Theory and Society*, 25, 5, 667–691.

Pakulski, J., and Waters, M. (1996b). *The Death of Class*. London: Sage.

Paldam, M. (2000). Social Capital: One or many? Definition and measurement. *Journal of Economic Surveys*, 14, 5, 629–653.

Palmer, M., and Harley, D. (2011). Models and measurement in disability: an international review. *Health Policy and Planning*, 27, 5, 357–364.

Palmore, E. (2001). The ageism survey: First findings. *The Gerontologist*, 41, 5, 572–575.

Patsios, D. , Hillyard, P. , Machniewski, S. , Lundstrom, F. and Taylor, D. (2012). Inequalities in old age: the impact of the recession on older people in Ireland, North and South, *Quality in Ageing and Older Adults*, 13, 1, 27–37.

Payne, G. (2007). Social divisions, social mobilities and social research: Methodological issues after 40 years. *Sociology,* 41, 5, 901–915.

Payne, G. (2013) Social divisions as a sociological perspective. In G. Payne (ed.) *Social Divisions, 3rd edition*. London: Palgrave Macmillan, pp 347–360.

Pedersen, A.W. (1999). *The Taming of Inequality in Retirement: A Comparative Study of Pension Policy Outcomes.* PhD thesis, European University Institute, Florence, Italy.

Peek, M.K., and O'Neil, G.S. (2001). Networks in later life: an examination of race differences in social support networks. *International Journal of Aging and Human Development*, 52, 3, 207–229.

Perrin, N., Dal, L., and Poulain, M. (2015). The objective approaches of ethnic origins in Belgium: methodological alternatives and statistical implications. In P. Simon, V. Piché, and A.A. Gagnon (eds), *Social Statistics and Ethnic Diversity: Cross-National Perspectives in Classifications and Identity Politics.* Cham: Springer, pp 191–208.

Petev, I. D. (2013). The association of social class and lifestyles: Persistence in American sociability, 1974 to 2010. *American Sociological Review*, 78, 4, 633-661.

Pettersson, I., Hagberg, L., Fredriksson, C., and Hermansson, L.N. (2016). The effect of powered scooters on activity, participation and quality of life in elderly users. *Disability and Rehabilitation: Assistive Technology*, 11, 7, 558–563.

Pew Research Center (2012). *Fewer, Poorer, Gloomier: The Lost Decade of the Middle Class.* Washington, DC: Pew Social and Demographic Trends.

Phelan, J.C., and Link, B.G. (2015). Is racism a fundamental cause of inequalities in health? *Annual Review of Sociology*, 41, 311–330.

Phoenix, A. (2016). Psychosocial intersections: Contextualising the accounts of adults who grew up in visibly ethnically different households, in H. Lutz, M.T. Herrera-Vivar and L. Supik (eds), *Framing Intersectionality: Debates on a Multi-Faceted Concept in Gender Studies.* London: Routledge, pp 137–152.

Piachaud, D. (1988). Poverty in Britain 1899 to 1983. *Journal of Social Policy*, 17, 3, 335–349.

Pickard, S. (2014). Frail bodies: geriatric medicine and the constitution of the fourth age. *Sociology of Health and Illness*, 36, 4, 549–563.

Pickard, S. (2016). *Age Studies: A sociological examination of how we age and are aged through the life course.* London: Sage Publications.

Pickard, S. (2019). Age war as the new class war? Contemporary representations of intergenerational inequity. *Journal of Social Policy*, 48, 2, 369–386.

Pietroski, P., and Rey, G. (1995). When other things aren't equal: saving ceteris paribus laws from vacuity. *British Journal for the Philosophy of Science*, 46, 1, 81–110.

Plagnol, A.C. (2011). Financial satisfaction over the life course: the influence of assets and liabilities. *Journal of Economic Psychology*, 32, 1, 45–64.

Platt, L. (2009). Social activity, social isolation and ethnicity. *Sociological Review*, 57, 4, 670–702.

Poggi, G. (2001). *Forms of Power.* Cambridge: Polity Press.

Pollert, A. (1996). Gender and class revisited; or, the poverty of patriarchy'. *Sociology*, 30, 4, 639–659.

Pongiglione, B., De Stavola, B.L., and Ploubidis, G.B. (2015). A systematic literature review of studies analyzing inequalities in health expectancy among the older population. *PLoS One* 10, 6, Article e0130747.

Portes, A., and Rumbaut, R.G. (2001). *Legacies: The Story of the Immigrant Second Generation.* New York: Russell Sage Foundation.

Poterba, J.M., Venti, S.F., and Wise, D.A. (2018). *Longitudinal Determinants of End-of-Life Wealth Inequality.* NBER Working Paper No 23839, National Bureau of Economic Research, Cambridge, MA.

Poulantzas, N.A. (1975). *Classes in Contemporary Capitalism.* London: New Left Books.

Präg, P., Mills, M.C., and Wittek, R. (2016). Subjective socioeconomic status and health in cross-national comparison. *Social Science and Medicine*, 149, 84–92.

Prus, S.G. (2000). Income inequality as a Canadian cohort ages: an analysis of the later life course. *Research on Aging*, 22, 3, 211–237.

Pullin, G. (2009). *Design Meets Disability.* Harvard, MA: The Massachusetts Institute of Technology Press.

Putnam, R.D. (2000). *Bowling Alone: The collapse and revival of American community.* New York: Simon & Schuster.

Pyke, K.D., and Bengtson, V.L. (1996). Caring more or less: individualistic and collectivist systems of family eldercare. *Journal of Marriage and the Family*, 58, 2, 379–392.

Rahman, F. (2019). *The Generation of Poverty: Poverty over the Life Course for Different Generations.* London: Resolution Foundation.

Rallu, J.-L. (2017). Projections of older immigrants in France, 2008–2028. *Population, Space and Place*, 23, 5, e2012.

Ramirez-Valles, J., and Diaz, R.M. (2005). Public health, race, and the AIDS movement: the profile and consequences of Latino gay men's community involvement. In A.M. Ransome (ed), *Work, Consumption and Culture: Affluence and social change in the twenty-first century.* London: Sage.

Rehnberg, J. (2019). What levels the association between income and mortality in later life: age or health decline? *Journals of Gerontology: Social Sciences*, doi:10.1093/geronb/gbz082 Advance Access publication June 8, 2019.

Reinharz, S. (1986). Friends or foes: Gerontological and feminist theory. *Women's Studies International Forum*, 9, 5/6, 503–514.

Reus-Pons, M., Vandenheede, H., Janssen, F., and Kibele, E.U. (2016). Differences in mortality between groups of older migrants and older non-migrants in Belgium, 2001–09. *European Journal of Public Health*, 26, 6, 992–1000.

Ricci, C.A. (2016). Perceived social position and income inequality: do they move together? Evidence from Europe and the United States. *LIS Working Paper Series, no 667.* Luxembourg Income Study (LIS), Luxembourg.

Richards, N., Warren, L., and Gott, M. (2012). The challenge of creating 'alternative'images of ageing: Lessons from a project with older women. *Journal of Aging Studies,* 26, 1, 65–78.

Rieker, P.P. and Bird, C.E. (2005). Rethinking gender differences in health: Why we need to integrate social and biological perspectives *The Journals of Gerontology: Series B,* 60, 2, S40–S47.

Rocca, W.A., Boyd, C.M., Grossardt, B.R., Bobo, W.V., Rutten, L.J.F., Roger, V.L., and Sauver, J.L.S. (2014). Prevalence of multimorbidity in a geographically defined American population: patterns by age, sex, and race/ethnicity. *Mayo Clinic Proceedings* 89, 10, 1336–1349.

Rockwood, K. (2005). What would make a definition of frailty successful? *Age and Ageing,* 34, 5, 432–434.

Roebuck, J. (1979). When does old age begin? The evolution of the English definition. *Journal of Social History*, 12, 3, 416–428.

Roger, K.S., and Medved, M. (2010). Living with Parkinson's disease – managing identity together. *International Journal of Qualitative Studies on Health and Well-being*, 5, 2, 5129. doi:10.3402/qhw.v5i2.5129

Roger, K.S., Wetzel, M., Hutchinson, S., Packer, T., and Versnel, J. (2014). 'How can I still be me?' Strategies to maintain a sense of self in the context of a neurological condition. *International Journal of Qualitative Studies on Health and Well-being*, 9, 1, 23534. doi:10.3402/qhw.v9.23534

Romo, R.D., Wallhagen, M.I., Yourman, L., Yeung, C.C., Eng, C., Micco, G., Pérez-Stable, E.J., and Smith, A.K. (2013). Perceptions of successful aging among diverse elders with late-life disability. *The Gerontologist*, 53, 6, 939–949.

Rose, D., and Harrison, E. (2007). The European socio-economic classification: a new social class schema for comparative European research. *European Societies*, 9, 3, 459–490.

Rose, D., Harrison, E., and Pevalin, D. (2014). The European Socio-Economic Classification: a prolegemon. In D. Rose and E. Harrison (eds), *Social Class in Europe: An Introduction to the European Socio-Economic Classification*. Routledge/ESA Studies in European Societies. London: Routledge, pp 3–38.

Rose, D., Pevalin, D.J., and O'Reilly, K. (2005). *The National Statistics Socio-economic Classification: Origins, Development and Use.* Basingstoke: Palgrave Macmillan.

Rosenfeld, D.L., and Burrow, A.L. (2017). The unified model of vegetarian identity: a conceptual framework for understanding plant-based food choices. *Appetite*, 112, 78–95.

Ross, C.E., and Wu, C.-L. (1996). Education, age, and the cumulative advantage in health. *Journal of Health and Social Behavior*, 37, 104–120.

Rothman, R.A. (2015). *Inequality and Stratification: Race, Class, and Gender*. London: Routledge.

Rowntree, B.S. (1941). *Poverty and Progress. A second social survey of York*. London: Macmillan.

Rowntree, B.S., and Lavers, G.R. (1951). *Poverty and Progress: A Third Social Survey of York*. London: Longmans.

Ruspini, P. (2010). *Elderly Migrants in Europe: An Overview of Trends, Policies and Practices, Preliminary Report*. Occasional Paper, Sofia: CERMES – Centre for European Refugees, Migration and Ethnic Studies, New Bulgarian University. www.cermes.info/upload/docs/Elderly_migrants_in_Europe_paolo_ruspini_14_07_10.pdf

Russell, C. (2007). What do older women and men want? Gender differences in the 'lived experience 'of ageing. Current Sociology, 55, 2, 173–192.

Ryan, L. (2008) Social networks, social support and social capital: The experiences of recent Polish migrants in London. *Sociology* 42, 4, 672–690.

Sabariego, C., Oberhauser, C., Posarac, A., Bickenbach, J., Kostanjsek, N., Chatterji, S., Officer, A., Coenen, M., Chan, L., and Cieza, A. (2015). Measuring disability: comparing the impact of two data collection approaches on disability rates. *International Journal of Environmental Research and Public Health*, 12, 9, 10329–10351.

Said, E.W. (1995). *Orientalism: Western Conceptions of the Orient* (First published 1978). Harmondsworth: Penguin Books.

Salecl, R. (2011). *The Tyranny of Choice*. London: Profile Books.

Sanders, J.M. (2002). Ethnic boundaries and identity in plural societies. *Annual Review of Sociology*, 28, 1, 327–357.

Santoni, G., Marengoni, A., Calderón-Larrañaga, A., Angleman, S., Rizzuto, D., Welmer, A-K, Mangialasche, F., Orsini, N. and Fratiglioni, L. (2017) Defining health trajectories in older adults with five clinical indicators, *The Journals of Gerontology: Series A*, 72, 8, 1123–1129.

Savage, M. (2000). *Class Analysis and Social Transformation*. Milton Keynes: Open University Press.

Savage, M. (2015). *Social Class in the 21st Century*. London: Penguin Books.

Savage, M. (2016). End class wars. *Nature*, 537, 475–479.

Savage, M., Warde, A., and Devine, F. (2005). Capitals, assets, and resources: some critical issues. *British Journal of Sociology*, 56, 1, 31–47.

Sayer, A. (2005). *The Moral Significance of Class*. Cambridge: Cambridge University Press.

Scambler, G., and Higgs, P. (1999). Stratification, class and health: class relations and health inequalities in high modernity. *Sociology*, 33, 2, 275–296.

Scambler, G., and Scambler, S. (2015). Theorizing health inequalities: the untapped potential of dialectical critical realism. *Social Theory and Health*, 13, 3–4, 340–354.

Schafer, M.H. (2013). Structural advantages of good health in old age: investigating the health-begets-position hypothesis with a full social network. *Research on Aging*, 35, 3, 348–370.

Schoeni, R.F., Freedman, V.A., and Martin, L.G. (2008). Why is late-life disability declining? *The Milbank Quarterly*, 86, 1, 47–89.

Schöllgen, I., Huxhold, O., and Tesch-Römer, C. (2010). Socioeconomic status and health in the second half of life: findings from the German Ageing Survey. *European Journal of Ageing*, 7, 1, 17–28.

Schultz, T.W. (1961). Investment in human capital, *The American Economic Review*, 51, 1, 1–17.

Scott, J.W. (1986). Gender: A useful category of historical analysis. *The American Historical Review,* 91, 5, 1053–1075.

Seidman, S. (1997). *Difference Troubles: Queering Social Theory and Sexual Politics.* Cambridge: Cambridge University Press.

Seidman, S. (2016). *Contested Knowledge: Social Theory Today* (3rd edition). London: John Wiley.

Shakespeare, T. (1996). Disability, identity and difference. In C. Barnes and G. Mercer (eds), *Exploring the Divide*. Leeds: The Disability Press, pp 94–113.

Shakespeare, T. (2012). Still a health issue. *Disability and Health Journal*, 5, 3, 129–131.

Shakespeare, T., and Watson, N. (2001). The social model of disability: an outdated ideology? *Research in Social Science and Disability*, 2, 9–28.

Shaw, B.A., Krause, N., Liang, J. and Bennett, J. (2007). Tracking changes in social relations throughout late life. *The Journals of Gerontology: Series B*, 62, 2, S90–S99.

Shaw, R.L., Gwyther, H., Holland, C., Bujnowska-Fedak, M., Kurpas, D., Cano, A., Marcucci, M., Riva, S., and D'avanzo, B. (2018). Understanding frailty: meanings and beliefs about screening and prevention across key stakeholder groups in Europe. *Ageing and Society*, 38, 6, 1223–1252.

Shildrick, T., and MacDonald, R. (2013). Poverty talk: how people experiencing poverty deny their poverty and why they blame 'the poor'. *The Sociological Review*, 61, 2, 285–303.

Shorrocks, A.F. (1975) The age–wealth relationship: a cross-section and cohort analysis. *Review of Economics and Statistics*, 57, 2, 155–163.

Shragge, E. (1984). *Pensions Policy in Britain: A socialist analysis.* London: Routledge.

Siebers, T. (2001). Disability in theory: From social constructionism to the new realism of the body. *American Literary History*, 13, 4, 737–754.

Simon, P., Piché, V., and Gagnon, A. (2015). The making of racial and ethnic categories: official statistics reconsidered. In P. Simon, V. Piché and A. Gagnon (eds), *Social Statistics and Ethnic Diversity: Cross-national Perspectives in Classifications and Identity Politics.* Champagne, IL: Springer, pp 1–14.

Simon, P. (2017). The failure of the importation of ethno-racial statistics in Europe: debates and controversies. *Ethnic and Racial Studies*, 40, 13, 2326–2332.

Simpson, L. (2002). 'Race' statistics: their's and our's. *Radical Statistics* 79/80. www.radstats.org.uk/no079/simpson.htm

Singh-Manoux, A., Adler, N.E., and Marmot, M.G. (2003). Subjective social status: its determinants and its association with measures of ill-health in the Whitehall II study. *Social Science and Medicine*, 56, 6, 1321–1333.

Skeggs, B. (1997). *Formations of Class and Gender: Becoming Respectable.* London: Sage.

Slorach, R. (2016). *A Very Capitalist Condition: A History and Politics of Disability*. London: Bookmarks Publications.

Snow, D.A., and Anderson, L. (1987). Identity work among the homeless: the verbal construction and avowal of personal identities. *American Journal of Sociology*, 92, 6, 1336–1371.

Social Security Administration (2016). *Income of the Aged Chartbook, 2014.* SSA Publication No 13-11727. SSA, Washington. www.ssa.gov/policy/docs/chartbooks/income_aged/2014/iac14.pdf

Sokhi-Bulley, B. (2016). *Governing (Through) Rights.* London: Bloomsbury Publishing.

Soom Ammann, E., and van Holten, K. (2013). Getting old here and there: opportunities and pitfalls of transnational care arrangements. *Transnational Social Review: A Social Work Journal*, 3, 1, 31–47.

Springer, K.W. and Mouzon, D.M. (2011). "Macho men" and preventive health care: Implications for older men in different social classes. *Journal of Health and Social Behavior*, 52, 2, 212–227.

Stanworth, M. (1984). Women and class analysis: a reply to John Goldthorpe. *Sociology*, 18, 2, 159–170.

Steinbach, A. (2018). Older migrants in Germany. *Journal of Population Ageing*, 11, 3, 285–306.

Stern, Y. (2007). The concept of cognitive reserve: a catalyst for research. In Y. Stern (ed), *Cognitive Reserve: Theory and Applications.* New York: Taylor and Francis, pp 1–4.

Stevens, N.L., and van Tilburg, T.G. (2011). Cohort differences in having and retaining friends in personal networks in later life. *Journal of Social and Personal Relationships,* 28, 1, 24–43.

Stiglitz, J.E. (2012). *The Price of Inequality: How Today's Divided Society Endangers Our Future.* New York: W.W. Norton.

Stiglitz, J. (2014). Inequality is not inevitable. *New York Times*, 27 June, 1–3. http://opinionator.blogs.nytimes.com/2014/06/27/inequality-is-not-inevitable/?ref=opinion

Stockhammer, E. (2012) Financialization, in J. Toporowski and J. Michell, (eds) *Handbook of Critical Issues in Finance.* Cheltenham: Edward Elgar, pp 121–126.

Stockhammer, E. (2015) Rising inequality as a cause of the present crisis, *Cambridge Journal of Economics,* 39, 3, 935–958.

Stockwell, E.G. (1963). A critical examination of the relationship between socioeconomic status and mortality. *American Journal of Public Health and the Nation's Health*, 53, 6, 956–964.

Storm, I., Sobolewska, M., and Ford, R. (2017). Is ethnic prejudice declining in Britain? Change in social distance attitudes among ethnic majority and minority Britons. *British Journal of Sociology*, 68, 3, 410–434.

Strauss, W., and Howe, N. (1992). *Generations: The History of America's Future, 1584 to 2069.* New York: Harper Collins.

Strauss, W., and Howe, N. (2000). *Millennials Rising: The Next Great Generation.* New York: W.W. Norton.

Strmic-Pawl, H.V., Jackson, B.A., and Garner, S. (2018). Race counts: racial and ethnic data on the US census and the implications for tracking inequality. *Sociology of Race and Ethnicity*, 4, 1, 1–13.

St Sauver, J.L., Boyd, C.M., Grossardt, B.R., Bobo, W.V., Rutten, L.J.F., Roger, V.L., Ebbert, J.O., Therneau, T.M., Yawn, B.P., and Rocca, W. A. (2015). Risk of developing multimorbidity across all ages in an historical cohort study: differences by sex and ethnicity. *BMJ Open*, 5 (2), e006413.

Sugisawa, H., Harada, K., Sugihara, Y., Yanagisawa, S., and Shinmei, M. (2018). Socioeconomic status disparities in late-life disability based on age, period, and cohort in Japan. *Archives of Gerontology and Geriatrics*, 75, 6–15.

Sullivan, L., and Meschede, T. (2014). Retirement security for households of color: disparities during the life course compounded in old age. In D. Mitra and J. Weil (eds), *Race and the Life Course: Readings from the Intersection of Race, Ethnicity and Age*. New York: Palgrave Macmillan, pp 223–245.

Sullivan, L., and Meschede, T. (2016). Race, gender, and senior economic well-being: How financial vulnerability over the life course shapes retirement for older women of color. *Public Policy and Aging Report*, 26, 2, 58–62.

Sutin, A.R., Stephan, Y., Carretta, H., and Terracciano, A. (2015). Perceived discrimination and physical, cognitive, and emotional health in older adulthood. *American Journal of Geriatric Psychiatry*, 23, 2, 171–179.

Sylv, S. (2003). *Retirement is Twice as Much Husband on Half as Much Money*. New York: Athena Press.

Tajfel, H., and Turner, J.C. (1979). An integrative theory of intergroup conflict. Reprinted in M.J. Hatch and M. Schultz (eds), *Organizational Identity: A Reader.* Oxford: Oxford University Press, 2004, pp 56–65.

Tarrant, M. (2016). 'Thinking you're old and frail': a qualitative study of frailty in older adults. *Ageing and Society*, 36, 7, 1483–1500.

Taylor, M.G. (2008). Timing, accumulation, and the black/white disability gap in later life: a test of weathering. *Research on Aging*, 30, 2, 226–250.

Taylor, R.J., Chatters, L.M., Woodward, A.T., and Brown, E. (2013). Racial and ethnic differences in extended family, friendship, fictive kin, and congregational informal support networks. *Family Relations*, 62, 10, 609–624.

Tennstedt, S., and Chang, B.H. (1998). The relative contribution of ethnicity versus socioeconomic status in explaining differences in disability and receipt of informal care. *The Journals of Gerontology Series B: Psychological Sciences and Social Sciences*, 53, 2, S61–S70.

Terry, D.F., Sebastiani, P., Andersen, S.L. and Perls, T.T. (2008). Disentangling the roles of disability and morbidity in survival to exceptional old age. *Archives of Internal Medicine*, 168, 3, 277–283.

Tesch-Römer, C. and Wahl, H.W. (2017). Toward a more comprehensive concept of successful aging: disability and care needs. *The Journals of Gerontology: Series B*, 72, 2, 310–31.

Thewissen, S., Kenworthy, L., Nolan, B., Roser, M., and Smeeding, T. (2015). Rising income inequality and living standards in OECD countries: how does the middle fare? *LIS Working Paper Series, No 656*. Luxembourg Income Study (LIS), Luxembourg.

Thomas, C. (2007). *Sociologies of disability and illness: Contested ideas in disability studies and medical sociology*. London: Macmillan.

Thomas, C., and Milligan, C. (2015). How can and should UK society adjust to dementia? *Joseph Rowntree Viewpoint*. York: Joseph Rowntree Foundation.

Thompson Jr, E.H., and Bennett, K.M. (2017). Masculinity ideologies. In R.F. Levant and Y.J. Wong (eds), *The Psychology of Men and Masculinities*. Washington, DC: American Psychological Association Press, pp 45–74.

Tilly, C. (1998). *Durable Inequality*. Berkeley: University of California Press.

Tinson, A., Aldridge, H., Born, T.B., and Hughes, C. (2016). *Disability and Poverty: Why Disability Must Be at the Centre of Poverty Reduction*. London: New Policy Institute.

Titmuss, R.M. (1955). Pension systems and population change. *The Political Quarterly*, 26, 2, 152–166.

Tornstam, L. (1989). Gero-transcendence: a reformulation of the disengagement theory. *Aging Clinical and Experimental Research*, 1, 1, 55–63.

Torres, S. (2019a). *Ethnicity and Old Age: Expanding Our Imagination*. Bristol: Policy Press.

Torres, S. (2019b). Ethnicity, race and care in older age: what can a social justice framework offer? In S. Westwood (ed), *Ageing, Diversity and Equality: Social Justice Perspectives*. London: Routledge, pp 185–198.

Torres, J.L., Lima-Costa, M.F., Marmot, M., and de Oliveira, C. (2016). Wealth and disability in later life: the English Longitudinal Study of Ageing (ELSA). *PloS One*, 11, 11, e0166825.

Torres, S., and Hammarström, G. (2009). Successful aging as an oxymoron: older people – with and without home-help care – talk about what aging well means to them. *International Journal of Ageing and Later Life*, 4, 1, 23–54.

Townsend, P. (1964). *The Family Life of Old People*. Harmondsworth: Penguin Books.

Tsakloglou, P. (1990). Aspects of poverty in Greece. *Review of Income and Wealth*, 36, 4, 381–402.

Tuckman, J., and Lorge, I. (1953). Attitudes toward old people. *Journal of Social Psychology*, 37, 2, 249–260.

Tulle, E. (2015). Theorising embodiment and ageing. In J. Twigg and W. Martin (eds), *Routledge Handbook of Cultural Gerontology*. London: Routledge, pp 125–135).

Tunstall, J. (1966). *Old and Alone: A Sociological Study of Old People.* London: Routledge and Kegan Paul.

Turner, B.S. (1984). *The Body and Society: Explorations in social theory.* Oxford: Basil Blackwell.

Turner, B.S. (1991). Recent developments in the theory of the body. In M. Featherstone, M. Hepworth, & B.S. Turner (eds), *The Body: Social process and cultural theory.* London: Sage Publications, pp 1–35.

Turner, B.S. (2006). *Vulnerability and Human Rights.* University Park, Pennsylvania: Penn State Press.

Turner, R.J., Brown, T.N., and Hale, W.B. (2017). Race, socioeconomic position, and physical health: A descriptive analysis. *Journal of Health and Social Behavior*, 58, 1, 23–36.

Twigg, J., and Martin, W. (2015). The field of cultural gerontology: An introduction, in J. Twigg and W. Martin (ed), *Routledge Handbook of Cultural Gerontology.* Abingdon: Routledge, pp 1–23.

United Nations (2006). *Convention on the Rights of Persons with Disabilities.* New York: United Nations. www.un.org/disabilities/documents/convention/convoptprot-e.pdf

US Census Bureau (2015). *Income and Poverty in the United States: 2015* www.census.gov/data/tables/time-series/demo/income-poverty/cps-pov/pov-02.html

US Census Bureau (2016a). American Community Survey: disability characteristics, Table S1810. https://factfinder.census.gov/faces/tableservices/jsf/pages/

US Census Bureau (2016b). American Community Survey: age by disability status by poverty status, Table B18130. https://factfinder.census.gov/faces/tableservices/jsf/pages/

Uslaner, E.M., and Conroy, R.S. (2003). Civic engagement and particularized trust: the ties that bind people to their ethnic communities. *American Politics Research*, 31, 4, 331–360.

Van Deth, J.W. (2003). Measuring social capital: orthodoxies and continuing controversies. *International Journal of Social Research Methodology*, 6, 1, 79–92.

Van Emmerick, I.J.H. (2006). Gender differences in the creation of different types of social capital: A multilevel study. *Social Networks*, 28 (1), 24–37.

Van Kippersluis, H., Van Ourti, T., O'Donnell, O., and Van Doorslaer, E. (2009). Health and income across the life cycle and generations in Europe. *Journal of Health Economics*, 28, 4, 818–830.

Van Ourti, T. (2003). Socio-economic inequality in ill-health amongst the elderly: should one use current or permanent income? *Journal of Health Economics*, 22, 2, 219–241.

Van Zon, S.K., Bültmann, U., Reijneveld, S.A., and de Leon, C.F.M. (2016). Functional health decline before and after retirement: a longitudinal analysis of the Health and Retirement Study. *Social Science and Medicine*, 170, 26–34.

Vargha, L., Gál, R.I., and Crosby-Nagy, M.O. (2017). Household production and consumption over the life cycle: National Time Transfer Accounts in 14 European countries. *Demographic Research*, 36, 905–944.

Vaupel, J.W., Manton, K.G., and Stallard, E. (1979). The impact of heterogeneity in individual frailty on the dynamics of mortality. *Demography*, 16, 3, 439–454.

Veenhoven, R. (2002). Why social policy needs subjective indicators. *Social Indicators Research*, 58, 1/3, 33–46.

Verbrugge, L.M., and Yang, L.S. (2002). Aging with disability and disability with aging. *Journal of Disability Policy Studies*, 12, 4, 253–267.

Victor, C.R., Burholt, V., and Martin, W. (2012). Loneliness and ethnic minority elders in Great Britain: an exploratory study. *Journal of Cross-Cultural Gerontology*, 27, 1, 65–78.

Villa, P.-I. (2016). Embodiment is always more: Intersectionality, subjection and the body. In H. Lutz, M.T. Herrera Vivar and L. Supik (eds), *Framing Intersectionality: Debates on a Multi-Faceted Concept in Gender Studies.* London: Routledge, pp 171–186.

Vinokurov, A., and Trickett, E.J. (2015). Ethnic clusters in public housing and independent living of elderly immigrants from the former Soviet Union. *Journal of Cross-Cultural Gerontology*, 30, 4, 353–376.

Vogel, L. (2013). *Marxism and the Oppression of Women: Toward a unitary theory*. Amsterdam: Brill.

Von Kondratowitz, H.J. (1994). The medicalization of old age: continuity and change in Germany from the late eighteenth to the early twentieth century. In M. Pelling and R.M. Smith (eds), *Life, Death, and the Elderly: Historical Perspectives*. London: Routledge, pp 134–164.

Wade, P. (2005) Hybridity theory and kinship thinking. *Cultural Studies*, 19, 5, 602–621.

Wadsworth, M. (2011). Intersectionality in California's same-sex marriage battles: a complex proposition. *Political Research Quarterly*, 64, 1, 200–216.

Walby, S. (1990a). *Theorising Patriarchy.* Oxford: Blackwell.

Walby, S. (1990b). From private to public patriarchy: the periodization of British history. *Women's Studies International Forum*, 13, 1/2, 91–104.

Walby, S. (2009). *Globalization and Inequalities: Complexity and Contested Modernities.* London: Sage.

Wallerstein, I. (1989). 1968, revolution in the world-system. *Theory and Society*, 18, 4, 431–449.

Walker, A. (1981). Towards a political economy of old age. *Ageing & Society*, 1, 1, 73–94.

Walker, A. (1983). The social production of old age. *Ageing & Society*, 3, 3, 387–395.

Walks, A. (2013). Income inequality and polarization in Canada's cities: an examination and new form of measurement. *Research Paper 227*. University of Toronto, Cities Centre, Toronto.

Wang, J., Caminada, K., and Wang, C. (2017). Measuring income polarization for twenty European countries, 2004–13: a Shapley growth-redistribution decomposition. *Eastern European Economics*, 55, 6, 477–499.

Wang, J., Caminada, K., Goudswaard, K., and Wang, C. (2015). Decomposing income polarization and tax-benefit changes across 31 European countries and Europe wide, 2004–2012. *MPRA Paper No 66155*. University of Munich, Munich. https://mpra.ub.uni-muenchen.de/66155/

Wang, J., Caminada, K., Goudswaard, K., and Wang, C. (2017). Income polarization in European countries and Europe wide, 2004–2012. *Cambridge Journal of Economics*, 42, 3, 797–816.

Wanka, A., Wiesböck, L., Allex, B., Mayrhuber, E.A.-S., Arnberger, A., Eder, R., Kutalek, R., Wallner, P., Hutter, H.-P., and Kolland, F. (2018). Everyday discrimination in the neighbourhood: what a 'doing' perspective on age and ethnicity can offer. *Ageing and Society*, 39, 9, 2133–2158. https://doi.org/10.1017/S0144686X18000466

Warde, A., Silva, E., Bennett, T., Savage, M., Gayo-Cal, M., and Wright, D. (2009). *Culture, Class, Distinction*. London: Routledge.

Warmoth, K., Lang, I.A., Phoenix, C., Abraham, C., Andrew, M.K., Hubbard, R.E., and Tarrant, M. (2016). 'Thinking you're old and frail': a qualitative study of frailty in older adults. *Ageing & Society*, 36, 7, 1483–1500.

Warnes, A.M., and Williams, A.M. (2006) Older migrants in Europe: an innovative focus for migration studies. *Journal of Ethnic and Migration Studies*, 32, 8, 1257–1281.

Webber, D., and Mallett, L. (2018). *Effects of Taxes and Benefits on UK Household Income – Flash Estimate: Financial Year Ending 2018*. London: ONS. www.ons.gov.uk/peoplepopulationandcommunity/personalandhouseholdfinances/incomeandwealth/bulletins/nowcastinghouseholdincomeintheuk/financialyearending2018

Weeden, K.A., and Grusky, D.B. (2012). The three worlds of inequality. *American Journal of Sociology*, 117, 6, 1723-1785.

Weibel-Orlando, J. (1988) Indians, ethnicity as a resource and aging: you can go home again. *Journal of Cross-Cultural Gerontology*, 3, 4, 323–348.
Wemrell, M., Merlo, J., Mulinari, S., and Hornborg, A.C. (2016). Contemporary epidemiology: a review of critical discussions within the discipline and a call for further dialogue with social theory. *Sociology Compass*, 10, 2, 153–171.
Whelan, C.T., Russell, H., and Maître, B. (2016). Economic stress and the great recession in Ireland: polarization, individualization or 'middle class squeeze'? *Social Indicators Research*, 126, 2, 503–526.
WHO (2006). *World Health Survey, 2002–2004*. Geneva: World Health Organization. www.who.int/healthinfo/survey/en/
WHO/World Bank (2011). *World Report on Disability*. Geneva: World Health Organization.
Whitehead, M. (1992). *Inequalities in Health: The Black Report: The Health Divide*. Harmondsworth: Penguin Books.
Wilmoth, J.M., London, A.S., and Heflin, C.M. (2015). Economic well-being among older-adult households: variation by veteran and disability status. *Journal of Gerontological Social Work*, 58, 4, 399–419.
Wilkinson, R., and Pickett, K. (2010). *The Spirit Level: Why Equality Is Better for Everyone*. London: Penguin UK.
Winant, H. (1986). *Racial Formation in the United States: From the 1960s to the 1980s*. New York: Routledge and Kegan Paul.
Wolf, N. (1991). *The Beauty Myth: How Images of Beauty Are Used against Women*. New York: Random House.
Wolfe, P. (2016). *Traces of HISTORY: Elementary Structures of Race*. London: Verso Books.
Wolff, E.N. (2016). Household wealth trends in the United States, 1962 to 2013: what happened over the Great Recession? *RSF: The Russell Sage Foundation Journal of the Social Sciences*, 2, 6, 24–43.
Wood, E.M. (1998). *The Retreat from Class: A New 'True' Socialism*. London: Verso.
Wright, E.O. (1979). *Class, Crisis and the State*. London: New Left Books.
Wright, E.O. (2005). Foundations of a neo-Marxist class analysis. In E.O. Wright (ed), *Approaches to Class Analysis*. Cambridge: Cambridge University Press, pp 4–30.
Wrong, D.H. (1968). Some problems in defining social power. *American Journal of Sociology*, 73, 6, 673–681.
Wrzus, C., Hänel, M., Wagner, J. and Neyer, F.J. (2013). Social network changes and life events across the life span: a meta-analysis. *Psychological Bulletin*, 139, 1, 1–28.

Yan, T., Silverstein, M., and Wilber, K.H. (2011). Does race/ethnicity affect aging anxiety in American baby boomers? *Research on Aging*, 33, 4, 361–378.

Yoo, S.H., and Sung, K.-T. (1997). Elderly Koreans' tendency to live independently from their adult children: adaptation to cultural differences in America. *Journal of Cross-Cultural Gerontology*, 12, 3, 225–244.

Yu, H.W., Chen, D.R., Chiang, T.L., Tu, Y.K., and Chen, Y.M. (2015). Disability trajectories and associated disablement process factors among older adults in Taiwan. *Archives of Gerontology and Geriatrics*, 60, 2, 272–280.

Yuval-Davis, N. (2006). Intersectionality and feminist politics. *European Journal of Women's Studies*, 13, 3, 193–209.

Yuval-Davis, N. (2008). Belonging and the politics of belonging. *Patterns of Prejudice*, 40, 3, 197–214.

Yuval-Davis, N. (2010). Theorizing identity: beyond the 'us' and 'them' dichotomy. *Patterns of Prejudice*, 44, 3, 261–280.

Yusif, S., Soar, J., and Hafeez-Baig, A. (2016). Older people, assistive technologies, and the barriers to adoption: a systematic review. *International Journal of Medical Informatics*, 94, 112–116.

Zaidi, A., and Burchardt, T. (2005). Comparing incomes when needs differ: equivalization for the extra costs of disability. *Review of Income and Wealth*, 51, 89–114.

Zajicek, A.M., and Calasanti, T.M. (1998). Patriarchal struggles and state practices: A feminist, political-economic view. *Gender & Society*, 12, 5, 505–527.

Zimmermann, K.F. (2007). Migrant ethnic identity: concept and policy implications. *IZA Discussion Paper No 3056*. IZA, Bonn. https://ssrn.com/abstract=1022951

Zubair, M., and Norris, M. (2015). Perspectives on ageing, later life and ethnicity: ageing research in ethnic minority contexts. *Ageing and Society*, 35, 5, 897–916.

Index

Page numbers in **bold** refer to tables and in *italics* to figures.